AN ETHICAL
PHILOSOPHY OF LIFE

PRESENTED IN ITS MAIN OUTLINES

BY

FELIX ADLER

"An Ethical Philosophy of Life" by Felix Adler. ISBN 978-0-9897323-3-8.

Manufactured in the United States of America.

PREFACE

THIS book records a philosophy of life growing out of the experience of a lifetime. The convictions put in it are not dogmatic, for dogma is the conviction of one man imposed authoritatively upon others. The convictions herein expounded are submitted to those who search, as the writer has searched, for light on the problems of life, in order that they may compare their experience with his, and their interpretations of their experience with his interpretation.[1]

It is a great hope that some of the readers of this book may find the general world-view expounded congenial, and for them also real and true. It is believed that others may find the practical suggestions as to the conduct of life in which the theory issues helpful in part, if not in whole, as many of us accept from the teachings of the Stoics, or of other thinkers, practical precepts, without on that account adopting the philosophy from which these precepts are derived.

The book is divided into four parts: the first an autobiographical introduction describing the various stations on the road by which the author arrived at his present position, and offering incidental appreciations and appraisements of the Hebrew religion, of Emerson, of the ethics of the Gospels, of Socialism and of other social reform movements.

The second part expounds the philosophical theory.

The third part contains the applications of the theory to the more strictly personal life, under the captions of the Three

---

[1] In view of the writer's connection with the Ethical Culture Societies it is fitting to state expressly that the philosophical positions herein set forth are not to be taken as an official pronouncement on behalf of the Ethical Culture Movement. The Ethical Societies as such have no official philosophy. *See* Book IV, Chapter *9*.

Shadows of Sickness, Sorrow and Sin, and also to the principal so-called Rights to Life, Property, Reputation.

The fourth part applies the theory to the social institutions, to the Family, the Vocation, the State, the International Society, and the Church, these institutions being considered as an expanding series through which the individual is to pass on his pilgrimage in the direction of the supreme spiritual end.

The principal problems considered are:

1. How to establish the fundamental ethical dictum that every human being ought to count, and is intrinsically worth while. This dictum has been denied by many of the greatest thinkers, who assert the intrinsic inferiority of some men, the intrinsic superiority of others. The practice of the world also runs most distinctly contrary to it. How then is it to be validated?

2. The problem of how to attach a precise meaning to the term "spiritual," thereby divesting it of the flavor of sentimentality and vagueness that attaches to it.

3. How to link up the world's activities *in* science, art, politics, business, to the supreme ethical end.

4. How to lay foundations whereon to erect the conviction that there verily is a supersensible reality.

For the repetitions that occur throughout the volume indulgence is requested. In presenting an unfamiliar system of thought they may sometimes assist the reader in retaining the thread.

The work is conceived as a whole, and should be read through before any part of it is more minutely examined. The theory of Part II especially should be read in the light of the applications submitted in Parts III and IV.

Table of Contents

An Ethical Philosophy of Life
INTRODUCTION

An *Ethical Philosophy of Life* was written early in the 20th Century by a man of the 19th. It has been 40 years since David Muzzey wrote a preface to this same book. The contents are now dated in terms of language and style. Yet under the cover of Germanic sentence structure and questionable moralizing on specific issues lies the most systematic explanation Felix Adler ever gave of his religious vision. For the Ethical Culture Movement, which he founded, this book is both a source of historical perspective on our evolutionary faith, and a resource of social and ethical questions which still live today.

My personal feelings are mixed, about this book and its author. Every day I follow my vocation within the institution Adler created. His portrait looks down at me from the wall of my Ethical Society. He is in some senses my teacher, my father, a pioneer of my ethical community. Yet I know that if we ever, by some warp in time, were to meet, I would not enjoy the experience, and he would not find me acceptable as a colleague. Neither of us could fail to notice the distance between us. He would not approve of a Leader who was female, or once divorced, or lacking a doctoral degree. He was unhappy with pacifists who more than once created divisions in the Movement. I, on the other hand, am troubled both personally and institutionally by the stance of an authoritarian with fixed (and Victorian) judgements on political, social, personal, and sexual morality.

Yet there is still something in Adler's religious vision, expressed in the Ethical Culture Movement as a living community, and in this book as a personal document, that transcends the divisions of language, style, generation, and encapsulated opinion. That something was a moral fire, a constitutive drive, however poorly formulated in old rules, that yearned toward the humane and creative community of the future. Whatever perspectives had to change, whatever opinions had to be sacrificed, whatever work was required, it was the future development of a distantly apprehended "ethical manifold" by which the truth or usefulness of all else was to be measured. Adler did not hold any principle to be final, however much he believed in it (held it in his heart), even the unique worth of the human person. That principle of worth, he said, is something we choose. We attribute worth and by so doing, we make an ethical social order possible. Human worth is not a truth we prove, but a condition we require.

Which means the Felix Adler and I might ultimately share together in the realization of a great ethical social evolution, the definite description of which might be as much a surprise to me as my opinions would be to him. And it may come about not by toleration of human differences, but by encouragement of them. Not by rhetoric, but by recognition of each other's humanity. Not by rules for restraint, but by nurture and growth. All these possibilities are present in the quest Adler recounts here. This is a beginning rather than an end of a spiritual journey.

Adler was a process theologian a century ahead of his time; he was a patronizing sexist. He was a self-critical pilgrim; he was pompous. He was a careful rational analyst of data; he was sentimentally and emotionally invested in traditional opinions. His religious vision, his ethical manifold ideal, is sketched in this book like an old map—the edges of which are marked "Terra Incognita." The brown ink is faded, the paper is brittle, the scale is disproportional, and the sea serpents who raise their heads from the waters surrounding terra firma are perhaps poorly rendered, perhaps misidentified, perhaps imaginary. But I love the old map. It belonged to my grandfather. I find it honest. I find it evocative.

I do not choose to travel with all of Adler's baggage, or always with his original version of the map. But I am deeply moved to know how important, how necessary, how self-creating he felt the journey to be. Because it is the journey of my life, and of the community of people I love and need. Because the Terra Incognita of ethical human relationships is where we are all going. Because we are all spiritual immigrants.

Sorrow, sickness, and sin remain with us in their varying forms. The issues raised by this book are still worth the attention we may give them in our Ethical Society discussion groups. But beyond discussion, there is the living development, the laboratory community which Adler wrote of, in which we attempt to live, and not just to name, the means by which we move into the future. This book is a valuable old map. The man who drew it would have wanted us to appreciate its value, and to make the journey. And he would have wanted us to draw a new map, a better map, of the new world.

Like all immigrants, with or without maps, we will change the new world where we go.

Judith E. Espenschied, Leader
PHILADELPHIA ETHICAL
SOCIETY
Summer 1986

BOOK I

AUTOBIOGRAPHICAL INTRODUCTION

CHAPTER 1

PRELUDE

WHAT this book offers is a system of thought and of points of view as to conduct, as these have jointly grown out of personal experience. It will be useful to introduce them with an autobiographical statement. The ideas which follow are such as have been found by me, the author, to be fruitful. Certainly I claim for them objectivity; but I do so because of what I have found them to mean in my own life. He who has been scorched by lightning knows that the effects of the lightning will be felt by all who are exposed to the same experience. I narrate my experience; let others compare with it theirs.

There is, however, a serious, and most embarrassing difficulty in the way of discussing the phases and vicissitudes of one's ethical development. Self-appraisement is necessarily involved in the narration. The outstanding subject of ethics is the self and its relations. The physicist, the chemist, the biologist* however the methods they use may differ in other respects, agree in the endeavor to eliminate the personal equation. The psychologist likewise does his best to see the procession that moves across the inner stage like an interested but detached spectator. In the case of ethics, however, the personal factor cannot be eliminated, because the personal factor is just the Alpha and the Omega of the whole matter; and if this be left out of account, the very object to be studied disappears.

Ethical standards are exacting, separated often from performance by the widest interval. To set up a standard, therefore, is to reflect upon oneself, to expose oneself to the backstroke of one's own deliverances, to be plunged perhaps into deep pits of self-humiliation. How shall anyone have the courage to face so searching a test, or the hardihood to discuss with a lofty air, and to recommend to others ideals of conduct against which he knows that he daily offends ? How can anyone teach ethics or write about it? The words of the Sermon on the Mount, "Judge not that ye be not judged," seem to apply very closely. Do not judge others, do not lay down the law for others, because in so doing you will be judged in the inner forum, becoming a repulsive object in your own eyes, or standing forth a whited sepulcher. In brief, to touch the subject of ethics is to handle a knife that cuts both ways, to cast a weapon which returns upon him who sends it.

The difficulty then which confronts the ethical writer is that the attitude of detachment possible in other branches of investigation is found to be impossible when one attempts to sound the profundities of that kind of inner experience which is called ethical. The self obtrudes itself at every point, and it instinctively refuses to be humbled. What may be denominated the struggle for self-esteem has indeed played a leading role both in the outer and inner history of mankind. This struggle, whose immense importance is often overlooked accounts for even more interesting facts than the biological struggle for existence. The desire to exercise power over others, often ruthless in the means adopted, is frequently nothing more than a miserable attempt to save self-esteem by covering up the inner sense of the weakness of the self. But the same struggle penetrates also into the realm of theoretical ethics with which we are concerned. Here it tampers with the standards which mortify self-esteem, by inventing such ethical theories as seem to make the problems of personality easy of solution, and by blinking the tragic facts of guilt, remorse, etc. Various ethical systems that are in vogue at the present time are, at least in part, exemplars of this process—the theory for instance that ethics is nothing more than a calculus of self-interest, or a matter of sympathetic feeling, or a balancing of the more refined against the grosser pleasures. The instinct of self-preservation, in the shape of the preservation of self-esteem, is quite incorrigible, and against its insidious suggestion we have reason to be particularly on our guard in the discussion which we are entering.

Are we then to refrain, out of sheer regard for decency, from touching on this subject at all? Is everyone who writes on ethics, or attempts to teach it, either a pedant or a hypocrite? But we cannot avoid discussing it, nor resist the impulse to teach and write about it, for it is the subject on which more than any other we and others sorely need help and enlightenment. And we shall get help in the endeavor to afford it to others. This, then, is my position: I do not presume to lay down the law for anyone. I find that I can set forth the better standards which in the course of trial and error I have come to recognize. I would not shamelessly expose mere private failures and failings after the manner of Rousseau in the "Confessions"; for there is a tract of the inner life which ought to be kept from publicity and prying intrusion. I shall then deal with deflections only in so far as they can be traced to false standards or principles, and as they tend to illustrate the flaw in those standards and principles.

What I state as certain is certain for me. It has approved itself as such in my experience. Let others consult their experience, and see how far it tallies with that which is here set forth. A distinction, however, I wish to call attention to between the theory as expounded in the second part of this volume, and the practical applications to be found in the third and fourth parts. Persons who are not trained in metaphysical thinking or interested in it, may do well to omit the reading of the second part. To those who are competent in philosophical thinking, and who disagree with the positions there taken, I may perhaps be permitted to suggest that one can dissent from a philosophy and yet find help in the applications to which it leads. And, after all, it is the practice that counts.

With these preliminaries, I now proceed to delineate briefly the stages of inner development which have led me slowly and with much labor to the system of thought described in the following pages.

One of the leading principles to which I early gave assent, and to which I have ever since adhered as a correct fundamental insight, is expressed in the statement that every human being is an end *per se,* worth while on his own account.[1]

Every human personality is to be safe against infringement and is, in this sense, sacred. There is a certain precinct which may not be invaded. The experience which served me especially as the matrix of this idea was the adolescent experience of sex-life,—the necessity felt of inhibiting, out of reverence for the personality of women, the powerful instincts then awakened.[2]

The fact that I had lived abroad for three years in frequent contact with young men, especially students, who derided my scruples, and in the impure atmosphere

[1] Though I must at once mention the first great error which accompanied the true insight, the shadow which went alongside of the light, namely, my understanding of the above principle mainly in a negative sense. My ethics was largely what may be called non-violation ethics.

[2] The relation of chastity to the birth of the idea of personality among the Hebrews I have touched upon elsewhere. The Hebrew people abhorred promiscuity, or the dishonoring of oneself by indiscriminate mingling. It is instructive that this did not stand in the way of polygamy. Those persons whom the Hebrew received, so to speak, into the sphere of his personality, did not imperil his sense of personal intactness. And personal intactness seems to have been the determining motive in the severe attitude taken toward prostitution. The fact that the worship of other gods, the worst of crimes in the eyes of the Hebrew legislator, was described as "whoring after other gods" is particularly significant. The sacred, sensitive self, the holy thing whatever it might be, which the Hebrew discovered within his own sex experience, was thereafter attributed also to others, and especially to those who had the same aversion to promiscuity as he. Hence perhaps the limited ascription of holiness to members of the Hebrew people.

of three capital cities of Europe, Berlin, Paris and Vienna, where the "primrose path" is easy, tended to make the retention of my point of view more difficult, and at the same time to give it greater fixity, also to drive me into a kind of inward solitude. I felt myself in opposition to my surroundings, and acquired a confidence, perhaps exaggerated, to persevere along my own lines against prevailing tendencies.

I ought next to mention the decay of theism which took place in my mind in • consequence of philosophic reading. Already at an early age I had stumbled over the doctrine of Creation. I remember asking my Sunday School teacher—How is creation possible? How can something originate out of nothing? The answer I received was evasive, and left me uneasy and unsatisfied. On another occasion I ventured to suggest to the same authority—a revered and beloved authority— that the conception of God seemed to me too much like that of a man, too much fashioned on the human model; and he amazed me beyond words by replying that he himself sympathized more or less with the ideas of Spinoza. This chance remark set me thinking, and seemed to open wide spaces in which my mind felt free to travel—though I never tended in the direction of Spinoza.[3]

My thoughts were driven still further by reaction

[8] Pantheism has always seemed to me the least satisfactory of theological or ethical solutions. The system of thought which will be found later on in this volume may have a certain superficial resemblance to Pantheism, but in reality is as far from it in origin and purpose as pole from pole.

against the narrow theology of the lectures on Christian Evidences as taught at that time in Columbia College, where I was a student. And all these influences came to a head in the atmosphere of the German university at Berlin. There I heard Zeller, Duhring, Steinthal, Bonitz. Above all I came into contact with Herman Cohen, subsequently and for many years professor of philosophy at the University of Marburg, and undertook to grapple in grim earnest with the philosophy of Immanuel Kant. The net outcome was not atheism in the moral sense,—I have never been what is called an atheist,—but the definite and permanent disappearance of the individualistic conception of Deity. I was attracted by the rigor, the sublimity, of Kant's system, and especially by his transcendental derivation of the moral law. The individualistic basis of his ethics, which is quite uncongenial to me, I ignored, and for a time simply accounted myself a follower of Kant. Very often since then I have discovered that men, unbeknown to themselves, are apt to sail under false flags, ranking themselves Kantians, Socialists, or what not, because the system to which they give their adherence attracts them at some one outstanding point, the point namely, where it sharply conflicts with views which they themselves strongly reprobate; and they are thus led to overlook other features no less important in which the system is really uncongenial to them. Thus a person who recognizes the evils of the present wage system may label himself a Socialist, simply because Socialism is most in evidence as an adversary of the wage system, while he may by no means agree with the positive principles that underlie Socialism, when he comes to examine them dispassionately.

I thought at that time of the Moral Law as that which answers to or should replace the individualistic God-idea. I believed in an unknown principle or power in things of which the Moral Law is the manifestation, and I found the evidence of the moral law in man's consciousness. Matthew Arnold's "the power that makes for righteousness" is a phrase which at that time would have suited me,—though perhaps not entirely even at that time. I have since come to see that "making for righteousness" is a conception inapplicable to the ultimate reality, and is properly applied only to human effort; since purpose implies that the end sought has not as yet been realized, and non-realization and ultimate reality are contradictory ideas. The power that only makes for righteousness cannot be the ultimate truth in things. The utmost we can say is that the ultimate reality expresses itself in the human world as the power that inspires in men moral purpose.

To return to my personal experiences, there fell into my hands, while still a student abroad, a book by Friedrich Albert Lange entitled *Die Arbeiterfrage* (The Labor Question), which proved epoch-making in my life. Bacon says in his essay *Of Studies:* "Some books are to be tasted, others to be swallowed, and some few to be chewed and digested." He might have added that there are books that make a man over, changing the current of his existence, or at least opening channels which previously had been blocked.[4]

Die Arbeiterfrage is not a great book. In the literature of the subject it has long since been super-: seded. Yet it opened for me a wide and tragic prospect, an outlook of which I had been until then in great measure oblivious, an outlook on all the moral as well as economic issues involved in what is called the Labor Question. My teacher in philosophy, Cohen, once said to me sharply, that if there is to be anything like religion in the world hereafter, Socialism must be the expression of it. I did not agree with his statement that Socialism spells religion, and have not seen my way to this day toward identifying the two. But I realized that there was a measure of truth in what he said,—and that I must square myself with the issues that Socialism raises. Lange helped me to do this.

He aided me in other respects as well. His *History of Materialism* dispelled some of the fictitious glamor that still hung about the materialistic hypothesis at that time,—though the last chapter on the ultimate

---

[4] There are also passages in books that have the same revolutionizing effect (Cf. the passage quoted from St. Paul in St. Augustine's "Confessions"). However, it is curious to observe that the effect brought about may be quite out of proportion to the cause. The book or the passage may prove to be of inferior value, so far as its subject is concerned, and may yet serve suddenly to call attention to the subject itself, and give rise to trains of thought that eventually go far beyond the impetus that set them in motion. "Ripeness," says Shakespeare, "is everything,"—ripeness to receive the impetus. Relatedness to the state of mind of the recipient is the decisive factor, and this accounts for the astounding changes that result.

philosophy of life, in which he identifies religion with poetry, is distinctly weak. I read his book on the Labor Question with burning cheeks; no work of fiction ever excited me as did this little treatise. It was ethical in spirit, if not in its ruling ideas. It favored productive co-operation, and seemed to point a way to immediate action, as Socialism did not.

The upshot of it was that I now possessed a second object, namely, the laborer, to whom I could apply my non-violation ethics. I had always felt an instinctive, idealizing reverence for women, and this had its influence in the first practical outcome of the philosophy of life with which I started on my career. I would go out as the minister of a new religious evangel. Instead of preaching the individual God, I was to stir men up to enact the Moral Law; and to enact the Moral Law meant at that time primarily to influence the young men with whom I came into contact to reverence womanhood, and to keep inviolate the sacred thing, woman's honor. And now I had a second arrow in my quiver. I was to go out to help to arouse the conscience of the wealthy, the advantaged, the educated classes, to a sense of their guilt in violating the human personality of the laborer. My mother had often sent me as a child on errands of charity, and had always impressed upon me the duty of respecting the dignity of the poor while ministering sympathetically to their needs. I was prepared by this youthful training to resent the indignity offered to the personality of the laborer, as well as the suffering endured by him in consequence of existing conditions.

Accordingly, on returning from abroad, my first action consisted in founding among men of my own or nearly my own age a little society which we ambitiously called a Union for the Higher Life, based on three tacit assumptions: sex purity, the principle of devoting the surplus of one's income beyond that required for one's own genuine needs to the elevation of the working class, and thirdly, continued intellectual development. A second practical enterprise attempted was the establishment of a co-operative printing shop. This having failed because of the selfishness actuating the members, the Workingman's School was founded, with the avowed object of creating a truly co-operative spirit among workingmen.

I must, however, pause at this point to explain how the development described led me to separation from the Hebrew religion, the religion in which I was born, and to the service of which as a Jewish minister it was expected that I should devote my life.

CHAPTER II

THE HEBREW RELIGION

The separation was not violent. There was no sudden wrenching off. There were none of those painful struggles which many others have had to undergo when breaking away from the faith of their fathers. It was all a gradual, smooth transition, the unfolding of a seed that had long been planted. I have never felt the bitterness often characteristic of the radical, nor his vengeful impulse to retaliate upon those who had imposed the yoke of dogmas upon his soul. I had never worn the yoke. I had never been in bondage. I had been gently guided. And consequently the wine did not turn into vinegar, the love into hate. The truth is, I was hardly aware of the change that had taken place until it was fairly consummated. One day I awoke, and found that I had traveled into a new country. The landscape was different; the faces I encountered were different; and looking casually into a mental mirror, as it were, I perceived that I too had become different. And I was sure also that I had gained, not lost, that into my new spiritual home I had taken with me, not indeed the images of my gods, like Æneas, fleeing from Troy, but something for which those images had stood, and which in other ways would remain for me a permanent possession.

It has been said that the science of today lives only in so far as it supersedes the science of yesterday. Whatever may be true of science (and the statement is certainly not true without large qualifications—the science of Newton and Darwin has not been "superseded"—and it may even come to pass that outreachings of a more ancient science frustrated at the time will hereafter be taken up anew with fairer results than formerly were attainable), in religion at all events there is no such thing as the bare substitution of the new for the old. The religions of the past, at least the more advanced religions, are not simply to be cast on the scrap heap, or treated as exploded superstitions. There is in all of them a certain fund of truth which may not be allowed to perish, but should be rescued out of the wreck.

On the other hand, even the most advanced religions contain a large admixture of error, survivals of primitive taboos, mythological elements having their root in polytheism, while the very truths which I have just admitted to be infinitely precious require to be restated so as to fit them into a larger synthesis.

It is not easy to define my attitude toward the Old Masters, I mean the Old Masters in religion, the incomparably great religious teachers of the past, who tower above us like giants. My attitude is one of profoundest reverence—toward the Hebrew prophets and Jesus especially. The Hebrew religion first sounded the distinctively spiritual note. Zoroaster had emphasized the struggle of the powers of Light and the powers of Darkness, but the conception of light in his system remained to a considerable extent materialistic. Buddha emphasized Enlightenment in the sense of escape from Illusion, and in conjunction with it sympathy for all who remain under the spell of illusion. Confucius endeavored to walk, and taught his followers to walk, with equipoise in the Middle Path; he emphasized what he thought to be the cosmic principle of balance or equilibrium. Plato, taking his stand on the highest terrestrial platform, caught, or believed himself to have caught, sight of transcendental beauty as the ultimate principle in things. But the prophets of Israel assigned to the ethical principle the highest rank in man's life and in the world at large. The best thing in man, they declared, is his moral personality; and the best thing in the world, the supreme and controlling principle, is the moral power that pervades it.

The predominance of the ethical principle in religion dates from the prophets of Israel. The religious development of the human race took a new turn in their sublime predications, and I for one am certainly conscious of having drawn my first draught of moral inspiration from their writings.[2]

But nevertheless I found myself compelled to separate from the religion of Israel. Now why was it

---

[2]I still go back to that fountain-head for refreshment and inspiration, much as a modern poet may go back to Homer, without attempting to copy him, or as a modern sculptor or architect may go back to the Greek artists without relinquishing his right and his duty to help in producing a different kind of art, which perchance may one day culminate in masterpieces like theirs, though his own performance be but the poor beginning.

necessary for me to take this step? Why not continue along the path first blazed by the Hebrew prophets—smoothing it perhaps and widening it? Why not separate the dross from the gold, the error from the truth, explicating what is implicit in that truth, and adapting it to the needs and conditions of the modern age? The answer is that the truth contained in the Hebrew, and as I shall presently show, in the Christian religion, is not capable of such adaptation. It claims finality. I have mentioned that there is an element of permanent value in both the Hebrew and the Christian religion, and that it should be restated and fitted into a larger synthesis. But this is impossible unless the Hebrew or Christian setting be broken, unless the element to be preserved is taken out of its context, and treated- freshly and with perfect freedom. A religion like the two I am concerned with is a determinate thing. It is a closed circle of thoughts and beliefs. It is capable of a certain degree of change but not of indefinite change. The limits of change are determined by its leading conceptions—the monotheistic idea in the one case, and the centrality of the figure of Christ in the other. Abandon these, and the boundaries by which the religion is circumscribed are passed.

The great religious teachers are men who see the spiritual landscape from a certain point of view, including whatever is visible from their station, excluding whatever is not. The religion which they originate is thus both inclusive and sharply exclusive. What they see with their rapt eyes they describe with a trenchancy

17

and fitness never thereafter to be equaled.[2] But in order to progress in religion it is necessary to advance toward a different station, to reach a different, a higher eminence, and from that to look forth anew upon the spiritual landscape, comprehending the outlook of one's predecessors in a new perspective, seeing what they saw and much besides.

Religious growth may also be compared to the growth of a tree. To expect that development shall continue along the Hebrew or Christian lines is like expecting that a tree will continue to develop along one of its branches. There is a limit beyond which the extension of a branch cannot go. Then growth must show itself in the putting forth of a new branch.

But let me now state with somewhat greater particularity the reasons that compelled me to depart from the faith of Israel, and to leave my early religious home, cherishing pious memories of it, but nevertheless firmly set in my course towards new horizons.[3]

---

[2] Compare the ejaculatory deliverance of Isaiah, the Sermon on the Mount, and the Parables of Jesus. Who can attempt in language to express what they saw as they did?

[8] No seriously religious person will attempt to strike out into a new path unless he be under inward coercion to do so. The advantages of what is commonly called historic continuity (I have just shown wherein real continuity consists, that of growth along the trunk, and not of growth along the branch) are great. There is for one thing the support derived from leaning on an ancient tradition, the proud humility felt in passing on the torch that had been held *by* mighty predecessors, the self-dedication to that which is larger than self, *i.e.,* to an institution and ideas that existed in the world before one was born, and will exist after one is gone. There is the strength drawn from contact with a large and powerful organization, power-

1. The difficulty created by the claim that Israel is an elect people, that it stands in a peculiar relation to the Deity. This claim, at the time when it was put forth, was neither arrogant nor unfounded. It was not arrogant because the mission was understood to be a heavy burden not a privilege: or if a privilege at all, then the tragic privilege of martyrdom, a martyrdom continued through generations. And the claim was not unfounded or preposterous at the time when it was put forth because the Hebrews were in reality the only people who conceived of morality in terms of holiness. It was not absurd for them to assert their mission to be the teachers of mankind in respect to the spiritual interpretation of morality, since there was something, and that something infinitely important, which they actually had to teach. Moral thinking and moral practices of course had existed from immemorial times everywhere, but the conception of morality as divine in its source, as spiritual in its inmost essence,—this immense idea was the offspring of the Hebrew mind. On the other hand, I asked myself, has not the task of Israel in this respect been accomplished? Have not its Scriptures be-

ful both in sustaining one's efforts, and in restraining and correcting them when need be. There are, on the other side, the perils of innovation, the errors into which one is led for lack of restraint and correction, the too great dependence on self, the spiritual loneliness and the lack of many gracious and useful aids to the religious life such as a noble ritual, majestic music, the fit emotional expressions of religious feeling, which are not to be had for the asking, the fine embellishments that are precious in their way, and that, like the fruits in the Gardens of the Gods, ripen slowly, and may not be extemporized or anticipated.

come the common property of the civilized nations? And does not that teacher mistake his office who attempts to maintain his magisterial authority after his pupils have come to man's estate, and are capable of original contributions? The "nations" are not to be looked upon in the light of mere pupils. The ethical message of Israel so far as it is sane is universalistic. It is founded on the conviction that there is a moral nature in every human being, and that the moral nature is a spiritual nature. And if this be so, then the utterances, the insights, the new visions with which the spiritual nature is pregnant, cannot be supposed to be restricted to members of the Jewish people. If the teaching function is to be maintained it must be exercised by all who have the gift. If there is to be an elect body (a dangerous conception, the meaning of which is to be carefully defined), it must consist of gentiles and Jews, of men of every race and condition in whom the spiritual nature is more awakened than in others, peculiarly vivid, pressing towards utterance.

2. Aside from the spiritual interpretation of morality, the mission of the Jewish people has been said to consist in holding aloft the standard of pure monotheism as against trinitarianism. But pure monotheism is a philosophy rather than a religion. Taken by itself it is too pure, too empty of content to serve the purposes of a living faith. The attributes of omniscience, omnipotence, etc., ascribed to Deity are highly abstract, too abstruse to be even thinkable, save indirectly, and they certainly fail to touch the heart. As a matter of fact it was the image of the Father projected upon

the background of these abstractions, that made the object of Jewish piety. Jahweh is the heavenly spouse; Israel is to be his faithful earthly spouse. The Children of Israel are pre-eminently his children. Other nations likewise are his children,—some children of wrath to be cast out and destroyed like the rebellious son in Deuteronomy, others to be eventually gathered into the patriarchal household. But this view comes back to the same general conception of the relations of Israel to other nations which has just been discussed. Moreover, the Father image, as representing the divine life in the world, even when extended so as to include all mankind on equal terms, is open to a serious objection.[4]

3. If, nevertheless, the Jews have a mission, is it perhaps this: to rehabilitate the prophetic ideal of social

[4] See Chapter IX on the Religious Society in Part IV of this volume. It gives rise to the belief that men as individuals or collectively are the objects of a special Providence, and that the universe is so arranged as to be adapted to man's needs, not to say his wishes; whereas the facts show that man must adapt himself to the universe, and find his physical safety and his ethical salvation in so doing. The belief in the Father who allows not one hair of our heads to fall unnoticed raises expectations to which actual experience fails to correspond.

As to the issue between monotheism and trinitarianism, it has long since become obsolescent, if not obsolete. The forward-looking men and women of our time are absorbed in far other issues—Is the mechanical theory propounded by science the ultimate account of things? Is the world in which we live a blind machine? Is man a chance product of nature, like the beasts that perish? Not is God one in unity or is He a Triune God, but, is there a God at all? Is there a supersensible reality? Is religion capable of a new lease of life, and of giving a new lease of life to us who now are spiritually dead?;

justice? Is it not social justice that the world is crying for today? Were not the prophets of Israel the great preachers of righteousness in the sense of social justice? Did they not affirm that religion consists in justice and in its concomitant mercifulness, but above all in justice? Did not Isaiah say: "When ye come to tread my courts, who has demanded this of you? Go wash you, make you clean. Put away the evil that is in your hands. Cease to do evil; learn to do good." And later on, "That ye let the oppressed go free, and that ye break every yoke." These are solemn, marvelous words assuredly! They have been ringing down through the ages, and still find their echo in our hearts. And yet the justice idea of the prophets is inadequate to serve the purpose of social reconstruction today. To go back to it would mean repristination, not renovation; It is sound as far as it goes, but it does not *go* far enough. It is negative, rather than positive; it is based on the idea of non-violation. What we require today is a positive conception, and this implies a positive definition of that holy thing in man that is to be treated as inviolable. To the mind of the prophets justice meant chiefly resistance to oppression, since oppression is the most palpable exemplification of the forbidden violation. The prophets in their outlook on the external relations of their people stood for the weak, the oppressed, against the strong, the oppressor. They stood for their own weak little nation, the Belgium of those days, against the two over-mighty empires, Egypt and Assyria, that bordered it on either side. In the internal affairs of Israel they espoused the cause of the weak against the rich and strong: "Woe unto them that add house to house and field to field, that grind the faces of the poor." Ever and ever again the same note resounds, the same intense, passionately indignant feeling against violation in the form of oppression. But this aspect of justice, as I have said, is the negative aspect,—inestimably important, but insufficient. Where oppression does not occur, have the claims of justice ceased? Is there not something even greater than mere non-infringement, greater than mercifulness or kindness, which in justice we owe to the personality of our fellows, namely, to aid in the development of their personality? Righteousness, yes, by all means,—but does the righteousness of the prophets of Israel exhaust or begin to exhaust the content of that vast idea?

The universalistic ethical idea in the Hebrew religion is bound up with and bound down by racial restrictions. The issue between monotheism and trinitarianism is no longer a vital issue of our day. The Father image as the symbol of Deity raises expectations which experience does not confirm. The ideal of social justice as conceived by the prophets of Israel is a valid but incomplete expression of what is implied in social justice. These are weighty considerations that make it difficult to retain the belief in the elect character attributed to the people of Israel. There is one other, of very deep-reaching importance, that must be noticed. An elect people is supposed to be an exemplary people, one that sets a moral example which other nations are expected to copy. But it has become more and more clear to me that the value of example in the moral life has been overestimated and misunderstood. No individual, for instance, can really serve as an example to others so as to be copied by them. The circumstances are always somewhat different, the natures are different, and the obligations, finely examined, are never quite the same. In fact, the best that anyone can do for another by his example is to stimulate him to express with consummate fidelity his different nature in his own different way. I do not of course deny that there are certain uniformities, chiefly negative, in moral conduct, but I have come to think that the ethical quality of moral acts consists in the points in which they differ rather than in those in which they agree. The ideally ethical act, to my mind, is the most completely individualized act.

And what is true of individuals is no less true of peoples. No people can really be exemplary for other peoples, and in this sense elect. Every people possesses a character of its own to which it is to give expression in ways which I shall indicate in the last part of this work. But the way rightly adopted by one nation cannot be a law or a model for its sister nations. If the ideal of the modern Zionists were realized, if the Jews were to return to Palestine, to speak once more the language of the Bible, to cultivate their distinctive gifts, they would not therefore produce a pattern which could be copied in Japan, or among the 400 millions of China, or in the United States, or among the Slavic or Latin peoples.

In concluding these reflections, I may not conceal from myself or from others that the objection to the

24

function of exemplariness, if sustained, affects at the root both the theology and the ethics of the past. If no individual can be in the strict sense an example to others, neither can an individual Deity be an example to be copied by men, neither can Christ be the perfect exemplar to be imitated. There can be no single perfect exemplar. Virtues that bear the same name are not therefore the same virtues. Often it is only the name that is the same, not the substance; and where they are in a broad way the same, yet there remains a difference of accent. The natures of men are unlike. Their moral destiny is to work out the unlikeness of each in harmony with that of the others. The moral equivalence of men, rather than their moral equality, is for me the expression of the fundamental moral relation.[5]

At the early stage of my career to which I am still

[5] Of many ethical types of behavior no examples whatever as yet exist, for instance, of the ethically-minded employer or merchant, ethically-minded in thought and in practice. The standard of ethical behavior which we apply is at present higher and more exacting. The standard itself indeed is in process of being defined, and there are no illustrations of it, or none but very imperfect ones, on which to dwell with satisfaction. But the same is true of other vocations. We are very thankful for any examples that can be found. They seem to prove that that which ought to be can be. But we may not lean on them too hard. They are never quite adequate, even in their limited sphere; and there is ever an Ought-to-be beyond that which has been even partially realized, beyond that which has even as yet been conceived. To make too much of example is to check moral progress. Along with a due appreciation of past moral achievements, there should be encouraged a spirit of brave adventure, a certain intrepidity of soul to venture forth on voyages of discovery into unknown ethical regions, taking the risks but bent upon the prize.

adverting it was urgently put to me that with all the changes that had taken place in my inner life, I need not separate myself from the religion of the Fathers, nay, that I might remain a servant and teacher of religion within the Jewish fold, gradually weaning away from the beliefs which they held those whom I might contrive to influence, and drawing them up— such was the phrase used—to my own "higher level." But this advice was repelled by every inmost fibre of my being, and could not but be utterly rejected. I was to publicly represent a certain belief with the purpose of undermining it. I was to trade upon the simplicity of my hearers in order to rob them of what they, crudely and mistakenly perhaps, considered their most sacred truth, by feigning provisionally, until I could alter their views, to be in agreement with them. Would this be fair to them or to myself? Was I to act a lie in order to teach the truth? There was especially one passage in the Sabbath service which brought me to the point of resolution: I mean the words spoken by the officiating minister as he holds up the Pentateuch scroll, "And this is the Law which Moses set before the people of Israel." I had lately returned from abroad where I had had a fairly thorough course in Biblical exegesis, and had become convinced that the Mosaic religion is so to speak a religious mosaic, and that there is hardly a single stone in it which can with certainty^ be traced to the authorship of Moses. Was I to repeat these words? It was impossible. I was certain that they would stick in my throat. On these grounds the separation was decided on by me, and became irremediable.

CHAPTER III

EMERSON

I FIND on looking backward that my development proceeded with the help of a series of definitions fixing my attitude toward teachers who made a special appeal to me, and toward great historic tendencies past and present. I was helped both by what I was able to appreciate in them, and, where I diverged, by what they forced me to think out for myself. Here let me acknowledge a passing debt to Emerson. As in the case of Kant, a strong attraction drew me toward Emerson with temporary disregard of radical differences, —although the spell was never so potent or so persistent in the latter instance as in the former. I made Emerson's acquaintance in 1875. I came into touch with the Emerson circle and read and re-read the *Essays*. The value of Emerson's teaching to me at that time consisted in the exalted view he takes of the self. Divinity as an object of extraneous worship for me had vanished. Emerson taught that immediate experience of the divine power in self may take the place of worship. His doctrine of self-reliance also was bracing to a youth just setting out to challenge prevailing opinions and to urge plans of transformation upon the community in which he worked. But I soon discovered that Emerson overstresses self-affirmation at the expense of service.

For a time indeed I reconciled in my own fashion the two contrary tendencies. The divine power, I argued, flows through me as a channel—hence the grandeur which attaches to my spiritual nature. But the divine power manifests itself in redressing the wrongs that exist in the world, and in putting an end to such violations of personality as the sexual and economic exploitations which disgrace human society. So for a time I continued to walk on air with Emerson, and had my head in the clouds,—the clouds in which Emerson enveloped me.

Out of this false sense of security, this quasi-pantheistic self-affirmation, the experiences of the next few years effectually roused me. I came to see that Emerson's pantheism in effect spoils his ethics. Be thyself, he says, not a counterfeit or imitation of someone else. Be different. But why! Because the One manifests itself in endless variety. Penetrating below the surface, however, one finds that in this kind of philosophy the value of difference, to which I attach essential importance on ethical grounds, is nothing more than that of a foil. According to Emerson life is a universal masquerade, and the interest of the whole business of living consists in the ever-renewed discovery that the face behind the different masks is still the same. Difference is not cherished on its own account. And here, as in the case of the uniformity principle of Hebraism, I found myself dissenting.

Emerson is a kind of eagle, circling high up in the ether—*non soli cedit.*

Emerson with his oracular sayings might have served

as a priest at Dodona or led the mysteries at Eleusis. Yet, withal, he is genuinely American,—a rare blend of ancient mystic and modern Yankee,—a valued poet too, but as an ethical guide to be accepted only with large reservations.

CHAPTER IV

THE TEACHINGS OF JESUS

AT about this time I began to occupy myself more
seriously than I had done before, with the study of the
New Testament. I had, I think a great advantage in
my approach to it, for the very reason that I had not
been brought up in the Christian tradition. I came
from the outside, with a mind fresh to receive first-hand
impressions. I had not had instilled into me from
childhood the kind of hesitant awe that prevents impartial appraisement of excellences and of possible deficiencies. On the other hand, as a searcher I was
deeply interested to ascertain what Christianity could
give me, and to what extent it could further my spiritual development. I had not the enforcedly apologetic
attitude; I did not come prepared to accept without
question nor yet to find fault; I came to test for my own
use. Here am I, with life and its problem before me—
how can the teachings of Jesus help me in my search,
in my dire perplexities?

I must say to begin with that I was particularly
struck with the originality of Jesus' teachings, a quality
in them which to my amazement I had found disputed,
not only by Jews, but by representative Christians. In
Jewish circles it is not uncommon to speak almost con-
descendingly of Christianity as of a daughter religion

commissioned to spread abroad the truths of Judaism, with such alloy as may be needed to suit them to the apprehension of the gentiles. But Christian teachers likewise—I remember particularly a recent sermon to that effect—have taken the ground that Jesus added nothing new to the ethical insight of mankind. His work, it is said, consisted merely in supplying a sufficient motive for performing the duties which everyone knows, but which, lacking this motive, we are supposedly impotent to practice. This strange misapprehension of the intimate nature of Jesus' contribution to ethical progress is largely due, I take it, to the poverty of our moral vocabulary. Language puts at our disposal only a few terms, such as Justice, Righteousness, Love,—which must needs stand for a great variety of moral ideas. Thus Justice in Plato's use of the word, implies that "a shoemaker shall stick to his last," that those who perform the humble functions shall be content to perform them in due subservience to their superiors. A very different meaning was attached to justice by the Hebrew prophets as I have explained in the last chapter. Again, a quite different conception of justice is framed and stressed by modern social reformers. Now it is this ambiguity of the moral vocabulary that conceals the novelty of Jesus' precepts. Thus, to mention only a single capital instance, it has been asserted that the Golden Rule as taught by Jesus is not original, but substantially the same rule that had been laid down by Confucius 500 years before the time of Jesus. But on closer scrutiny it will be seen that the two Golden Rules are by no means the same. As propounded by the Chinese sage the rule appears to mean: Keep the balance true between thyself and thy neighbor; illustrate in thy conduct the principle of equilibrium. As impressed upon his disciples by Jesus it means: Look upon thy neighbor as thy other self; act towards him as if thou wert he.

To return to my point, the impression of novelty which I received in reading the Gospels was definite and striking. The mythological idealization of Jesus, indeed, I put aside as a thing that did not concern me. On the other hand, to say with certain modern liberals that he was just a man, an infinitely gracious personality, one who exemplified in his life the virtues of forgiveness and self-sacrifice, did not satisfy me either. Buddha too had taught forgiveness: "For hatred is not conquered by hatred at any time; hatred is conquered by love." It could not then be the bare precept of forgiveness that lets light on the secret of Jesus. And self-sacrifice—"Greater love hath no man than this, that he should lay down his life for his friend"—had been practiced within and without the pale of Hebraism.

That he continued the work of his Hebrew predecessors I made no doubt. On the Hebrew side he was a prophet, or rather, a saint in Israel. But I had just as little doubt that he took a step beyond his predecessors, that his teachings bear upon them the signature of originality.

To put my thought briefly, I came to conclude that the ethical originality of Jesus consists in a new way of dealing with the problem of evil, that is, of evil in the guise of oppression. The prophets, his predecessors, as we have seen, identified injustice with oppression; and in the first flush of their moral enthusiasm the more optimistic among them believed that justice as they conceived of it would presently triumph and that oppression would cease altogether—"Arise, shine, for thy light is come." God would miraculously interfere, and bring about on earth a state of righteousness. But years and centuries passed by, and oppression, far from ceasing, became under the ruthless administration of Rome ever more grinding and terrible. The yoke of Rome weighed upon the Jews as it did upon other peoples ; but perhaps, because they were more independent in spirit, it galled them more sorely. The fiery zealots among the Jews persisted in hoping that by supreme desperate efforts, God coming to their aid, they might yet succeed in shaking off this yoke—efforts which culminated in the horrors of the last siege of Jerusalem. Jesus was not of their way of thinking. He seems indeed to have believed that the end of the existing order, was near. It was too incredibly bad to last. The world would be consumed by fire. A new earth and a new heaven would appear. But in the meantime how accommodate oneself to the intolerable fact of oppression? Jesus said, Resist not evil in the guise of oppression, it is irresistible. He mentions in particular three forms of intolerable oppression: a blow in the face, the stripping of a man of his garment, and the coercing him to do the arbitrary bidding of another. He says, Resist not evil, resist not oppression. Shall then evil triumph? Is the victim helplessly at the mercy of the injurer? Shall he even be told that in a servile spirit he must accept the indignities that are put upon him? No; this is not the meaning. Quite a different meaning is implied. And here the teaching of Jesus takes its novel turn. There is a way, he says to the victim, in which you can spiritually triumph over the evil-doer, and make your peace with irresistible oppression. Use it as a means of self-purification; pause to consider what the inner motives are that lead your enemy, and others like *him, to do* such acts as they are guilty of, and to so violate your personality and that of others. The motives *in them* are lust, greed, anger, wilfulness, pride. Now turn your gaze inward upon yourself, look into your own heart and learn, perhaps to your amazement, that the same evil streams trickle through you; that you, too, are subject, even if it is only subconsciously and incipiently, to the same appetites, passions, and pride, that animate your injurers. Therefore let the sufferings you endure at the hands of those who allow these bad impulses free rein in their treatment of you lead you to expel the same bad impulses that stir potentially in your breast; let this experience fill you with a deeper horror of the evil, and prove the incentive to secure your own emancipation from its control. In this way you will achieve a real triumph over your enemy, and will be able to make your peace with oppression. There' are other intolerable evils in the world besides oppression which nevertheless must be tolerated. The method of Jesus can be applied to these also. This method I regard as a permanent contribution to the ethical progress of humanity.

A second original trait in Jesus' teaching I found in

his conception of the spiritual nature, and of his doctrine of love as dependent on that conception. The conception or definition is still negative as in the non-violation ethics of the Hebrew prophets. The spiritual element in man is hidden. It cannot be apprehended as to what it is substantively. The attributes ascribed to it are the effects in which it manifests itself; this goes without saying. To define the spiritual nature means to describe these effects, these manifestations. According to the Hebrew predecessors of Jesus the spiritual power is to be conceived of as that which prompts a man to respect the holy precinct of personality in others and in himself. What the holy thing is remains unknown. This view leads to acts of justice and mercy, as above explained. According to Jesus the spiritual essence in man bids him expel the inner, impure impulses that lead to external violations. In brief, the spiritual power is conceived of in terms of purity. It is the pure thing in man that thrusts out as alien to itself whatever is impure—whatever is of the world, the flesh, and, in mythological language, whatever is Satanic. In this sense I say that the definition is negative. It marks out, indeed, a definite line of conduct; and it even leads, as we shall presently see, to active efforts in a specific direction. A negative principle may have certain positive results. But in the main, nevertheless, the teaching of Jesus enlightens us as to what shall not be rather than as to what shall be. From the Hebrew prophets we learn that there shall not be violation of personality or injustice, the positive concomitant being mercy; from Jesus' teachings we learn that there shall not be impurity in the inner forum, the positive by-product being the doctrine of love.

Taking over the Hebrew heritage, Jesus affirmed that the spiritual nature exists in all human beings. In every man there is presumed to be this inner power to reject the unclean admixtures, to ward off and repel the carnal solicitations, to withdraw from the "world," and to move upward toward the source of purity, which is God. The spirituality of man consisting of purity, the Father-God, the Father of Lights, is likewise conceived as the absolutely pure, in this sense as the most holy. In every man there is a ray of the eternal light emanating from the eternal luminary, and all men are one in so far as their rays converge at the focus of Godhead. To love men is to be conscious of one's unity with them in the central life, and to give effect to this consciousness. Hence Christian love, the love that Jesus taught, is no earthly love, no mere sentiment, or outreaching of the human affections. On the contrary, the natural human ties are repeatedly set aside in the *logia*. To love another is to love him in God. Later the current phrase became, to love him in Christ; that is, to think of him, and act towards him, as if he possessed the same capacity for purity with oneself.

The love of others in God or Christ encouraged a particular kind of earthly beneficence, and it especially inspired the followers of Jesus with an unparalleled zeal in works of remedial (though never of preventive) charity. This may at first sight seem paradoxical. The young man is advised to dispossess himself of all he has, and in the same breath is told to distribute his possessions among the poor. Why not rather scatter them to the winds? Why should not the poor too cease to toil and spin and take heed for the morrow? For their simple necessities God would provide. The two-fold attitude, however, is easy to understand if we remember that certain acts of helpfulness have a symbolic significance, as attesting the value we set upon the person to whose needs we minister, much as a flower offered to a beloved person emblematically intimates our sense of the beauty and worth of the one to whom the tribute is' offered. Christian charity, on its earthly side, has a similar meaning and purpose. It is intended to efface the indignity to which human beings are subjected when reduced to extreme indigence or allowed to suffer without relief, for it is the disdain of the spiritual personality thus evinced which Jesus disallows. He bids his followers intimate by earthly tokens their consciousness of the super-earthly worth of their fellow-beings. But the pursuit of riches as such he nowhere encourages —quite the contrary. And it is certainly a mistake to represent Jesus, as has recently been done, as a kind of precursor of modern Socialism, and to think of him as one who, if he had lived in our time, would have laid stress on equality of opportunity for all to gain earthly possessions. He who advocated wealth for none could not be supposed to have sympathized with a social movement whose first object it is to secure wealth for all.

It is this interpretation of love that helped me to understand the interior meaning of the doctrine of the forgiveness of enemies as taught by Jesus, and to perceive wherein it differs from the apparently identical mode of behavior enjoined by Buddha and the Stoic Seneca. It plays a capital role in Jesus' teaching. As illustrated by the proto-martyr Stephen it probably effected the conversion of Paul. Jesus says: "Bless them that curse you." But how is it possible to bless those that curse us? How, for instance, was it possible for Stephen to bless the men of blood at the very moment when they were crushing him under stones? To bless them that curse you, to bless them that despitefully use you, means to distinguish between the spiritual possibilities latent in them and their overt conduct, to see the human, the potentially divine face behind the horrible mask, and to invoke the influence of the divine power upon them in order that it may change them into their purer, better selves.

With complete and eager appreciation of the points of excellence contained in these teachings, with a reverence which it is impossible to express in words for their incomparable Author, and with a large sense of the beneficent influence which they have exercised on human history, I still could not avoid the question, so vital for me, Have these ethical teachings of the great Master the stamp of finality upon them? Has Jesus really spoken the last word in ethics? Is nothing left for us but further to expand and apply the truth which he laid down once and for all? When theology goes, the last stand of apologetic writers is apt to be made on the ethics. The instinct to claim finality for the religion in which one has been brought up asserts itself in the claim that the moral teachings at least are unexceptionable and valid for all time to come. The searcher who is in great moral perplexities and who seeks help for others and himself, is bound to ask and will ask in no captious spirit, is this so?

The decisive point is whether the ethical teachings of Jesus supply a principle which enables us to work with zest in the world, to take the keenest interest in all the manifold activities of human society, to embrace the world with the view of penetrating it with a spiritual purpose and of thus transforming it. Do these teachings exhibit a way of making the world and the flesh instrumental to the spirit, or do they serve to turn us away from the world and its interests, to abandon the world in despair? Is the conception of spirituality as purity adequate? Purity is certainly one aspect of morality; is it the sole or the principal factor in it? The other-worldly attitude in the Gospels is certainly clearly marked. It is the background on which the ethical precepts stand forth. Tyrrel has argued as against Harnack for the close connection between the thought of Jesus and the apocalyptic vision. I asked myself, Can the apocalyptic vision, that is to say the other-worldliness, be dissociated from the ethics, or is the relation between them necessary?[1] If the world is speedily, almost immediately, coming to an end, then it is justifiable to prefer celibacy to marriage, to ignore the state, to counsel disregard of the toiling and the

[1] am aware that a highly esteemed school of modern theologians maintain that the apocalyptic element is a secondary and even an embarrassing feature for Jesus. But I am unable to convince myself of the justice of this view.

39

spinning. All of this is warranted on the assumption that the order of things in which these institutions and activities have their place is about to disappear.

But if this expectation is deceived, if things continue in their ancient course, if the world and the flesh persist, taking on ever new and more baffling shapes, how is a system of ethics which is based on the assumption of one state of things to be reconciled with a state of things exactly the opposite? How shall an ethical person conduct himself in a world which his philosophy of life teaches him to reject, but with which the necessities of his existence compel him to come to terms day by day and hour by hour? There must then be compromise. And the history of Christianity up to the present moment is the record of such compromises. Monasticism was one of the earliest. A distinction was made, so to speak, between perfect and imperfect Christians, between a class of men and women who lived in ascetic seclusion, as if the world did not exist, and another class, the greater number, who managed ethically as best they could, dependent on the supererogatory merits of the real Christians or saints to eke out their unholiness. Another species of compromise is illustrated, especially in Protestant countries. It appears as a division between the contracted sphere of holiness and the circumambient sphere of the practical life, in both of which, however, the same individual has his place. Chastity, forgiveness of personal enemies, and the like virtues are to be practiced in the contracted sphere of private life, the ability to practice these virtues being derived from mystical identification with Jesus. In the Christian's public life no such identification is possible, and he is left to be consciously or unconsciously unholy. As a politician, as a competitor in the struggle for wealth, he remains without ethical direction. The ethical ideal of the Gospels requires for its setting the apocalyptic vision. It derives its cogency from the belief that the world is about to perish. Can it serve as a sufficient guide to those who must live in the world, and affirm their ethical personality in dealing with it? In politics, in business, in science, in art, must .we not somehow see our way to the conception that these great interests are not alien to the spiritual nature, introducing perchance impure admixtures into it, but rather can be made subservient or instrumental to it? Yes; but instrumental in what way? At this point, not only the Christian system, but every one of the systems of ethics that have arisen since then has failed. And it is, moreover, perfectly evident that the instrumental function of the sex relation or of the pursuit of knowledge or of patriotism cannot be' determined unless we first answer the one question which the ethical writers are in the habit of evading—Instrumental to what end? What is the ethical end? Instruments are means to ends—how can the means be rightly appraised without a definite conception of the end ? And if the end be the affirmation of our ethical personality, of our spiritual nature, of that holy thing in us without which man loses his worth (and without which the rule of nonviolation itself falls to the ground, since where there is nothing inviolable there can be no infringement), it is plain that we must seek a positive definition of the spiritual nature which shall serve as a principle of regulation where the empty concept of purity has manifestly failed.

Christian ethics has promoted the moral development of mankind in a thousand ways. It has helped even by its mythological embodiment of a transcendental idea to place the individual more firmly on his feet. It has emphasized the inner springs of conduct; it has given prominence to certain principal virtues of the private life; but, like every product of the mind and aspirations of man, it exhibits the limitations of the time and of the social conditions under which it arose. The conditions have since changed. Society has become infinitely more complex, and in consequence new moral problems have forced themselves upon men's attention; and with the help of Christianity itself the human race has advanced beyond the point of view for which Christianity stands.[2]

Speaking again only for myself I could not assent to the position that finality appertains to the ethical teachings of the Gospel, that they or their Author have spoken the last word in ethics. I could not persuade myself that this is so because I failed to get from these teachings, inestimably precious as they are, an answer to the question that most pressed upon me—Instrumental in what sense, instrumental to what end?

[2] See the similes used in the previous chapter on the growth of the tree as manifested in the putting forth of a new branch, and the ascent of an eminence which includes the part of the spiritual landscape previously seen, but also that part which from the previous station was excluded.

CHAPTER V

SOCIAL REFORM

MY position at that time may be summarized as follows.: There is a divine power in the world, not individual, manifest in the moral law as revealed in human experience. The moral law involves recognition of the presence of a something holy in each human being. Since the world presents innumerable examples of the grossest violation of human personality (e.g., prostitution and exploitation of laborers), the business immediately in hand is to make an end of these violations. There was as yet in my mind no positive definition of personality. Clarification and further development were promoted by the necessity of grappling with the problems of poverty and with the attempted solutions of the Socialists and of other social reformers. At this period, the notion of personality in my mind being still without determinate content, empirical matter intruded, and a species of millennialism for a time vitiated my thinking. In order to set up a goal for humanity, I dallied with Utopias, and flattered my imagination with the vision of something like a state of ultimate earthly felicity. The cheap cry of "Let us have heaven on earth" was also on my lips, though the delusion did not last long and perhaps never penetrated very deeply.

The problem of poverty, as mentioned above, engrossed me early. I acted as chairman of the meeting at which Henry George was first introduced to the public in New York City. But Henry George's remedy,—a single draught of Socialism with unstinted individualism thereafter—never attracted me, while his descriptions of the misery of the poor, eloquent as they were, and fitted to awaken persons unacquainted with actual conditions, conveyed to me no novel message. I had before then been profoundly stirred by the chapters in Karl Marx's *Kapital* in which he collects from the English Blue Books frightful evidence of the mistreatment of laborers and especially of children in the early part of the nineteenth century. My errands in the tenement slums of New York had also made me fairly familiar with the bitter facts, and throughout my life I have been in touch in a practical way with the appalling complexus of misery and wrong which we abstractly designate as the Labor Question. I shall not here take time to discuss Socialism or other social reform movements in detail. My intention is to sketch a certain philosophy of life, and to trace the steps by which I reached it. My reaction against Socialism and related movements, however, was a prime factor in this inner development; and it is of this reaction and the causes of it that I must speak.

The evils inherent in poverty are, in the first place, obviously, the privations entailed by it; secondly, the fact that the greater part of the life of the poor is consumed in efforts to provide the bare necessaries, the mind being thus kept in bondage to bodily needs and prevented from rising to other interests more appropriate to rational beings; thirdly, the fact that the first two wrongs are caused, not wholly it is true, but yet in a large measure, by fellow human beings.[1] The sting in poverty is not so much the hardships suffered, as the contempt for the manhood of the poor, exhibited by their exploiters,—the inequity being thus turned into iniquity.

Now my reaction against Socialism was and is that it neglects the third, the moral evil, and stresses only the first and second. I am now speaking of Marxian Socialism, with which in its rigid form I early acquainted myself. The Marxian Socialist does not deny the pain felt in consequence of the inequity, nor the desire of those who suffer to become the equals of their masters; but he regards this desire as a fact of nature explicable on deterministic grounds, a consequence of improvement in the technique or tools of industry. He does not deny that there are so-called moral ideas, but he considers them epiphenomena or by-products of economic development. The tendency toward equilibrium of power in human society, termed democracy, is to him just a fact and nothing more. The mere desire for it

---

[1] I say *caused*, but perhaps not deliberately intended, although there are instances of the latter. An act is diabolical when maliciously designed to inflict a wrong on another; as rape for the purpose of dishonoring a family. It is cruelly selfish but not fiendish when it springs from scorn of others as if they were only fractional human beings. The Brahmin's attitude towards the lower castes, the attitude of the feudal lord toward the serf, of Shakespeare's nobility toward the common citizens, and of some modern theorists toward the democratic multitude, are instances in point. In such cases the moral sense itself is astray, but there is perhaps no deliberate sinning against the light.

45

apart from the rightness of the desire is the efficient cause which leads to social readjustments. But evidently this account of the matter will be persuasive only in case the efficient cause proves to be really efficient, that is to say, in case the desire for equilibration is on the point of effectuating itself. If it is not, if the desire of the masses for power is thwarted, if the realization of their hopes is indefinitely postponed, then the foundations of the theory are undermined. Hence Marxian Socialism has been coupled with and depends on a belief which is a kind of materialistic parallel of the apocalyptic vision of Jesus,—the belief that the end of the present world (the world of the wage system) is close at hand, only with the difference that the end is to be brought about not by divine interference but automatically by the acquisition of power on the part of the masses.

To me neither hunger nor the bondage of the mind to physical necessities nor the bare fact of inequity seem sufficient to justify the demand for social reconstruction, apart from moral right. If there be no such thing as morality, or if morality be but an epiphenomenon of economic conditions, what warrant have the hungry or the disadvantaged for complaining? Animals, too, hunger and sicken. If man be like them a mere chance product of nature, why should he not share their fate? Let the weak succumb! Surely the bald fact that the democratic masses today chafe under the yoke of their masters and demand a better state of things, is no *more* a ground of obligation for the former than the tendency toward an ultimate equilibrium in nature of which scientists speak can be a ground of obligation. The tendency will effectuate itself or not as the acting forces determine. There is in truth no such thing as obligation from this point of view. Then why not fold our arms and wait for what will happen? The notion of democracy currently held is obnoxious to the same criticism. Leave out the moral basis in the claim to equity, and nothing remains but the brute fact that men, being egotists, fret under the exercise of superior power by their fellow egotists. But let Nietzsche or some one else demonstrate that certain higher values, higher merely because subjectively relished as higher, are incompatible with equilibrium of power, and he will be justified at least in his own eyes in scoffing at equality and scourging the democratic dogs back to their kennels. No one denies that the masses have the desire to be treated as the equals of their masters (very inconveniently for the latter), but it is quite another matter whether their desire ought to be gratified. Social reconstruction, in other words, must be motivated by other considerations than those by which according to Marx the great change is to come about.

I have not stopped to consider whether the Socialistic scheme is workable, whether the run of mankind are capable of cooperative effort on a large scale without the preeminent leadership of master minds; whether Socialism, if carried out, would really breed, as it is expected to, the sentiment of ideal brotherhood; whether the sentiment of brotherhood itself, unless it be rooted in the closer family and national ties, is morally sound, whether the emotional forces that sweep through and overwhelm large aggregations of men, can he bridled and sufficiently enlightened to promote the ends of Socialism. All such questions as these touch the feasibility of the ideal proposed; my own reaction was and is against the ideal *itself.* Instead of pronouncing as some do that mankind are not yet ripe to carry out so high an ideal, I found myself seriously challenging and finally rejecting the very ideal on the ground that it is not a genuine moral ideal at all. It is ethically spurious, because it omits the notion of right and substitutes for it that of power.

A different objection lies against certain modifications of Socialism and against many of the social reform movements of our time. In these movements the idea of personality is not absent as in Marx's theory. The inherent dignity of every human being is deeply felt, and *per contra* the indignity of the present condition of the greater number. Man is worth while; and for the sake of the worth in him, the unfavorable circumstances which stifle the promise of his nature are to be changed. My objection in this case is that the higher spiritual nature of man, or the notion of personality, is left indefinite and remains vaguely in the background. It supplies indeed the initial motive for practical efforts; but the instrumental relation of the goods of life to the supreme good is not apprehended positively. And thus the door is left open, as we shall presently see, for corrupting influences to enter in.

There seems, it is true, at first sight, considerable warrant for demanding certain instant reforms without troubling about ulterior spiritual ends. We are confronted in modern society with evils which seem to require immediate abolition. Exploitation is palpably one of them. It is the clearest possible case of trespass on personality. Why not then demand respect simply for personality in general, without inquiring into the nature of personality ? Is it not beyond all question dishonoring to human nature that some should be on the verge of starvation while others are even themselves injured by excessive possessions; that the energies of children should be exhausted by premature toil; that adults should be worked like beasts of burden? Why not leave in abeyance the definition of the supreme end, and concentrate effort on the removal of these incontestable evils ?

My answer to this is, in the first place, that we cannot gain the best leverage even for these initial reforms without a high and defined conception of man as a spiritual being. Efforts directed toward improving even material conditions are apt to be fluctuating, spasmodic, and are ever in danger of dying down, unless material improvement is seen in its relation towards something else that commands the highest respect—implicit respect. Sympathy alone is altogether inadequate. It often works grave harm; it is notoriously intermittent, at one time broadly expansive and then again contracting upon the nearest objects. Furthermore, we can at best sympathize genuinely with only a very limited number of persons. If anyone were to open his heart to the sufferings of all the millions of human beings at present engaged in conflict on the battlefields of Europe; if he were to try to realize the indirect consequences of this war; if he were to take a still wider sweep and embrace in his imagination the populations of India, China, and the races of Africa, the effect upon him would be simply paralyzing. The possible effect of one's sympathetic action upon this huge volume of human suffering would appear so insignificant as to make exertion on his part seem quite irrational. We are assisted by sympathy in the matter of social reform by the narrowness of our horizons; and even within these narrow boundaries the efficiency of the motive depends largely upon the transciency of the sympathetic mood. Sympathy as a permanent attitude would disintegrate the self.[2]

The second answer is that by ignoring the ultimate end we *install proximate ends in its place.* The reform movements of our day abstain from attempting to set up an ultimate good. They are content, as they say, "to evaluate the tangible goods ready at hand." In consequence these tangible goods inevitably usurp the place of the supreme good. Begin as we may with the high notion of personality, we become materialists before we have proceeded very far, and we infect the laboring masses with our materialism if we omit to define the relation of proximate ends to the ultimate aim. For remember that the ultimate end is that which prescribes the limits within which the nearer aims are to be sanctioned,—the limit for each being the degree in which it conduces toward the highest end. Without a goal set

[2] I have not touched upon the further question to what extent we can really compass the happiness, except at rare moments, even of a single human being. The altruistic philosophy is apt to confound the removal of manifest evils with positive benefaction. But the removal of one kind of evil lets in new kinds; and wherein then consists the gain so far as happiness is concerned?

up, without an explicit conception of its regulative function, the proximate ends abound, and are likely to expand *ad indefinitum*. This is evident, for instance, in the case of wealth-getting. The poor have not enough wealth, the rich have too much. "Let us then redress the balance by at least securing enough for the poor. The necessary limitations we can discuss after they shall have at least reached the limit of sufficiency." But we are thus kindling the desire for wealth; and this desire and its possible gratifications are boundless. It is in the nature of desire to be prolific of new desire, and to aim unceasingly at new satisfactions. First, a decent dwelling, sufficient food, education for the children, are wanted, then luxury, then millions, then multi-millions. Secondary motives take the place of primary ones. Wealth becomes a token; the satisfactions it gives are no longer related to actual wants or needs, but solely to a fantastic desire for preeminence. Has not this been the actual history of many of those who have risen from poverty to great riches? But the same desires are present, though suppressed, unsatisfied, in the masses, who look up to the few with admiration or envy. And suppressed desires are often even more insidiously poisoning, more contaminating in their effects than satisfied desires.

The psychological fact is that human volition as expressed in action is always determined by some end. A means is never adopted without there being some object or purpose in view. Leave out the ultimate aim and the means become themselves the ends. A decent subsistence should be treated as related to the ultimate end,—

a decent living, for example, as a means to fit the worker for the duties of fatherhood and citizenship.

It may again be urged that what has been said is true only of the ambitious minority, and that the masses would be quite content with a decent subsistence if only that much could be assured them. But the prevalence of cheap imitations of luxury among the poor points in the opposite direction. At least in a democratic community, the ambitions of the few are apt to be contagious. And where this is not the case, as in some of the older countries of Europe, a certain sordid Philistinism is apt to manifest itself. The life of the middle class in Europe is without the restless brilliance that characterizes the upward-striving class in America,—is not daringly but meanly materialistic. Redeeming features are, of course, not wanting, yet how anyone can conceive the social ideal as a state of things in which the laboring people shall be raised to the level at present occupied by the "middle class" is difficult for me to understand. Nor is it a sufficient rejoinder to say that the present complexion of the middle class, its narrowness and Philistinism, are due to isolation from the social classes beneath them, and that the broad sentiment of universal fellowship and fraternity, when it shall have come to prevail, will purify the atmosphere on the middle level. I have sufficiently indicated my doubts as to the efficiency and soundness of what is called fraternalism.

In brief, if we are to preserve a man's respect for himself as a moral being, we must find a ground on which he can maintain his self-esteem apart from the material conditions in which he is placed, and in the interval before the desirable material changes can possibly be accomplished. This interval is certain to be long. The betterment of social conditions is sure to be gradual. The slum ought to be abolished immediately, but until it goes we must find a reason to respect the man in the slums even now, and a reason why he should respect himself even now. This reason can only be derived from the spiritual nature of man, from the spiritual end for which he exists; and on this account, above all others, it is indispensable that the spiritual end be defined. How painfully social reformers may be led into error by slighting this consideration is seen in the readiness with which some have subscribed to the amazing opinion that the issue between chastity and dishonor for the working-girl depends ultimately on the amount of her wages.

There are two fallacies that affect the social reform movements of today. The substitution of power for right is one* What I venture to call the fallacy of pro-visionalism is the second. This is the fallacy of the opportunist movements. "Lead the laboring classes pro-* visionally up to the level of sufficiency, or of decent existence, and then we shall see." But man does not act without ends, and unless we define the ultimate end, we give license to the proximate ends. In other words, we simply cannot act provisionally. We cannot ignore our spiritual nature without offending against it. We may start with the idea of serving it, but without explicit definition of it we shall presently find ourselves disgraced in all sorts of idolatries.

What I am trying to show is how I came to perceive

the inadequacy of the non-violation ethics. Its formula is: Admit the existence of personality; do not infringe upon it. In your actions for the good of others, try to abolish the manifest infringements or violations. Since there must be some positive content to the idea of good, accept the material or empirical goods as the provisional content with the general understanding that they are to be instrumental to the higher life but without troubling to define exactly how."

The aberrations to which this view leads on the side of action toward others I have pointed out. A word now as to the injurious effect on self. Of these the following are the most important:

1. The leader in social reform is apt to be regarded by his followers and to think of himself as a kind of savior. It is his sincere intention to save society from some of the glaring evils with which it is afflicted. But if salvation is sought in the betterment of external conditions, the social savior is apt to become the victim of a false sense of moral security. He is likely to be off his guard at the weak points of his own character, and to fall abruptly from high levels into the ditch.

2. The social reformer who adopts the fallacy of provisionalism is apt to be absorbed in the *mechanical* details of his work,—the settlement or the municipal reform society, or the charitable association tend to become highly organized and efficient pieces of machinery. But moral idealism declines in proportion as this kind of efficiency increases,—the salt loses its savor.

3. The social reformer who sets his heart on external changes is apt to become *impatient* to bring about those

changes. For since he attempts to work from without inwardly, and not at the same time from within outwardly, he has nothing to show for his pains unless the desired outward changes are actually effected. In this way may be explained a certain dictatorial manner, a certain arbitrariness sometimes observed in social workers of whose earnestness and devotion there can be no question, the preposterous outcome being that in attempting to carry out plans of reform in a democratic community such reformers offend against the very principle of democracy by over-riding the personality of others.

4. The Social reformer who concentrates his attention on external changes is apt to be ambitious of large results, to measure betterment by statistical standards. Though quality be not overlooked, *quantity* is likely to be over-emphasized.

5. The painful spectacle is sometimes presented of a leader in social movements who *goes to pieces morally in his private relations* (becomes a bad father, a worthless husband, an unscrupulous sponge on his friends, etc.). Absorption in extensive public movements has this danger in it that it often tends to make men neglectful of the nearer duties.

Facts of this kind, which came repeatedly under my observation in the course of years, drove home to my mind the conviction that the provisional method in social reform (the method of working for external changes without definition of the end) is morally perilous, both in its effects on those who are to be benefited, and in its reaction on the character of the reformer himself. I parted company with opportunism in every one of its forms; I became more and more imbued with the belief that no one can really help others who in the effort to do so is not himself morally helped, i.e., whose character is not improved in every respect, who does not become a *better* father, husband, citizen, a more upright man in all his relations in and because of his endeavors to benefit society. I became convinced that the ethical principle must run like a golden thread through the whole of a man's life, in a word, that social reform unless inspired by the spiritual view of it, that is, unless it is made tributary to the spiritual, the total end of life, is not, social reform in any true sense at all.[3]

The fundamental question, therefore, echoed and re-echoed with ever intenser insistence: "What then is the holy thing in others ? What is the supreme end or good to which all the lesser goods should be subordinate and subservient? And what is the holy thing in me?—for I

[8] To ward off the most serious misunderstanding, I must remind every reader of the chapter on Social Reform, as well as on the Hebrew religion and on the ethics of the Gospels, that I am narrating the phases of my own development. I am not attempting to do justice to all that is excellent in those great religions and in these great social movements; I am trying to show at what points, despite those excellences, I myself felt compelled to diverge from them, to push beyond them. In regard to Socialism.I-recognize the immense service it has performed in awakening the conscience of modern society to the sufferings of the working class. And in pointing out the dangers of opportunism, the fallacy of provisionalism,
I am speaking of dangers from which I felt that I must escape, not casting a slur on the noble personalities that have appeared in the field of social reform during my own time and among my friends and acquaintances. Such personalities, because of their inbred fineness, may be immune against tendencies which yet undeniably exist, and which therefore require to be explicitly apprehended.

may not spiritually sacrifice myself. My own highest good must be achievable in agreement with that of others. What definition of the essential end is possible that shall reconcile egoism and altruism-by transforming and transcending them? And if there be such end thinkable and definable, how establish the applicability of this end to empirical man, either in the person of others or in my own?"

I shall have to dwell on this subject at length in the sequel. Here at the outset I cannot forbear expressing my sense of the obliquities, the folly, the meanness, the cruelties which human nature often exhibits on the empirical side when dispassionately contemplated. That there are also finer traits in people, gleams of gold in the quartz, I do not deny. But even in the best exemplars of the race the alloy is not wanting. And it is an open question how far any human being, if his whole make-up and all the circumstances that influenced him be considered, can be called predominantly good, assuming that goodness is a matter of desert and not of chance. How, therefore, a being that to actual, impartial observation reveals himself as so dubiously worth while, can be regarded as possessing the quality of transcendent worth (which seems to be implied in the idea of personality as inviolable and precious) will be the starting point of my inquiry into the philosophical first principle in the second part of this volume.

CHAPTER VI

THE INFLUENCE OF MY VOCATION ON INNER

DEVELOPMENT

THE present chapter deals with my inner development as I believe it to have been furthered by my connection with the Society for Ethical Culture. The functions intrusted to me in this connection were, first, various forms of so-called philanthropic activity. The effects of the experience gathered in them has been described in a preceding chapter; they may be summed up in the formula: littleness in the external results achieved, consciousness of moral danger to self.

Secondly, the ministerial function of offering "edification" in public addresses to Sunday assemblies, the solemnizing of marriages, and the conducting of funeral services,—while in addition a large part of my vocational life consisted in the building up of an educational institution.[1]

The Public Addresses. Edification, or building up, as I understood it, involved the profoundly difficult task of supplying a working philosophy of life without traveling into the field of metaphysics, teaching the practicable counterpart of a connected system of thought concerning the problems of life,—the system being so firmly knit as to make the appropriate feelings and im-

[1] See the published accounts of the Ethical Culture School.

pulses more or less natural to its exponent. In my case, not having fallen heir to such a system, the task of edification became doubly difficult. It meant from the beginning unceasing self-edification, with a view to edifying others.[2] Setting out with a general scheme along Kantian lines, I proceeded to fill in the outline in the course of my public teachings, with the result that the content filled in eventually disrupted the scheme, and compelled a thorough-going reconstruction. The Holiness conception had been my starting point. I never gave it up. I was attracted to Kant because he affirmed it. I broke with him because he does not make good his affirmation.

[1] began with Kantianism, which is predominantly individualistic, and I found that in dealing with the problems of the family, with the labor question, and in the attempt to reach an ideal of democracy beyond the materialistic conception of it which is at present current— I was introducing into my initial sketch elements incompatible with individualism, and necessitating formulation in social terms. And since I retained and stressed the notion of personality, I had to seek a way of interpreting the term Social spiritually, as Kant had undertaken to interpret the term individual spiritually. I certainly could not fall in with Darwinism or other evolutionary interpretations of sociality, inasmuch as they

[2] The word "edification" as commonly used has a sentimental flavor. It does not as a rule convey the idea of constructiveness at all. It frequently suggests a kind of warm, moist, semi-tropical atmosphere for the emotions of the hearer to simmer in. But in its genuine meaning of "building up" it is too valuable a word to lose.

all leave out the concept of inviolable personality, the indefeasible factor in my ethical thinking.

These things are here alluded to in order to emphasize the influence of the public Sunday addresses delivered by me regularly for more than forty years in stimulating, I had almost said forcing, my ethical growth. To care for anyone else enough to make his problem one's own is ever the beginning of one's real ethical development. To care for a group of people in the sense of being challenged to suggest to them ideas and ways of behavior that shall really be of use to them in the storm and stress of life, is the most searching incentive to self-development imaginable. It is more powerful than the desire to get truth for one's own sake. The closet philosopher may be serious enough in his search for truth, and he may succeed in constructing a symmetrical system which at the time seems complete. Will it stand wear and tear? Will it in the bitter moments of his life hold together? If not, he has failed; but then he only is the loser, it is only his ship that has gone down. But the situation is different when a company of people venture with you on the same voyage, and trust to you as in a way their pilot.

The challenge that comes from the expectant eyes of those who are in trouble, of those whose relations to their friends or the members of their family have become tangled, the challenge that comes from the larger public towards which every public speaker has a certain ethical duty—all these challenges press home the question: are the things that you believe true, so true that you may confidently expect them to be confirmed by the experience of those who in some measure depend upon you? Are they genuinely of use?

There is also another kind of challenge that in a way is even more taxing and searching: the silent appeal that comes from those who are spiritually dead, from those who are sunk in sloth or sensuality, or who waste their precious days in the pursuit of trivial, frivolous ends, and from the insensitive consciences of the self-righteous and the self-complacent. In the Bible we read that the prophet Elisha once threw himself on the body of a dead child, in order with his own life to kindle there the life that seemed extinct. In some such way in public addresses, in which it is not the word but the personality behind the word that counts, the speaker is bound to throw himself body and soul, as it were, upon those who are spiritually numbed, and to *enhance the life within himself* in order to stir up life in them. All of which means that the task of edifying others involves continuous efforts at self-edification.

The Solemnizing of Marriages. In solemnizing marriages I had the experience that some of those at which I had officiated ended disastrously,—there had been no real marriage at all. Though such instances were not numerous in my own experience, yet the statistics of divorce prove that the number of unfortunate marriages in this and other countries is very large, and is increasing. What are the foundations of a permanent relation such as would tend to the development of personality in and through marriage? was the question urged upon me. Here is a social tie in which two individuals, and later the offspring, are combined in the closest propinquity.

How can an ethical theory of marriage be reached, that is, a theory dependent on the idea of the joint realization of the highest end of life by the members of the family group? This ethical theory of marriage will be set forth in a subsequent part of this volume. Here I wish again to mark the retroactive effect of the function I was called upon to exercise in the Ethical Society on the development of theory. The most incisive effect of my practical experience, however, was the being compelled to encounter the effect of *frustration*. How reluctant is the natural man to face this fact! How he shrinks, and puts up screens between his face and the head of Medusa! In my earliest marriage addresses I remember how I used to describe the relation as one in which each of the partners receives the cup of happiness at the hands of the other. The second time I performed the ceremony, the bride was the only child of excellent friends, whose life was completely wrapped up in their one daughter. She was a charming young girl, and the bridegroom was a fine-grained person entirely devoted to her. That marriage feast I shall never forget. A little less than a year after, the young wife having died in child-birth, I was called in to speak at her bier. Where, then, was the exchange of happiness? How suddenly had the house of bliss fallen into ruins! A similar experience that touched me even more deeply was that of a friend, the first one among my associates who believed with me in the possibility of a religious society without a dogmatic creed. The course of love in his case had not run smooth. The marriage between himself and the lovely young woman he wedded was the happy culmination of many trials, a haven of peace after storms. Hardly more than two years elapsed when he suddenly developed a fatal form of mental disease, and lingered for ten years in a long, slow, degrading decline. I thus became acquainted with frustration in one of its most woful shapes. I remember how the poor young wife, during those ten years, widow in all but name, sought alleviation in various directions for her intolerable grief. Work to occupy her mind was one; caring for the needs of the poor another. I remember also how futile these devices seemed. She had lived "on the heights"; she must now descend to lower levels; she had had first best, she must now put up with second or third best. Gladly indeed would she have exchanged places with some of the poor women whom she assisted, could she have kept her husband at her side as they had theirs. It was well enough for her to try to alleviate the troubles of these people, but what were their sorrows compared to hers? And to keep the mind occupied by work, what was it at best but a temporary anodyne? When the work was over, in the still, lonely hours of the night, the storm of grief would break with all the greater violence. I had not taught these my friends a really valid spiritual conception of the purpose of marriage: I had failed in that: and when they were in need of it they did not have it to support them. They had looked on marriage as a scene of felicity; they had not been taught to make allowance for the frustration.

I had not made preparation for the palpable frustrations just mentioned, nor yet for others, for the discovery that the beloved person is faulty, that the nimbus of divine personality does not coincide with the character. And especially did the lack of any explicit idea of personality prove fatal in those cases where the frustration is most serious, where real or apparent incompatibilities appear, or where actual degeneration occurs, and the hope of regeneration becomes remote.

Bereavement was the second shape in which the fact of frustration most often came home to me. Hundreds of times I have spoken to people in the moment of the last leave-taking. The usual consolations, aside from those that depend on mythological beliefs, are: Submit to the inevitable; clinch your teeth and face the storms of fate. Remember the debt you owe to the living. There is work that remains for you to do. See to it that you do not by excessive grieving destroy your capacity for work. Instead of indulging in sorrow for your own loss, take upon yourself the sorrows of others. In particular it is uplifting for one who has been more severely afflicted to take upon himself the sorrow of those whose burden is lighter. Be grateful for what you have possessed. Think not so much of what you have lost, as of what you were privileged for a season to call your own. Make the virtues of those who are no longer living a force for good in your own life. Paint the portrait of your friend incessantly. Retouch it. Eliminate what was of merely transient value in him. Remember him in the light of his best qualities, and live so as to be able to endure his purified glance. Or, in the case of those whose lives were stained, seek to expiate their faults in your life. Purify and perpetuate them in this way in yourself. Memory is not a mere passive receptacle, it is rather a creative faculty. Let it play upon the lives that are no longer sensibly present, and thus maintain the connection with them. A friend living across the sea, whom you will never see again, may yet be a living presence for you if you continue by the aid of memory to be in communication with him. In the case of the departed, likewise, their effectual influence may remain none the less real.

These various modes of consolation have each a certain value. To the one last mentioned I attach the greatest value. Bereavement is a challenge for a fresh start in spiritual development. It should not mean putting up with the second best, but reaching out toward first best. The object to be achieved by the ethical teacher on such occasions is to help the bereaved to tie anew the threads that have been sundered, or rather to substitute a more ethereal but firmer tie for the contacts mediated by the senses. But this task of the reweaving of ties, spiritually, not sensibly, depends entirely for its success upon a spiritual conception of personality. And if this be lacking, the attempt is hopeless. Frustration itself must be recognized as partial if it is to lead beyond itself. There must be found in man that which cannot be defeated if the defeat is not to be accepted as final.

A third kind of frustration was brought home to me by the problem of specialization, as it presented itself in the course of my efforts to work out an ethical theory true to the facts of life. To discharge competently my own special function, I saw that I ought to be acquainted with the best ethical thought of the past. This meant an exhaustive study of the philosophical systems of which the ethical thought of the philosophers is the fruit. I ought further to be familiar with the great religions, in which so much of the ethical insight of mankind is incorporated. I ought to acquaint myself with the moral history of mankind in so far as it is accessible, including that of the primitive races. I ought to gain a survey of the variations of moral opinion that have so staggered belief in the possibility of ethical truth. I ought to master at least the general principles of the physical and biological sciences, since it is impossible that the first principles of ethics should not be related to the governing principles that obtain in other departments of knowledge. I ought in addition to master in their ethical aspect the economic and political problems of the present day, as well as the psychology of individual and social life, in order to be able to apply with some degree of competence the directives of ethics to actual conduct. There are in addition other subjects, such as jurisprudence, poetry and the fine arts, that have ultimate relation to ethics, and that may not safely be neglected. Behold, then, the problem of specialism in one of its most appalling forms. For how can any one individual hope to adequately fill out such a programme? And what I have said is but my own personal illustration of a general problem that more and more besets every reflective person in our time. And it is a problem that has direct bearings upon the question of human personality. The personality is not a detached and isolated thing. It is a center that radiates out in every possible direction, and depends for the release of its energy on the influences received in turn from all directions. On the one hand, to have a footing at all in reality one must be a specialist, and the fields of specialism are becoming more and more restricted. To know one thing well is the indispensable condition of the sense of mastery, yes, of self-respect. And yet it seems to be becoming increasingly clear that one cannot really master a single specialty without knowing of other specialties whatsoever is related to one's own. Narrowness, and loss of power, and consequent decay of the special function itself, seems the one alternative. Dilettantism, the other. But again I ask, who can actually fill out such a programme? The frustration of effort thus appears, in its intellectual guise, as one more manifestation of that general fact of frustration which we meet with wherever we turn.[3]

On the side of character the same reflections occur. Unity in the direction of distinctiveness or uniqueness is the end and aim. But instead of unity of character, conflict of inner tendencies, ever-recurrent rupture of provisional harmonies, a duality of self or multiplicity of selves, are the facts attested by one's inner experience. And frustration here, at the core of a man's being, is perhaps more painful and more seemingly contradictory of the very ideal and purpose of ethical development than in any of the forms previously recorded.

The last instance of frustration that I will mention appears in connection with the cosmic relation of our race. The thought of the death of the individual may be

[8] A new conception of culture is needed, based neither on exclusive specialism, nor on the ambition to know everything after the manner of Goethe in his early days, and such a conception of culture must supply the foundation of an educational philosophy.

overcome by the idea of perpetuity in the lives of successors. The death of the human race, its eventual extinction, is capable of no such assured compensation. We are ethical beings, committed to the pursuit of an ideal end, yet the cosmic conditions are such as to make the end unattainable within the limits of a finite world. This unattainableness of the end it is true is the very ground and foundation of the supersensible interpretation of ethical experience. Yet this thought itself can only be made good by a positive interpretation of personality (of the spiritual nature), which we are yet to seek. As viewed empirically, the human generations are but accidents of nature, waves on the sea of life, passing shadows. And viewing ourselves in this manner our self-respect goes to pieces. The idea of obligation vanishes. Man's claim to infinite worth is bitterly mocked. Unless we can reach the spiritual view of life, the frustration of purpose in the large, that is, of humanity as a whole, is final.

These then, summarily stated, are the problems with which an ethical philosophy of life has to deal.

1. How to remedy the belittlement of man, the infinitesimal insignificance of him as a creature of time and space, when compared with the immensities of the world around him—its spatial and temporal immensities. What is man in the presence of these myriads of worlds, of this unending procession of time that he should attribute to himself significance, nay, worth? Is he perhaps an infinitesimal member of an Infinite?—preserving in this way the sense of his littleness, and of the vastness that bears down upon him, and yet maintaining

himself irrefragably at his station, as indispensable to the perfection of the whole.

2. How to discover a way of retaining the connection between man and the lower forms of life that preceded him, not doing violence to the facts which the evolutionists have brought out, and yet at the same time assuring man's spiritual distinction? Does he perhaps possess in his ethical nature a window, so to speak, through which he can catch at least a glimpse of the ultimate reality, of the infinite life which is the real life, behind the picture screen of sea and mountain, plants and animals?

3. How to overcome the various types of frustration mentioned above: frustration on its intellectual side, or the reconciliation of specialist efficiency with breadth and relatedness; frustration on the character side.

Frustration in the social relations, as in marriage, or as in the case of defective children.

Frustration through bereavement, or the privation suffered by the going out of our life of lives with which we are inseparably connected by ethical as well as affectional ties.

Frustration in the attempt to carry out projects of social betterment; on what moral ground to assert the possible moral value of life in the slums today, and at the same time to put forth and to stimulate the most assiduous efforts to abolish the slum; on what grounds to affirm that the best life is possible under the worst conditions, and yet not to cease or for an instant relax the effort to change the conditions.

The problem of how to support and console the wretched multitudes of mankind in the interval that must elapse before the reform of conditions can take real effect; the problem of support and consolation in fatal sickness, on the deathbed, and in the harrowing recollection of irremediable and irrevocable wrong done to others; the problem raised by the prospective extinction, or the possible old age and degeneration before extinction of mankind—all these problems should be taken together, not one, for instance the so-called social problem, accentuated, leaving the rest out of sight. From one peg they all hang, on one cardinal idea they all depend—the idea of personality as positively defined, of the holy thing as not merely inviolable without regard to its content, but inviolable because of a certain positive content. The ascription of worth to man, in this sense, is the fundamental problem of all, and to the full discussion of this we shall turn in the constructive part of the volume which is now to follow.

BOOK II

PHILOSOPHICAL THEORY

CHAPTER I

I begin my statement of the ethical ideal with a critique of Kant. The reason for this is that Kant stands forth preeminent among all philosophers as the one who emphatically asserts that the attribute of inviolability attaches to every human being, in his formula that *every* man is to be treated as an end *per se,* and never to be used as a mere tool by others. The formula as thus worded by him is subject to grave objections which will be dealt with later on. But the grand conception of the moral worthwhileness of all men is specially connected with the name of Kant. Did he succeed, on the basis of his system, in establishing this conception? He seems to make it the corner-stone of his ethics. Is the corner-stone secure?

Referring again to my individual development, I should find it difficult to express how much Kant's *Metaphysik der Sitten* and *Kritik der praktischen Vernunft* at one time meant to me.

The one ethical fact of which I was so to speak perfectly assured, the "inviolability" so often mentioned in previous chapters, is extremely hard to justify to the thinking mind. The empirical school of philosophers scoff at the very notion of it. The practice of the world is a perpetual, painful evidence of small attention paid to it, and even idealistic philosophers from Plato down have found it quite possible to construct quasi-ethical systems based on the idea, not of human equality, but of the inferiority of the greater number. In Kant, however, one encounters an epoch-making philosopher who not only accepts as a fact the idea of inviolability, and of the kind of equality that goes with it, but who undertakes to set it forth in such a manner as to command the assent of the reason. For a long time I believed that he had succeeded in his great enterprise; and it was only after years of discipleship, not indeed without suppressed misgivings, that I began to see that I had been mistaken.

My eyes were opened when I realized certain extremely questionable moral consequences to which his doctrine led him: for instance, his unspeakable theory of marriage, his defense of capital punishment, the stiff individualism of his system, and his failure to establish an instrumental connection between the empirical goods, of wealth, culture, and the like, and the supreme good or supreme end as defined by him. I was forced by these unsound conclusions to ask myself whether the foundations of the system are sound. Surely if it is true of any system of thought, it is true of an ethical system that it must be judged by its fruits. The Kantian system is indeed vastly impressive, and even sublime in some of its aspects. We travel on the road along which Kant leads with a certain sense of exaltation, but when at the end of our journey we find that we have reached a goal at which we cannot consent to abide, it is imperative to inquire whether the point of departure was well taken.

The point of departure in Kant's exposition is the existence in all men of a sense of duty. Moral relations subsist only between moral beings. All men possess a sense of duty,—therefore all men are moral beings, therefore all are morally equal,—therefore no one may be used as a mere tool for the benefit of others, but is to be treated as worth while on his own account. Thus runs the argument.

The sense of duty is the consciousness of being bound to render implicit obedience to a categorical imperative. Our rational nature tells us categorically what is right to do. Our rational nature issues absolute commands. The sense of duty is man's response to them. Kant does not for a moment imply that either he or anyone else has ever adequately obeyed. The moral dignity, the moral equality of men, does not depend on the obedience but on the consciousness of the obligation to obey—on acknowledged subjection to the command. The actual moral performances of some men are certainly better than those of others; but of no one, not even of the best of men, can it be shown that the moral principle in its purity, that is, unadulterated by baser incentives, was ever the actuating motive of his conduct. The different members of the human species differ morally in degree, but are of the same moral kind, being distinguished from the lower animals not because they obey the moral law, but because they recognize the obligation to obey it. This sort of consciousness may be dim in some, but it exists in all. The most brutal murderer is dimly aware of the holy law which he has transgressed.

The great dictum of the universal moral equality of

mankind is thus made to depend on an assumed fact. If this fact can be successfully disputed, the dictum itself is imperilled. It has been disputed, not flippantly, but most seriously, and it is in my opinion obnoxious to fatal objections. I do not indeed believe it possible to establish the negative, to wit, that the sense of duty does not lurk somewhere, is not latent somewhere in the consciousness of persons morally the most obtuse; but I hold it to be impossible to prove the affirmative, to wit, that a sense of duty does exist in all human beings, even in the most degraded. Kant's dictum of equality depends on making good the affirmative proposition, but this he has failed to do.

One circumstance especially which at first sight seems favorable to Kant's contention turns against him. He has been assailed on the ground that his categorical imperative is a fiction, that no such an imperative plays a role in the actual experience of men. On the contrary, the actual experience of men is replete with categorical imperatives. Nothing in the life of man plays a greater role than these imperatives. The danger that threatens Kant's demonstration is due to the number of rival categoricals that compete with his, and from which the one he sets up is not with certainty distinguishable. To put the matter simply, what is called in technical language a categorical imperative is nothing else than a way of acting somehow felt by the individual to be obligatory upon him, whether he likes it or dislikes it. It is a constraint in which he is bound to acquiesce, a public rule of some sort which overrides his private propensities.

Constraints of this sort are numerous. Many of them

no one would think of designating as moral. Some are distinctly antimoral. I will mention a few:—for instance, the rules of behavior derived from the *tabu* notion. Certain kinds of food may not be eaten; certain objects like the Ark of the Covenant in David's time may not be touched.[1] Strict *tabus* obtain in regard to marriage such as the rules of endogamy and exogamy. Certain persons may not even be looked at. A feeling of horror is felt toward those who transgress these rules; and the transgression of them is often considered far more reprehensible than a moral sin. It would evidently be absurd to characterize a Hottentot or a Fiji Islander as the moral equal of a civilized man on the ground that, like the latter, he possesses the sense of duty, consisting in his case of an unquestioning acknowledgment of the categorical imperative of *tabus.*

Gang loyalty is another instance in point. In one of our prisons a certain convict is at present paying the penalty of a crime which was really committed by one of his pals. He could have got off scot free if he had "squealed." But "squealing" is contrary to the honor code of the gang and he preferred to sacrifice his liberty rather than prove recreant to the claims of gang loyalty. There are some writers who hold that this is an instance of morality, genuine as far as it goes, but restricted within too narrow a circle. The fact that it is restricted within too narrow a circle, that fidelity to a few is compatible with violent hostility against the community at large, seems to me to prove that the moral quality is absent. Morality is either universal or nothing. Gang

[1] See II Samuel, VI, 6, 7.

loyalty is a social phenomenon, but not an ethical phenomenon. The distinction between the two terms will be enforced later on. In any event the sense of constraint is manifest. The moral character of the constraint I deny.

Another example of an imperative which is categorical enough but at the same time non-ethical is furnished by Darwin's well-known explanation of the original of conscience. He assumes that certain ways of behaving which our ancestors found to be socially useful, have become registered as it were in our organisms, and constitute a kind of race-consciousness which persists in each individual. This latent consciousness is potent as a tendency, though often not masterful enough to repress the recalcitrant egoistic impulses. A conflict ensues. The deep ingrained tendency makes itself felt. And as social beings we are aware that we ought to side with it. But the egoistic impulses break out on the surface of consciousness and vehemently urge us in the opposite direction. The feeling of obligation, and thereafter of remorse, are the record of the inner struggle. I do not here undertake to discuss at length the truth of Darwin's theory. There are a number of weak spots in it, to which I shall merely allude in passing. First, he speaks of acts found to be socially useful in primitive communities. Is it possible to show that the same or similar acts retain their utility in a developed industrial society like that of the present day? Is not the term "socially useful" extremely vague, and can the notion implied in it be expanded without the assistance of a truly ethical principie?[a] Then again, why should the thing called social utility overawe the individual mind and thwart individual purpose? Why should not the daring egotist affirm his right to he and flourish in the present hour, in the teeth of social utility? It will be said that the claims are insistent, that the tendency is ingrained, that it has become instinctive in him, and that he cannot release himself from the control it exercises over him. But instincts can be weakened and in time extinguished, like the fear of the dark, when the absence of an objective cause is recognized. Why should not the altruistic impulse likewise, by the method of Freudian analysis, if you please, be exposed to the light, and the egotist thereby be enabled to disembarrass himself of the interference of dead ancestors in his life purposes, and to proceed on his way undisturbed by any inward qualms?

These examples serve to illustrate the point with which we are here concerned, namely, that the presence

[2] Primitive communities valued cooperation because it was socially useful. But there are different kinds of cooperation. Which kind shall we of today adopt? The mere idea of cooperation affords no clue. The self-sacrifice of the individual to the whole of which he is a part is socially useful. But on what occasions and to what degree is it useful? Altruism is socially useful. We are to serve others. But what in them shall we serve? Their physical needs, their intellectual needs, all their needs together? Is that humanly possible? Here again an ethical principle is required to define the quality and the limits of the service. The latent race-consciousness of which Darwin speaks affords no light on the ethical problems proper. The concept of social utility, if not valueless, is at best only of subsidiary value in any attempt to solve these problems. So far from reading once and for all the riddle of conscience, Darwin has not read aright the terms of the riddle.

and operation of undoubted constraints does not establish the existence in all men of the sense of duty on which Kant founds universal moral equality. Kant would indeed object that all these so-called constraints or imperatives are hypothetical, and not really categorical. By an hypothetical imperative he understands one in which the command depends upon an "if"—*if* there be invisible spirits such as primitive men imagined, then the rules of *tabu* follow. *If* the safety of the gang is an object of commanding interest, then gang loyalty is obligatory. *If* the preservation and prosperity of human society in general (a society superior to that of ants and of bees indeed but like them a product of nature and not radically distinct from them) be regarded as the supreme end of desire and endeavor, then the rules of social behavior are to be obeyed. But, he would say, none of these objects are fit to rank so high. They all are optional ends. An hypothetical imperative is one in which the end pursued is optional, the imperative extending only to the means. If the end be desired, then it is reasonable, and in so far imperative, that we adopt the means that lead to its attainment. An imperative truly categorical, however, is one in which the obligation extends to the end proposed as well as to the means. It is not left to our inclination to embrace or to refuse the end, it being of such a kind as absolutely to constrain us to accept it.

But if this be so, then in this first part of our criticism we turn upon Kant and declare that he has nowhere given us reason to believe that the acceptance of an absolute end is implied in the kind of constraints to which the generality of men submit. And again if such acceptance cannot be proved, then the universal moral equality of men based by him on the presence in all of the sense of duty disappears, and his lofty ethical structure breaks down at this point.

CHAPTER II

CRITIQUE OF KANT (CONTINUED)

I now proceed to the second point of criticism, which strikes at the heart of Kant's ethics. Man according to Kant is worth while on his own account (an end *per se),* never to be used as a mere tool or thing. He is a person, an object towards whom we are bound to evince absolute respect. Yet Kant immediately goes on to say that there is no object in all the world, neither man nor any other, that is worth while on its own account, that deserves such respect. Kant's views of actual human nature are tinged with somber pessimism. (Compare the chapter on Radical Evil in his *Religion Within the Limits of Pure Reason.)* A strange paradox is thus presented to us. Man is to be accepted as a worth while object, and yet there is no worth while object. How does Kant seek to escape from this predicament? He says, not the man primarily, but something that happens in the man, is supremely significant: certain acts are worth while on their own account, —the agent only in so far as he performs such acts (or, let us add with a sigh, as he tries to perform them) —namely, acts which have as their sole motive respect for universal law. Then he informs us that similar processes occur in other agents, in fellow human beings, or, more precisely, that these others are capable of trying to act as I myself feel bound to try to act. Consider how far fetched is the argument, on what wavering foundations has been placed the ethical pronouncement of human worth and human equality in which our interest is so profoundly engaged. We do wish to be assured of this cardinal truth. No other truth is practically and theoretically of greater importance. As against the iniquitous practices of the world, as against the exploitation of labor, as against the degradation of woman, as against political tyranny whether exercised by kings or by mobs, we raise up for our shield the indefeasible worth of men —not of some men but of all men. And now, behold! the thinker to whom we owe the forcible expression of this truth seems to have left it in the air. I scrutinize my neighbors, and find in their behavior no sure sign of real worth. I fall back on myself and I discover what? The idea of an act which, if I could perform it, would stand on its own merits (would be self-justified). I then find that I am bound to try to perform such acts. I cannot affirm that in a single instance I have ever performed such an act. I next infer—on what tenuous ground has been shown in the last chapter—that my fellow beings have the same inner experience as mine. And it is for this reason that by a circuitous inference I declare them to be worth while objects.

That Kant has formulated a truth of -the utmost importance for mankind (that no man is to be treated as a mere tool), seems to me incontestable. That he has not made good his own proposition is my contention, and that the whole problem must therefore be taken up *de novo*. It will assist us in doing so to expose the flaw in his categorical imperative, or the formal principle of universality and necessity applied to human actions, which in his view imprints upon them the character of absolute rightness.

Note that Kant approaches the problems of ethics from the side of physical science, and with the bias of the physical scientist. The ethical principle he sets up, the bare idea of universal necessity or of law in general, is derived by way of abstraction from the particular laws of nature. It is a physical principle in disguise. To understand Kant's system, it is simply indispensable to keep this point in mind. He was pre-occupied during the major portion of his life with profound speculations on scientific subjects. The title of the *Critique of Pure Reason* might not be inappropriately changed into "A treatise on the fundamental assumptions of science, as handled by Newton and his successors." He was undeniably interested in ethics. His ultimate aim was to clear the way for the confident holding of ethical principles. (See the Preface to the *Critique of Pure Reason.*) But he could not divest himself of the prejudice of his temperament and of his lifelong pursuit. He is not singular in this respect. To borrow the first principle of ethics from some other field is a common and apparently ineradicable error. Mechanics, aesthetics, and recently biology, have been laid under contribution for this purpose. A consistent attempt to study ethical phenomena on their own ground, to mark off what is really distinctive in the data of ethical experience, and then to search for some principle which shall serve to give a coherent account of them, has to my knowledge never yet been undertaken. Always ethics has been treated as an annex to some other discipline. Always we behold the attempt to assimilate before the distinctive traits and characteristics have been carefully investigated. Never yet has the independence of this wonderful aspect of human nature been truly acknowledged. Kant indeed freed ethics from its long tutelage to theology; but he left it still in subjection, subject to his own favorite study, physical science.

But though the notion of necessity, together with that of universality, which he derived from physics was employed by him as a fundamental principle of rightness in conduct, the principle itself insensibly, and as it would seem unbeknown to himself, underwent a remarkable change in the course of his undertaking to give it a new application. The following brief comments will serve to elucidate this point.

In physics, whenever an antecedent phenomenon has been exactly described, and a sequent phenomenon is defined in the same fashion, the connection is pronounced to be necessary—as for instance the transformation of mechanical energy into heat, and conversely. A single carefully guarded experiment may suffice to establish the necessary nexus between two phenomena. And after having established the necessity, we are confident of the universality. If exceptions should occur and contravene the supposed law, the calculations or the observations are to be corrected. But never in physical science do we start from universality and predict necessity therefrom. Kant in his ethics invariably couples together the two terms Universal and Necessary. But he reverses the procedure of science, he begins with the universality and thereupon affirms the necessity.

Universality is for him the test of moral necessity. If an act can be universalized, the performance of it, according to him, is morally necessary. For instance, the question is asked, Is it right to kill? Look at the act of killing, says Kant, and see whether it can be universalized, that is to say, whether if everybody felt at liberty to kill, the act of the murderer would or would not be self-defeating? He kills in order to *affirm* his life at the expense of another's. If his action were to be generally imitated, his own life would be forfeit, or at least in danger, and he would be annulling what he intends to affirm. Hence murder is morally wrong: to sacredly respect the life of others is right.-

But not only is the order reversed, so that necessity follows on the heels of universality, but the very meaning of the term necessity is altered. *A logical necessity is substituted for a physical necessity.* The idea of necessity as handled by physical science denotes the connection between one thing and something else. It is not the thing itself but its relation to some other thing that is necessary. It is not the phenomenon A nor the phenomenon B, in the case of a cause and its effect, that is declared to be necessary, but the sequence of B on A, the circumstance that B is tied up to A, must follow in its wake. But the term Necessity as used by Kant in his *Ethics,* denotes a relation of a thing to itself. It is in fact equivalent to self-consistency, which is a logical notion derived from the principle of self-identity. A is A, and it is not thinkable that it should be non-A. Similarly Kant says: If a man desires to affirm his life, that is, to be self-preserving, it is not thinkable, it would not be rational or logical on his part, to perform an act which would be self-defeating. Kant does not say that a man might not irrationally take another man's life, regardless of the consequences to himself; he says that as a rational intelligence acting on purely logical motives he could not do so.[1] To repeat, then, physical necessity is a relation of one thing to another thing: the logical necessity involved in self-consistency is a relation of a thing to itself.

My next contention, and this touches the root of the matter, is that the notion of end is incompatible with self-consistency as the paramount principle in ethics. For a self-consistent rational being is a being in harmony with himself, one who if this harmony should in some unaccountable way ever be broken would by his own endeavor seek to return to himself. (Kant declares that the morality of any one man cannot be affected by his fellows, by any influence from the outside; it must be his own act.) But an end presupposes some outside object as a means: means and ends are inseparable correlatives. On the other hand, an entity which merely affirms itself, or if somehow alienated from self endeavors without assistance from beyond its sphere

[1] He also assumes a society not only of rational intelligences determined by the same rational motives, but equal in ability to carry out their motives. (See my article in *Mind* [new series, Vol. XI, No. 42, p. 162], reprinted in the volume dedicated to William James, by the Philosophical Faculty of Columbia University.)

to return to itself, is no true end at all, and cannot be designated as such. It is no end because it employs no means.

What warrant then has Kant for introducing the foreign notion of end into a world of pure self-consistency? When we use the term Necessity in relation to physical phenomena, as of cause and effect, we assert unalterable sequence, unity of temporal and spatial differentiae. When we use the same term as Kant uses it, we assert the unity of a thing with itself. But this in the nature of the case does not admit the intrusion of the alien concept of the outside. The spiritual, society or pattern to which human society ought to be conformed, is according to Kant a society of ends, of ends *per se.* This is his great pronouncement. But the very idea on which he lays so much stress, the idea of end, on closer scrutiny of his premises disappears. The entities composing that society are self-sufficing, and moreover intrinsically unrelated to each other. Rational self-preservation is the only character that can be predicated of any of them.

I have laid stress on the fact that Kant derived his ethical principle from his physics. The passage in which he speaks of the ethical order as a universal and necessary order like that of nature is to my mind conclusive. I now urge in addition that this sort of second nature superimposed upon existing nature would not have to our contemplating minds a dignity superior to that of physical nature. The moral order as thus exhibited would not possess the worth we attribute to it as exalted above what is called the natural order. The falling stone is a perfect illustration of physical necessity. Necessity passed through human consciousness, or bathed in human consciousness, is not on that account a more eligible principle. Nay, since human consciousness interferes and causes contingent actions, due to passion, appetite, etc., the moral order constructed by men should be even less worth while than the physical order of nature, if indeed necessity be the touchstone of worth.[2]

To summarize: according to Kant man as an object is unfit to warrant the claim of unconditional obligation on the part of others toward himself. An abstract principle must be sought. This principle is universality, and necessity based on universality. Respect for this purely abstract notion is that which alone imparts a moral quality to so-called moral acts. We start, according to Kant, with the declaration that man is an end *per se*. But we reject him as an object, and take refuge in a formal principle. We then assume that every human being is conscious of the working within himself of this formal principle and acknowledges his subjection to it, whether he is able to analyze it out or not. And thus indirectly we derive out of emptiness a ray of glory which we allow to fall upon each and every man.

The question now is, since this approach to the ethical

[2] Surefootedness, or certainty in thinking and in acting seems to have been the chief desideratum at which Kant aimed. As against scepticism or mere empirical groping this element of the inner life is obviously of exceeding value. But it is far from being the only element to be taken into account.

problem manifestly fails, must we not begin at the opposite end, and take the attribution of worth to men, however unworthy they may actually be, as our starting-point?

CHAPTER III

PRELIMINARY REMARKS ON WORTH, AND ON THE

REASONS WHY THE METHOD EMPLOYED BY

ETHICS MUST BE THE OPPOSITE OF THAT EM-

PLOYED BY THE PHYSICAL SCIENCES

THE moral equality of men is a corollary of the attribution of worth to all men. Did we not ascribe worth to them, there is no reason why we should not make servile use of them. But there are admittedly formidable difficulties in the way of attributing worth to human nature.

The first and most obvious of these is the existence of repulsive traits in human beings, such as sly cunning, deceit, falsehood, grossness, cruelty: *homo homini lupus!* Secondly, there is the prevalent error of employing ethical terms, like good and bad, to denote the merely attractive and repellent traits.[1] Attractive traits, such as gentleness, sweetness, kindness, a sympathetic disposition, are, in those fortunate enough to possess them, pleasing accidents of nature. We delight in them, but have no reason to ascribe the superlative quality of worth to those who possess them. If the evil that men do revolts us, the so-called good in them does not give us the right to surround their heads with the nimbus of worth. Thirdly, and perhaps even more deterrent than

[1] See the more extended remarks on this subject in Book III.

91

the ever-present spectacle of evil and the inadequacy of so-called goodness, is the commonplaceness, the cheapness of men.

It must be admitted that, with rare exceptions, our estimates of others are apt to be low rather than lofty. Can we ascribe worth to those whom we hold cheap? The reason of our habitual under-estimation of fellow men I think is that we regard them from the standpoint of the use to which we can put them, and do not see them from the inside, as it were, in the light of the marvelous energies of which human nature is the scene. The grossest matter, the most ordinary physical happenings, reveal to the instructed eye of the scientist the play of forces which it taxes the most powerful intellects in some measure to apprehend and describe. Yet these miracles escape the dull senses of those of us who deal with the forces of nature from the point of view of their immediate use. We turn on the electric light, but have little more than a crude surmise of the things that the word electricity meant to Faraday, Clerk Maxwell, or Hertz. And as we turn on the electric light, so we turn on our fellowmen, as it were, to use them. The thought of the poet—"What a piece of work is man, how infinite in faculty!" occurs to us only at scattered moments. And yet things transpire in the inner life of human beings far more marvelous than the chemical processes or the flux of electric waves, did we but attend to them. There is in particular one kind of energy to which the quality of worth may well attach itself. It is unlike the physical forces; it is not a transformed mode of mechanical energy. It is *sui generis,* underivative, unique; it is synonymous with highest freedom; it is power raised to the Nth degree. It is ethical energy. To release it in oneself is to achieve unbounded expansion. Morality, as commonly understood, is a system of rules, chiefly repressive. Ethical energy, on the contrary, is determined by the very opposite tendency; a tendency, it is true, never more than tentatively effectuated under finite conditions. And because the energy is unique, it points toward a unique, irreducible, hence substantive entity in man, from which it springs. This entity is itself incognizable, yet the effect it produces requires that it be postulated. The category of substance, which is almost disappearing from science, is to be reinstalled in ethics. Ethics cannot dispense with it. This, as a prelude, may suffice to indicate the path along which we shall proceed.

The Reason Why the Method of Ethics Must Be the Opposite of the Method Employed by the Physical Sciences

Physical science begins from the bottom and builds upwards. It analyzes phenomena into their elements, and thereupon seeks to combine these elements into structures that shall correspond to experience. In this business it never comes to a finish. Its analysis of the elements is provisional. Every element is hypothetical. Indeed it is plain in the nature of the case that no element can be ultimate. An element is a unit, and every empirical unit necessarily conceals in its bosom a plexus of which it is the unification. The very idea of

93

unit requires for its complement a manifold of some kind. In hypothetical units, or ideal constructs that have for their purpose to lead to the discovery and arrangement of real phenomena, science abounds. Atoms, electrons, energy conceived as a substance by Ostwald, Spencer's physiological units, are examples.

The results achieved by science are never more than approximations in the sense that the units, the bricks with which the house is built, are liable to be rejected, and the constructions achieved are subject to revision.

The point however which I wish to emphasize is that the scientist is satisfied of the truth, the reality of its partial results. Newton, for instance, in formulating the law of gravitation has, so to speak, marked off a strip of reality. The ground covered cannot be lost; when some natural law is enunciated, the proper conditions for its discovery and verification having been observed, a sure footing in reality has been gained, science standing to this extent on *terra firma*, though beyond the domain within which the law applies the phenomena may be heaving and billowing like the sea.

Now the question I am intent upon is, Why is it possible for science to be content with partial acquisition? Why does it profess to know positively a part without knowing the whole? And why can ethics not take a step without an ideal of the whole?

Kant's chief purpose in the *Critique of Pure Reason* was to vindicate the certainty of the physical knowledge of a part as being compatible with total ignorance of the whole. The older metaphysics was engaged in the attempt to supply the whole, to sketch it out in order to give certainty to the part that is within the reach of science. The older metaphysics said to science: You have in hand the conditioned, but remember the conditioned depends on the unconditioned. Unless, therefore, you round out what you possess, with the help of the unconditioned, the certainty you seem to have within the field of the conditioned disappears. Again, science traces causes, and the older metaphysicians insisted that the whole chain of causes hangs in air unless it be attached to a first cause. Now Kant's *Critique of Pure Reason* really amounts *in nuce* to this: you do not require the whole in order to explain the part. Link the partial phenomena together in a certain way, a way dependent on the joint action of the space and time intuitions and the categories, and you will gain the desired certainty. The certainty is in the linkage. We may add link to link of the chain of reality without troubling to consider by what piers it is supported or on what shore the piers rest—if indeed there be piers and shores at all. The bridge hangs over the River of Time and we can safely travel on it. How we get on to this bridge we do not know, and where we shall leave it we cannot know either.

It is a mistake to speak of Kant as a rationalist pure and simple. When he expelled the older metaphysics he antagonized pure rationalism. The older metaphysics held that the mere existence of the conditioned proves the existence of the unconditioned, requires the unconditioned. In Kant's answer to this lies the gist of his enterprise in philosophy: You are quite right, he says, that the *idea* of the conditioned requires the idea of the unconditioned, logically, rationally. But observe well, nature is not just logical or rational. There is an irrational element in it, namely, extended manifold and temporal sequence. Juxtaposition and sequence are irrational, because, if I interpret him rightly, in the case of each the relation presented to the mind is that of parts outside each other—in the one case alongside, in the other before and after; while in the logical or rational relation the parts are implicit in the whole as in the case of the premises of a syllogism and the conclusion, the relation of a genus to the species, the universal to the particular.

We have in nature, according to Kant, a partnership between the irrational and the rational factors. And thereupon he proceeds to argue that we impose laws on nature, understanding thereby that we get hold of reality or objectivity in so far as we are able to imprint the rational element upon the irrational. The positing of the thing *per se,* which has proved a stumbling-block to many, is no more than a confession that we shall never succeed entirely in this business of subjecting the irrational to the rational factor. The thing *per se* is the X that remains over when the rational function has done its utmost. A thing, a real object, is that which is imprinted with, penetrated with, rationality. The manifolds of space and time, of juxtaposition and sequence are incapable of completely receiving this imprint, that is, of completely responding to our quest for reality, and this their incompetency is expressed in the notion of the thing *per se.*

To return to the main question as to the difference between the method by which science proceeds and the reverse method prescribed to ethics, I ask, Why is absolute knowledge of nature impossible? The answer is, Because absolute knowledge would mean the completely rational construction of nature, and this is prevented by the irrational element existing in it. But why has the relative knowledge we possess the character of certainty? Why are we sure of the law of gravitation? ' Why are we justified in saying that science within certain limits plants her foot on *terra solida?* , Because at certain points the sense data do coincide with the rational requirements. There are recurrent phenomena of such a kind, coupled together in such a way, that each is capable of mathematical measurement, and that the sequence of the one after the other can therefore be predicted.

Nature might have been arranged quite otherwise. The time spans might have been so long, as to prevent our observing the recurrences. A day-fly cannot observe the periodicity of the earth's revolution around its axis. The fact however that there is this partial correspondence between human rationality and the unknown nature of things is a bare fact, incapable of explanation.[2] The answer, then, I take it, is: our knowledge of nature is relative, which means incompletely rational, because of the foreign element in nature unamenable to the opera-

[2] In Kant's view the rational element is projected on the irrational. In this way spatial juxtaposition is ideally transformed into a spatial continuum. In the same manner temporal sequence is ideally changed into a uniform temporal flux. Without the former, geometry could not have established its propositions; without the latter Galileo could not have measured the fall of the stone.

97

tion of the rational, the synthetic, function. This relative knowledge is none the less certain, that is, in some sense absolute, because of the partial coincidence of the phenomena of nature and the synthetic processes of the mind.

With this degree of certainty we must perforce content ourselves, in dealing with outside nature. In trying to understand and interpret that which is not ourselves, we hit upon barriers which cannot be transcended, upon a foreign factor which opposes itself to our endeavors. But it is otherwise in the sphere of conduct. Here, if there is to be certainty at all, in regard to right as distinguished from wrong, if there is to be such a thing as right in the strict sense, we cannot content ourselves with the paradoxical, relative-absolute just described. For here we not merely interpret but act, and we must possess an ideal plan of the whole if we are to be certain of our rightness in any particular part of conduct. For in *conduct there is no such partial coincidence between the rational and the irrational as in the case of physical law.* There is not a single partial rule of conduct, neither "Thou shalt not kill" nor "Thou shalt not lie," nor any other that, taken by itself, is of itself ethically right. It may be right, it may be wrong. It takes its ethical quality from the plan of conduct as a whole, and without reference to the whole it is devoid of rightness.[3]

[8] The ethical character of acts depends on the worth of the agent and the object. Is it right to kill or to enslave a fellow man? We do not hesitate to kill an animal, or to harness horses to vehicles, or to use them as beasts of burden. Why not kill men, or use them

I have thus indicated the ground of the distinction between the method of science and the method of ethics, a distinction, it is true, to which Kant himself did not adhere. Partial coincidence of the rational with the irrational is expressed in physical law; absence of such concurrence destroys any attempt to build up an ethical theory on the empirical method. We cannot plant our feet on the part, gaining there the sense of certainty: we must creatively conceive the ideal of the whole and educe every partial mode of ethical conduct from that.

But how shall we proceed in the construction of such an ideal, for it is obvious that knowledge, in the scientific sense of the word, is entirely out of the question?

as beasts of burden in like manner?—Only because they possess a worth which gives them a different standing.

Is it on grounds of sympathy that I should observe the so-called moral rules? But if I am not sympathetic by nature, why should I be subject to censure in case I refrain from displaying a tenderness which I do not feel? Why should I sympathize with the pleasures and pains of fellow human beings any more than with the pleasures and pains of inferior sentient creatures, unless men have worth? And worth, as will appear in the subsequent chapters, signifies indispensableness in a perfect whole. No detached thing has worth. No part of an incomplete system has worth. Worth belongs to those to whom it is attributed in so far as they are conceived of as not to be spared, as representing a distinctive indispensable preciousness, a mode of being without which perfection would be less than perfect.

So that morality depends on the attribution of worth to men, and worth depends on the formation in the mind of an ideal plan of the whole—or instead of a complete plan let me say more precisely a rule of relations whereby the plan is itself progressively developed.

CHAPTER IV

THE IDEAL OF THE WHOLE

TO recapitulate and at the same time to enlarge somewhat the points thus far covered in Book II: Kant proclaims man an end *per se*. This promises a philosophic basis for an ethical world-view. The promise is not kept. Kant takes as his point of departure absolute obligation, and attempts to deduce out of an empty formula a worth-while object. Kant's formula is: Treat man never merely as a means, but also as an end *per se*. But how far man may be treated as a means, and what the relation of the means to the end may be is left undetermined. An upper crust of morality is formed, as it were, upon the empirical flood of passions, desires, etc. A straight line is drawn beyond which the under world in every man may not *emerge*. But a truly instrumental view of the means as related to the end is not established. This is one of the great gaps in Kant's system. Note the almost puerile reason given for culture: we should cultivate our talents *weil sie zu allerliand Zwecken niitzlich sein mogcn*.

Kant's ethical order is a duplicate of the physical order. The notion of law is taken from physics, and expanded into the concept of law in general. Ethical behavior is represented as behavior motivated by the notion of lawfulness. Law is characterized by universality and necessity. Chapter II, however, shows that in physics universality is predicated on the ground of an ascertained necessary connection. In physics, necessity has its true meaning as pertaining to a relation between one thing and another. If the linkage can be established, the universality follows. In Kant's ethics, on the contrary, necessity is taken as the consequence of the universality and the proper meaning of necessity is lost. Self-consistency takes the place of the relation to something else. The ideal society, as described, would therefore be a society of self-preserving rational intelligences, ethically solipsistic.

Next we began the investigation into the idea of worth. Why do men hold themselves and others cheap? They regard each other from the point of view of the *use* to be made of others and of their own life, and not from the point of view of the energies deployed. The turning on of electric power was used as an illustration. Nevertheless, even exceptional men, men regarded as illustrating in the highest degree the mental energies implicit in human nature, would not possess the quality of worth, that is, of being ends *per se,* merely on the score of their scientific or their artistic activities. We cannot say that the world would be less perfect if there were no scientists to discover its laws. There is a supreme, a unique energy and it is to this that the quality of worth belongs.[3]

---

[3] To rate anyone as an end *per se* means that in a world conceived as perfect his existence would be indispensable. The world we know may not be perfect, is not perfect, but we do conceive of an ideal world that is. And to ascribe to anyone the quality of worth,

The ethical quality called worth is the supreme good, and must be accessible to all, even to those to whom the lesser goods are denied. Ethics is a system of thought which stands or falls with the contention that while the better may be within reach only of the exceptional few, the best is within reach of all.

In attempting to approach the task of building up a world-view based on ethical experience, it became unavoidable to consider the method by which the approach might be made, and for this purpose to contrast the methods of science and the methods of ethics. Science, as we have seen, collects its bricks and builds its house by composition. Science analyzes phenomena into units, which it then combines. The mystery is how science can achieve certainty in respect to certain phenomena of nature without previous knowledge of the whole of nature. Kant's answer is that there is partial congruity between the mental functions and the data that come to us from the unknown. Kant's *Critique of Pure Reason* faces in two directions. It expels the older metaphysics which assumed that the empirical world is rational throughout, or rationalizable, and which thence argued the existence of the unconditioned as necessarily implied in the existence of the conditioned, and of a first cause as actually implied in the chain of causes and effects. Kant contends that there is an irrational element, namely, bare juxtaposition (part outside part), and bare sequence (part before and after part), while the logical or rational relation implies that

to denominate him an end *per se,* is to place him into that world, to regard him as potentially a member of it.

the part is to be conceived as implicit in the whole. Juxtaposition and sequence, therefore, can never be completely rationalized. On the other hand, Kant undertakes to prove that whatever of reality we know is traceable to the projection of the rational factor upon the irrational. One might even say that, according to Kant, the mind itself produces the Lrational factor, since the intuitions of space and time are according to him, functions of the mind itself—the mind setting up a manifold so constituted as to receive sense impressions. At any rate the capital point to which we were led up was that science puts her foot on *terra firma* in a restricted area, without reference to what lies beyond, while if we are to proceed in ethics at all, we must begin with some ideal plan of the whole, since in ethics we are not interpreting a foreign nature, but act upon natures similar to our own; and since, in the case of conduct, there is no such partial concurrence of the rational and irrational as in physics, no one of the so-called moral modes of behavior being moral when taken separately. Hence the conclusion that there is no possibility of establishing the conception of worth unless we have some ideal of the whole in which and in relation to which the incomparable worthwhileness of a human being can be made good.

We need hardly again remind ourselves that this conception of worth, or of man as end *per se,* is not a mere abstraction, and that our interest in it is not academic. Every outcry against the oppression of man by man, or against whatsoever is morally hideous, is but the affirmation of the cardinal principle that a human being as such is not to be violated, is not to be handled like a tool, but is to be respected and revered as an end *per se*. But what do we mean by end *per se,* and how account for this notion? Does it come into our mind like a bolt from the blue, or is it revealed as prefigured in the human mind when we follow it into its intimate constitution?

Our knowledge of the world we live in is extremely limited—in its details it is confined to the planet we live on, extending to the myriads of celestial bodies beyond us only by means of scant generalizations. If we have knowledge of only so small a portion, how can we frame an ideal of the whole? At the same time we must remember that the world we actually know, this earth and yonder starry myriads, is in very truth *our* world, the world as it exists for us, a world which with the help of data coming to us from the unknown, we ourselves have built up on certain constructive principles ; and that these principles have been found, within certain limits, availing.[3] I say availing within certain limits. The defeat they meet with beyond those limits is due to the intractable elements of juxtaposition and sequence, of the time and space manifolds, which in themselves are incapable of being completely rationalized.

Now the ideal of the whole is a plan or scheme in which the constructive principles of the mind are conceived as having untrammeled course and unhindered

[2] For a creature endowed with different senses, and having a mind unlike our own, the world would be a totally different world.

application, and the task of world-building, or rather universe-building, is in idea carried out to completion.

The attempt to present an ideal forecast, or outline of the whole of reality, as it would satisfy a mind constituted like ours, an ideal landscape of this sort, is not at all to be confounded with the arrogation of *a priori* knowledge. *A priori* knowledge is supposed to be a kind of knowledge, and *knowledge* of the whole is utterly and confessedly beyond our reach. The phrase *a priori,* too, is objectionable and unfortunate for two reasons. First, as just said, because it has been supposed to be a kind of knowledge. By some theologians men were supposed to possess *a priori* knowledge of God.[3] Secondly, because the word *a priori* suggests precedence in time, and our knowledge of the human mind and of its irreducible capacities comes out only in the course of experience. Much that has been called *a priori,* that is implicit in experience, did not become explicit until after prolonged experience. The Greek thinkers before Aristotle doubtless thought in terms of syllogism, but it was not until Greek science had attained a certain ripeness that Aris-

[3] To deny such *a priori* knowledge of the object called God is not to deny that the production of this object is due to constructive principles of human thinking; while, in turn, to assert the functional derivation of the God-idea is not to validate that idea itself as permanent and inexpugnable. It may have owed its origin to a permanent disposition of the mind, and yet be fallible because of the historical conditions under which it arose and the defective data in which it was expressed. By way of illustration we might apply the same reflection to the Ptolemaic astronomy. The mathematical processes by which this astronomy was constructed may be traced lo permanent singularities of human thinking, yet the astronomical theory of Ptolemy is not on that account *a priori* true.

totle was able to dissect out the logic which had previously been employed more or less unconsciously.

Instead, therefore, of using the term *a priori,* which gives rise to the two-fold misapprehension of an *a priori* knowledge and of temporal precedence, and instead of throwing out the child with the bath, that is, of ignoring the independent part played by our mental constitution in building up experience, and in affording us the conviction of certainty, and of reality, it is highly desirable that a new term be found to take the place of *a priori.* The term "functional finality" suggests itself to me for this purpose.[4]

My field is ethics. I am entirely desirous of sticking to my own last, that is, dealing with such concepts as the data of my subject force upon me. I do not wish to trespass, or to seem to trespass, on the domain of my neighbors. Hence in dealing with functional finalities I must deal with them primarily as they appear in the field of ethics, that is, in the domain of the actions and reactions of human beings upon one another. Irreducible *prindpia* of ethics are the functional finalities, which prescribe rules for such intercourse, or better which create a scheme of ideal intercourse whereby

*It must, however, be understood that the formula in which a finality is expressed is not itself a final formula. The business of definition is precarious, liable to error and dogmatic abuse, and the formulas of finality are to be constantly subjected to revision. Possible and even probable abuse, however, does not warrant the negative attitude at present taken; it does not justify the revulsion of feeling against *A Priorism* which is just now general. Exasperation with absolutism does not of itself justify recourse to the opposite extreme of pragmatism.

the conduct of men shall be measured and determined.

I must, however, glance for a moment at fields outside my own, for the purpose not of controversy but of elucidation; not to deal with the subject matter of my neighbors, but to mark off my own more definitely. What then, I ask, is the most general expression by which to designate the singularities of the human mind, the principles on which it acts, its immutable modes of behavior, the invariants that recur amid all the complex varieties of its processes? The principal invariants are the positing of a manifold of some kind, and the apprehending of that manifold as coherent. The manifold is not given, but is posited by the mind. The positing is a mental function, just as much as the apprehending of the plurality as coherent is a mental function. The particular manifolds of space and time experience are said to be given, but they would not be received by the mind were not the function of manifold-positing prepared to apprehend them.

In recent physical science the notion of the manifold plays a conspicuous role. Subtle speculations are employed to define the kinds of manifold which the physicist finds opportune, and the kind of unity of which these manifolds are respectively capable. The two terms mentioned are themselves the most abstract conceivable, and naturally, that which is here taken to underlie all the constructive, world-building activity of the mind in every possible direction can only be expressed in the most sublimated language. But the notions themselves, or rather the acts of the mind, the functions designated, are rich and replete with concrete utility when applied to subject matter in the different fields.

Wherever we turn we find that the assurance of reality depends on the joint use of the two principles mentioned, the joint operation of the two kinds of mental action; that is to say—on the positing of a manifold and on the simultaneous apprehension of the subject matter to which it relates as coherent, as unified.

The simultaneity, the inseparableness of the two mental acts or functions in regard to the same subject-matter is the essential point on which hangs the web of the argument here submitted. Thus in geometry space must be regarded as a continuum, unbroken, uninterrupted at any point, and at the same time the same space must be treated as capable of puncture, of linear and superficial delimitations; that is to say, of division. That which is one must yet be apprehended as divided; that which is divided, or delimitated, must yet be apprehended as one. The difficulties that arise spring from the vain endeavor to separate the two inseparable acts—the act of apprehending the manifold of space *sub specie pluralitatis,* and the act of apprehending it *sub specie unitatis.* Hence arises the puzzling question: How can that which is continuous be divided, how can chasms between the parts of space, however infinitesimal, be bridged? Witness the problem of Zeno, and the pragmatist solution of it by a demonstration that satisfies us indeed as to the fact (which no one doubts), but leaves the mental puzzle as before; and also Bergson's Method of accounting for division by a comparison of the inner and the outer flux, wherein he seems to overlook the difficulty that for the purpose of comparison two points must be fixed, one in each flux, that is to say, the division in the flux must be regarded as already existing.

In the physical sciences we are compelled to assume on the one hand the atomic or granular constitution of matter, in other words, manifoldness. On the other hand, if "action at a distance" is to be escaped, we are bound to assume a continuum of some sort like the ether. Again, in the organic world there is the manifold of structures and functions, and the unity of organism. To whatever object of inquiry we give our attention, we find ourselves not only restricted fundamentally to the two functions described, but we discover that to their insunderable co-operation we owe whatever of truth we possess.

Now the business of ethics is to define its own subject-matter, that is to say the particular kind of manifold with which it deals, and the kind of unity of which that manifold is susceptible. But as I approach this first goal of my enterprise, there is one obstacle which I must try to remove out of the way of the reader, before I can hope to win him to a hospitable consideration of my conclusions. The jointness or inseparableness of the two acts out of which certainty or reality issues has created all the difficulties. The fact that the manifold must be regarded as remaining a manifold, unaltered in its character as such, not derivative from the One (there is no such One), and that the unity does not contrariwise result from the manifold in the sense of springing from or being derived from .it;—in other words that we must see the same landscape of things and events both *sub specie pluraHtatis* and *sub specie unitatis*—has been the stumbling-block. The history of philosophy might be written under the two headings: 1, monistic systems that undertake, collapsing in their futile effort, to derive the world and its plurality from the One, as if there were such an One, out of whose bosom philosophy might evoke the many (creational systems, pantheistic systems, emanation systems, evolution systems); 2, pluralistic systems that essay, with equal lack of success, to explain the unity as somehow the offspring of the plurality.

Why then have these systems flourished? Why are these vain undertakings still renewed? The reason is that we cannot understand the joint action of the two functions, and the very point where enlightenment is needed is for us to recognize that no fundamental truths can be understood by us, that we can only look at them, contemplate and accept them. The point, I say, where enlightenment is needed is that the habit of trying to understand is due to a prejudice, to what may be called the *superstition of causality.*

I shall have to explain this hardy assertion with some care to prevent misconception. Causality, it will be objected, is the one thread that leads us through the labyrinth of nature. The search for causes enables us to become at home in our world by foreseeing events. In what sense then can it be permissible to speak of the prejudice of causality, nay, of the superstition of it? With what warrant prescribe a limit to the aspirations of the human intellect to push its inquiries to the farthest limit, even so far as to understand the functional finalities themselves, if such there be?

The answer, succinctly put, is this: explaining or understanding things means tracing effects to their causes, and this is only one mode, a somewhat *disguised* mode, of the joint functional activity of which I have spoken. The manifold in this case is that of the temporal sequence of phenomena, of differences due to change of position in time; and the unity established between them (as for instance energy, of which the sequent phenomena represent the transformations) is an ideal, fictive unity, mentally superimposed (real despite its ideal or imaginary character, because of the necessity we are under to view the sequent phenomena *sub specie unitatis).* That there is nothing in the antecedent to compel the sequent to follow has been since the days of Hume a commonplace in philosophy. That nevertheless there is such a thing as the prediction of eclipses was made by Kant the basis of his doctrine of synthesis *a priori.* Be the terms used what they may, what counts is the fact that the *joint action of two functions, 'which itself is inexplicable,* not to be understood, that is, not to be referred back to a preceding cause (as if there could be such a thing as a cause why we think in terms of causality) is the foundation-of all so-called understanding.

Moreover causality is an incomplete example of the fundamental functional process. We never do thoroughly understand; we gain a certain relief, a certain increased ease of mind by pushing the problem back a step. And what I have called the prejudice of causality, is the unwillingness on our part to acknowledge the fact that we are face to face, in the case of causality, with the inexplicable; that that which helps us partially to understand (and serves for practical purposes well enough) is in its nature not to be understood, one of the modes in which the joint action of the functional finalities manifests itself.

An ultimate principle has been defined as one which is presupposed in every attempt to account for it. The functional finalities of which I speak bear the test of, this definition. The upshot of it all is that the constitutive principles of the human mind cannot be explained or understood, but can nevertheless be verified. And verification, in the last analysis, means exemplification. If we look at these ultimate truths, whether in geometry, in physics, or, as we shall later see, in ethics and aesthetics, as enunciated abstractly, baldly, we confront them blankly, we are as it were dumb-founded in their presence. They seem arbitrarily imposed upon us. And why? Because we are endeavoring to understand them. We have acquired the habit of trying to get hold of truth by referring back to some antecedent. And therefore we are uneasy and disconcerted. But the moment we see-fchem exemplified, as in the constructions of the geometer, in the laws or uniformities established by the physicist, etc., we are convinced. The subject-matter of ethics is different. The kind of exemplification is likewise different. But verification is exemplification in ethics as elsewhere; and this will be found to mean that the life, the ethical experience, must lead to the certainty.

And now we have reached the point where a brief discussion of the ethical manifold and its mode of unification comes up in proper order.

CHAPTER V

THE IDEAL OF THE WHOLE AND THE ETHICAL

MANIFOLD

THE ethical manifold, conceived of as unified, furnishes, or rather is, the ideal of the whole. The ethical manifold is the true universe, not "Universe" in the sense in which the word is too laxly used at present to designate those fragmentary and in many respects unconnected lines of experience which might better by way of discrimination be called World.

The ideal of the whole, as the terms imply, must fulfill two conditions: it must be a whole, that is, include all manifoldness whatsoever; and it must be ideal, or perfectly unified. In such an ideal whole the two reality-producing functions of the human mind would find their complete fruition.

Point 1.—The totality of manifoldness must be comprised.

Point 2.—The connectedness must be without flaw.

From point one it follows that the ethical manifold cannot be spatial or temporal, since juxtaposition and sequence lapse into indefiniteness, abounding without ceasing, but never attaining or promising the attainment of totality. Our first conclusion then is that the ethical manifold is non-temporal and non-spatial.

Furthermore it is necessary and decisive for the theoretical construction here attempted to keep sharply in view, that the manifoldness may not be derived from the unity, or conversely. The manifold remains forever manifold. This means that in the ethical manifold each member [1] will differ uniquely from all the rest, and preserve his irreducible singularity. The member of the ethical manifold was not created by *the* One or any One. He is not derived as effect from any cause. Causality does not apply to the ethical manifold, being a category of spatial sequence. The member of the ethical manifold, or the ethical unit, as we may now call him (I say him metaphorically and provisionally) is unbegotten, induplicable, unique. In the ethical manifold each infinitesimal member is indispensable, inasmuch as he is one of the totality of intrinsically unlike differentiae. A [1] duplicate would be superfluous. Inclusion implies indispensableness; no member acquires a place within the ethical universe save on the score of his title, as one of the possible modes of being that are required to complete the totality of manifoldness.

But the reality-producing functions of the mind are two, and they act jointly. The same manifold that is regarded as the scene of irreducible manifoldness, is also regarded *sub specie wnitatis*. The immense practical importance of holding fast to diversity as indefeasible, and at the same time stressing the unity, will amply appear in the course of the third Book. It is

[1] Say not *part* or *element*, but *member*, to distinguish the components of the ethical manifold from such concepts as are used in mathematics and physical science.

this insistence on the two aspects *jointly,* that distinguishes the theory here worked out from preceding ethical philosophies, and will be found to open new ethical applications to conduct. It is this insistence on the joint action of the two reality-producing functions that will enable us to see in the ideal of the whole *a pattern traced,* and to derive from this pattern of relations a supreme rule of conduct. If the differences that exist among the members of the manifold be slurred over, if the indefeasible singularity of each member be overlooked, if the many be derived from the One, since the One is an empty concept, we shall gain no light upon the conduct to be followed by each of the many. It is true that our notion of the distinctive difference or the uniqueness of each ethical unit is also empty as far as knowledge goes. The unique is incognizable. Yet we are able to apprehend, and do apprehend, a determinate relation as subsisting between the ethical units, and this relation supplies us with an ideal plan of the ethical universe and a first principle and rule of ethics. The relation is that of reciprocal universal interdependence.

Consider that an infinite number of ethical entities is presented to our minds—each of them radically different from the rest. In what then possibly can the unity of this infinite assemblage consist? In this— *that the unique difference of each shall be such as to render possible the correlated unique differences of all the rest.* It is in this formula that we find the key to a new ethical system, in this conception we get our hand firmly on the notion of right, and by means of it we

116

discover the object which Kant failed to find, the object to which worth attaches, the object which is so indispensable to the ideal of the whole as to authenticate unconditional obligation or rightness in conduct with respect to it. It is as an ethical unit, as a member of the infinite ethical manifold, that man has worth.[4]

In accordance with the above, the first principle of ethics may be expressed in the following formulas:

A. Act as a member of the ethical manifold (the infinite spiritual universe).

B. Act so as to achieve uniqueness (complete individualization—the most completely individualized act is the most ethical).

C. Act so as to elicit in another the distinctive, unique quality characteristic of him as a fellow-member of the infinite whole.

---

[4] The distinction between value and worth must be stressed for it is capital. Value is subjective. The worth notion is the most objective conceivable. Value depends on the wants or needs of our empirical nature. That has value which satisfies our needs or wants. We possess value for one another, for the reason that each of us has wants which the others alone are capable of satisfying, as in the case of sex, of cooperation, in the vocation, etc. But value ceases when the want or need is gratified. The value which one human being has for another is transient. There are, in the strict sense, no permanent values. The value which the majority have for the more advanced and developed members of a community is small; from the standpoint of value most persons are duplicable and dispensable. Consider only the ease with which factory labor is replaced, in consequence of the prolific fertility of the human race. The custom of speaking of ethics as a theory of values is regrettable. It evidences the despair into which many writers on ethics have fallen as to the possibility of discovering an objective basis for rightness.

A and B are comprised in C. I am taking three steps toward a fuller exposition of the meaning of the principle. To act as a member according to A is to strive to achieve uniqueness as declared in B. To achieve uniqueness as declared in C is to seek to elicit the diverse uniqueness in others. The actual unique quality in myself is incognizable, and only appears, so far as it does appear, in the effect produced by myself upon my fellows. Hence, to advance towards uniqueness I must project dynamically my most distinctive mode of energy upon my fellow-members.

Since the finite nature of man is a clog and screen, clouding and checking the action of man viewed as an ethical unit, it follows that no man will ever succeed in carrying out completely the rule which is derived from the ideal pattern. He will invariably meet with partial frustration in his efforts to do so, and yet in virtue of his ethical character he will always renew the effort. While in physical science the recurrence of phenomena supplies the occasion for exemplification or verification, in conduct, or the sphere of volition, not recurrence but the persistence of the effort after defeat is at least a help to verification, arguing in one's self a consciousness, however obscured, of the relation of reciprocal interdependence and of subjection to the urge or pressure thence derived.[3] It is our own reality-producing functions, exerted to their utmost, to which we are delivered over. Hence the final formulation: So act as to raise up in others the ideal of the relation of give and take, of

[3] But the verification itself is the clearer and more explicit vision of the ethical relation, as it ought to be.

universal interdependence in which they stand with an infinity of beings like themselves, members of the infinite universe, irreducible, like and unlike themselves in their respective uniqueness.

The simile that may be used is that of a ray of light which has the effect of kindling other rays, unlike but complementary to itself. Each ethical unit, each mem[1]- ber of the infinite universe, is to be regarded as a center from which such a ray emanates, touching other centers, and awakening there the light intrinsic in them. Or we may think of a fountain from which stream forth jets of indescribable life-power—playing out of it, playing into other life, and evoking there kindred and yet unkindred life-waves, waves effluent and refluent. Whatever the symbolism may be, inadequate in any case, the idea of the enmeshing of one's life in universal life without loss of distinctness—the everlasting selfhood to be achieved on the contrary, by means of the cross-relation—is the cardinal point.

I have here to answer one question. By what warrant do I ascribe worth to any human being? Where is the head deserving that this ray that streams out from me shall light upon it? What man or woman merits that he be invested with this glory? Does not the same objection opposed to Kant hold with respect to my own view? It is true that he found no object at all, and sought indirectly to draw from the empty notion of obligation the inference that man is an end *per se*. Perhaps it will be admitted that the supremely worthwhile object has now been found, the holy thing (holy in two ways, as being inviolable, reverence-inspiring, holding at a distance those who would encroach: and intrinsically priceless as a component of the ethical manifold, as indispensable in a perfect whole). But this object, you will say, is in the air, or in the heavens, and how shall it be made to descend on empirical man?

My answer is that certainly I do not discover the quality of worth in people as an empirical fact. In many people I do not even discover value. Judging from the point of view of bare fact, many of us could very well be spared. Many are even in the way of what is called "progress." And the suggestion of some extreme disciples of Darwin that the degenerate and defective should be removed, or the opinion of others that pestilence and war should be allowed to take the unpleasant business off our hands, is, from the empirical point of view, not easily to be refuted. I can also enter into, if I do not wholly share, the pessimistic mood with regard to actual human nature expressed by Schopenhauer and others. To the list of repulsive human creatures mentioned by Marcus Aurelius in one of his morning meditations,—the back-biter, the scandal-monger, the informer, etc.—might be added in modern times, the white-slaver, the exploiter of child-labor, the fawning politician, and many another revolting type. And even more discouraging in a way, than these examples of deepest human debasement—the copper natures, as Plato calls them, or the leaden natures, as we might call them—is the disillusionment we often experience with regard to the so-called gold natures, the discovery of the large admixture of baser metal which is often combined with their gold.

It is imperative to acquaint oneself, nay, to impregnate one's mind thoroughly with these contrary facts, if the doctrine of worth, the sanest and to my mind the most real of all conceptions, is to be saved from the appearance of an optimistic illusion.

The answer to the objection is that I do not *fmd* worth in others or in myself, I *attribute* it to them and to myself. And why do I attribute it? In virtue of the reality-producing functions of my own mind. I create the ethical manifold. The pressure of the essential rationality within me, seeking to complete itself in the perfect fruition of these functions, *i.e.,* in the positing of a total manifold and its total unification, drives me forward. I need an idea of the whole in order to act rightly, in such a way as to satisfy the dual functions within me. My own nature as a spiritual being urges me to seek this satisfaction. This ideal whole, as I have shown, is a complexus of uniquely differentiated units. In order to advance toward uniqueness, in order to achieve what in a word may be called my own truth, to build myself into the truth, to become essentially real, I must seek to elicit the consciousness of the uniqueness and the interrelation in others. I must help others in order to save myself; I must look upon the other as an ethical unit or moral being in order to become a moral being myself. And wherever I find consciousness of relation, of connectedness, even incipient, I project myself upon that consciousness, with a view to awaking in it the consciousness of universal connectedness. Wherever I can hope to get a response I test my power. Fields and trees do not speak to me, as Socrates said, but human beings do. I should attribute worth to stones and to animals could they respond, were the power of forming ideas, without which the idea of relation or connectedness is impossible, apparent in them. Doubtless stones and trees and animals, and the physical world itself, are but the screen behind which lies the infinite universe. But the light of that universe does not break through the screen where it is made up of stones and trees and the lower animals. It breaks through, however faintly, where there is consciousness of relation: and wherever I discover that consciousness I find my opportunity. It is quite possible that the men and women upon whom I try my power will not actually respond. The complaint is often heard from moral persons, or persons who think themselves such, that what they call the moral plan of rousing the moral consciousness in others will not work. Perhaps the plan they follow is not the moral plan at all, but the plan of sympathy or of some other empirically derived rule. But be that as it may, the question is not whether we get the response but whether we shall achieve reality or truth ourselves; in theological terms, save our own life, by trying to elicit the response.

And here one profoundly important practical consideration will come to our aid, namely, the sense of our own imperfection, coupled indeed with the consciousness of inextinguishable power of moral renewal. Instead of attributing the lack of response to the hopeless dullness of the person upon whom we labor, a sense of humility, based on the knowledge of our own exceeding spiritual variability—best moments followed by worst

122

moments, imperfect grasp on our own ideals, most imperfect fidelity in executing them—will lead us to turn upon ourselves, and far from permitting us to despair of others, will impel us rather to make ourselves more fitting instruments of spiritual influence than obviously as yet we are.[4]

i. The term "ethical unit" used above should be found useful. The chemists have found the concept of the atom useful, though no one has ever seen an atom. And all the sciences have recourse to similar inventions,—such as the electron, or the ion, or energy regarded as a substance, and in mathematics the sublimated, space-transcending concepts. Looking through the eyes of science, we are taught to see, underlying the grossest forms of matter, imaginary entities which are well-nigh metaphysical in nature. Science starts from the realm of the sensible, and constructs its super-rarefied devices on mechanical models. Then it leaves the field of the intuitively perceptible, and rises by the path of analogy into realms where the notions with which it operates are no longer imaginable. I do not wish, in speaking of an ethical, invisible, and unimaginable entity, to derive the postulation of this conception from science. The ethical concept transcends wholly the field of sensible experience. It is not discovered by way of analogy. It is frankly and overtly super-sensible. It is not exemplified in the effects it produces in the world of volition as the most nearly metaphysical concepts of science are exemplified in the field of phenomena by the recurrences or uniformities which they serve to account for. The ethical concepts are not verified by their results at all, not by recurrences of phenomena, but by the persistence of the effort to attain that which is finitely never attained, and *by the more explicit perception of the ideal itself* which follows the persistent effort; for as has been shown above, when face to face with fundamental truth, *seeing is believing.* But I allude to these matters in order to show that the movement in ethical thinking represented by the system which I propose is not contrary to the present-day movement in science, but in line with it, though beyond it. It does not ask leave of science; it does not base its certainty on scientific precedent; but neither does it expect a,veto from the lips of science. The worthwhileness of scientific endeavor itself depends at bottom on the sanction which i.e. ideal of the complete carrying out of the reality-producing functions lends to their incomplete execution in the world of the space and time manifold.

CHAPTER VI

THE IDEAL OF THE SPIRITUAL UNIVERSE AND

THE GOD-IDEAL

We have seen whence the ideal of a spiritual universe arises. It is unnecessary to prove that the universe is moral. What it is necessary to verify is that a universe exists; for "universe" is an ethical ideal, it is the ethical manifold, or, if we distinguish ethical as concerning relations between man and man, then we may use the term "spiritual" to designate that infinite system of interdependence in which men as ethical units have their place. We begin with the affirmation—Man is an end *per se*. This wonderful affirmation, which the democracies are darkly and confusedly trying to express in political and social arrangements, constitutes the problem of all problems. It is the great datum of ethics, of which ethical theory must give an account. All other data or problems that have been thrust into the foreground— freedom of the will, responsibility, altruistic self-sacrifice—are secondary, in the sense that they depend for their solution on a right conception of man as end *per se*. As possessing worth on his own account he is an ethical unit. Only as a member of the infinite spiritual universe does he possess the two-fold attributes implied in worth —inviolability with respect to outsiders and indefeasible, intrinsic preciousness. Therefore I say that around the

125

individual, the ethical unit, we build up as a necessary postulate the spiritual universe. Man ethically considered carries with him this infinite environment.

Does this universe exist or is it a mere figment? It is the product of the reality-producing functions in their ideal completion. It is the necessary postulate required if the idea of right is to have validity, and the idea of right is required by man in so far as he is an agent and not merely a spectator of life. The ethical manifold, the spiritual universe, exists in so far as there is a right.

Have we then reinstated the idea of God as existent? Not the idea of God as an individual. We have on the contrary set aside that idea by affirming that manifoldness cannot be derived from unity, that the positing of plurality is just as much a primary function of the mind as the positing of unity. We have discarded the God-idea as the *locus* of unity, since the unity subsists in the relation of the units. Strictly speaking, we have replaced the God-idea by that of a universe of spiritual beings interacting in infinite harmony.

But at this point I must go back for a moment to Kant, using his ideas once more as a foil to make my own more explicit. Wilhelm von Humboldt said of Kant that some of the things he had destroyed would never be rebuilt, and that some of the things he had built would never be destroyed.

For more than a hundred years the impression has prevailed that among the things forever destroyed by Kant are the proofs of the existence of God. He is represented as an intellectual giant whose blows have forever shattered the proofs on which the existence of a supersensible reality rested. Kant's mind was preeminently scientific. He was the philosopher who made explicit the principles underlying Newtonian science as Aristotle had made explicit the logic underlying the Greek science. His philosophy is essentially agnostic. The use that he continues to make of the God-idea can be dissociated from his system with advantage to the latter.[1]

[1] I do not however agree with those who regard the shreds of theology remaining in his system as a concession, not wholly ingenuous, to orthodoxy. He was brought up in the pietistic faith, and had probably not entirely outgrown the emotional impressions of those early teachings. The noumena, however, play a part in the system itself distinct from the theology, and are not to be taken as supersensible realities. They are limiting concepts intended to serve as incentives or lures, winning the mind to continue without cessation its advance along certain paths within the field of experience; but they are not supposed to give any clue as to what is beyond experience. That which is beyond the field of experience is simply unknowable. Thus the noumenon called "thing *per se"* is notice given to the mind not to be deterred in its proper business of unifying the space and time manifold by the difficulties which arise when the time and space manifold is taken as an ultimate account of reality. The thing *per se* is a welcome to science and not a bar set up in its path.

The noumenon of freedom is an incentive to man urging him to act as if he were capable of practicing the law of universality and necessity. In fact the phrase "as if" plays a leading role in the Kantian philosophy. The noumenon of God, as will presently be shown, is afflicted with this conditional "as if" character to even a higher degree. We are to assume God in order to look upon the vast field of possible experience as if it were unified, as if a being who himself stands for unity had been its creator. This assumption is supposed to be necessary in order to encourage the scientist in his search for the thread of unity, lest he flag by the way. As a matter of fact scientists have contented themselves with the simple

But did Kant indeed destroy the idea of a supersensible reality as existent, or are we warranted in undertaking to build anew the supersensible world.[2] *"Du hast sie zerstorrt, die schdne Welt, In deinem Busen bam sie 'wieder"*—not indeed in the realm of mere feelings, but in the sphere of will. The spell of Kant's shattering attack still rests upon the intellectual world today. The notion of a supersensible reality, if held at all, is held timidly, apologetically and is apt to be based on subjective emotional need. The wish is more or less admitted to be father to the faith—the will to believe is defiantly asserted in despair of sound foundations. A scientist like Dubois-Ileymond enumerates seven world riddles, or mysteries that cannot be explained, and after saying

assumption of the uniformity of nature as necessary to the prosecution of their investigations, and have as a rule troubled themselves little to hypostasize the notion of unity. Nor has recent progress in science been associated with and influenced by the belief in an individual Deity. The noumenon of God is unnecessary for science while in Kant's ethical application of it is positively harmful. He introduces the God notion as an artificial device for linking together happiness and virtue, a device quite inconsistent with the noble austerity of his ethical system, whatever its other defects may be.

The noumena, then, are apparitions that appear at the end of certain paths in the field of experience, far off where the sky and the ground seem to meet. These paths run off in different directions. At the end of each is one of these limiting apparitions, and the society of noumena is disconnected internally: there is no relation of unity between the unifiers.

[3] The difference between "supersensible" and "supernatural" is capital. I do not encourage relapse into supernaturalism. The supernatural is the opposite of the supersensible. It is an attempt to represent in natural or *sensible* guise what is supposed to be beyond the senses; and the naturalistic representation of the supersensible is then taken not metaphorically but literally.

that they cannot be explained, he seems to see that no alternative remains but to take refuge in resignation: "Ignoramus, ignorabimus 1"

That "explanation" is not the only avenue to truth, that the referring of effects to their causes is not the highest operation of the reality-producing functions, I have pointed out in a previous chapter. But Kant, as has been said, is supposed to have utterly annihilated the arguments intended to demonstrate the existence of God, and it will clear up the matter at issue if we consider wherein he actually succeeded and wherein he quite failed. As he himself declares, his method is regressive ; he does not attempt the progressive method path. He seeks to ascertain whether by going backward along the chain of effects and causes, or of conditions, he can somewhere find God as first cause or as unconditioned. He does not look forward looking to the ideals of the will. He does not enter into the realm of ends, where the necessity of determining action in obedience to some universal plan or scheme of relations might have forced itself on his attention. His approach, like his habit of mind, is scientific. He is not primarily an ethicist. Proceeding in this manner he shows that the notion of a first cause is untenable, and he attacks in particular the ontological argument by which every other argument supplements itself at the point where it breaks down.

Did Kant, however, annihilate the Ontological Argument? Yes, in the scholastic form in which it was held. No, in a form, based on the idea of the ethical manifold, in which it can be restated. In the scholastic form it runs: "There is such a thing as the idea of a perfect being. Existence is an element of perfection. If the perfect being did not exist it would be less than perfect. But the *ens realisdmum,* the perfect being, is present as an idea in the mind. Therefore it exists." The disproof of this amounts to the curt statement that what exists in the mind does not necessarily exist outside of it, or, as Kant put it: "The idea of 100 thalers in the head of a man is one thing, lacking no element of conceptual integrity; while the existence of the 100 thalers in the man's purse is an entirely different matter." The evidence of existence, in other words, depends on the synthesis of the data of sense as arranged in the space and time manifold in accordance with the categories of the understanding. Existence is temporal and spatial. To prove that God exists we should have to prove that he exists in the world of the senses. Of any other kind of existence we are agnostic. Kant's disproof of the Ontological Argument thus depends on his agnosticism.

But suppose that on ethical grounds we find ourselves compelled to affirm that there is an object which has worth, and that to account for the inviolableness, indispensableness and preciousness of this object we are compelled to give free rein to the reality-producing functions, and to place this object having worth as a member in a manifold not spatial and temporal but infinite: and suppose we say that the existence of this worth-endowed object, of this ethical unit with its compeers, is as certain as the notion of rightness is certain, have we not then without blame widened the conception of existence, and placed the Ontological Argument where Kant's disproof does not even touch it?[3]

One more important remark is here in place, suggested by Kant's designation of God as the ideal of reason, and by his designation of our highest nature as the rational nature.

Is "rational" equivalent to intellectual? If it be so, then feeling must be classed as irrational, and impulse likewise, since neither feeling nor impulse is subject to logical rules. And then the war will be on between the intellectualists or rationalists and the champions of irrational conceptions of life, since feeling and impulse actually make up the major part of life, and can neither be left out of account nor compressed into intellectualist formulas.[4]

Plainly, there is a deep misunderstanding between the two parties. Ac error is involved somewhere. It appears to consist in assuming that objectivity can be supplied only by the intellect, in overlooking the fact that

[4] He allows indeed the *Ens Realissimum* to remain, and calls it the ideal of the reason, the ideal of unity hypostasized, centralized in an individual, and somehow harboring within itself all real properties whatsoever. But it is quite impossible to conceive how all real properties can belong to a single individual. For the properties as we know them are incompatible with each other. Surely an individual cannot be both great and small, beautiful and ugly, of all colors and sounds, etc., etc. Or again if all properties were somehow assembled in one individual, since that individual is conceived of as an hypostasized unity, it would be impossible to speak of a relation between them, and yet upon the relation of the differentiae depends the ethical utility of the idea of a supreme reality.

* Compare, for instance, the anti-intellectualistic philosophy of Bergson, with its emphasis on planless spurts of energy, the irrationalist philosophy of Schopenhauer, etc.

the feelings and still more the volition possess intrinsic controls and norms of their own, that Science, the work of the intellect, and art and ethics, spring from a common root, namely, the reality-producing functions. The manifolds with which each of the three respectively deals are different, the methods of synthesis are different, but the root principle, synthesis of the manifold, is identical in all.

To describe our highest nature, therefore, as the rational nature is perilous, since the word rational suggests intellectual. Either we must strain the signification of reason to include feeling and will, which is contrary to common usage, or we should select some other term, such as *spiritual,* to designate that nature within us which operates in science and art and achieves its highest manifestation in producing the ethical ideal.

Finally, if what has been said regarding the ethical manifold holds good, then a genuine philosophy of life can only be reached by the ethical approach to the problems of life. This has never yet been consistently attempted. The approach has been made from the scientific or the logical side, or as in the case of Plato from the aesthetic, or as in modern times from the biological. Yet the ethical approach is full of promise. A philosophy of physical nature may be feasible without it, a philosophy of art may be possible without it, but not so a philosophy of life. It has not been tried because ethics has lain in the lap of theology, which was itself corrupted by the attempt to apply to ethical problems the inadequate principle of causality in the form of creation theories, while again in recent times, by way of reaction against theology, the solution of ethical questions is sought for in the empirical disciplines where a measure at least of objective certainty has rewarded the investigators. Even Kant, who asserted the independence of ethics, actually made it dependent on Newtonian science. The great task now is, strictly to carry out the idea of the independence of ethics, not indeed as if its principles were unrelated to those of science and art, but in the sense of independently investigating the problems *peculiar* to ethical consciousness. I am well aware that the attempt made in this volume to take the ethical line of approach to a general philosophy of life, is tentative and defective in a hundred ways, nevertheless it is an attempt in a new direction.

In the next book I shall take up the practical consequences that follow from the theory here advanced. Having delineated the ethical ideal, and discovered the invaluable fact that there is a structural plan contained in it, we shall see that our actual human duties may be derived by applying this ideal scheme to the quasi-organic groups already existing in human society. There are provocative correspondences to the ethical ideal in the social life of men; otherwise it would be impossible to apply it. There are human groups in which a quasi-correlative membership in a common life already exists. In the case of each of these groups we find some sort of empirical multiplicity which must be studied scientifically, and also an empirical motive which may be utilized in the interest of developing the ethical relation. The family is the first of these groups which offers a footing in the world of experience for the ideal. In the family natural affection is the motive; in the vocational group, the desire to express a talent or special gift; in the state, patriotism; in the church, the need felt to integrate all human ideals.

Thus the things of earth are to be used as instrumentalities by which we are to become aware of the spiritual reality. Only that the disparateness of the physical world and the ethical universe should ever be kept in the foreground. Every effort to solve the riddle by somehow identifying the two has failed. To account for the existence of a finite world of indefinite extensibility side by side with a universe *ex hypothesi* infinite is impossible. Instead of seeking to explain let effort go toward utilizing. Let the *world* be used instrumentally for the purpose of verifying the existence of *universe*.

For the average man, and indeed for all men, the test of the truth of a theory is in the practice to which it leads. Abstract metaphysical arguments appeal only to a few, and even for them the formula in its abstract guise is unconvincing. Look at the mathematical figure, and see whether the axioms hold good. Look at the sequent phenomena and see whether the so-called law of nature is exemplified. And so with respect to conduct: look at the ways of human behavior traced out in accordance with the plan of the ethical manifold, and see whether such behavior wins the approval of the spiritual nature implicit within you.[5]

[0] The above exposition is not a transcendental derivation of ethics. The ideal of the infinite society is a fulguration out *of* ethical experience, to be ever renewed *in it*. We build not only our world, but our universe.

NOTE I

There are various points at which the system sketched in the text deviates from current opinion, but in regard to the underlying proposition the reader's particular attention is called to the remarks on the "prejudice of causality" and to the statement that verification is exemplification.

How can ethical truth be verified? How can we be sure that ethical ideals are more than fine wishes, expressing subjective aspiration, but having no counterpart in the ultimate constitution of things? This is the dark doubt that haunts the minds of ethical writers, as well as of the average man. We ask to have the things we believe in, the objects of our supreme aspiration, verified. How can they be verified?

I think that we shall see light in this matter once we have grasped the thought that verification, both in science and in ethics, is nothing more than exemplification. In the case of causality, in science, verification does not consist in mere recurrence. For if we find, even by a single carefully guarded experiment, that a given phenomenon A is the true antecedent of B, then we take leave to predict that B will always follow A, without regard to the repetition of the sequence in our ex-

The ethical principle is not a working hypothesis, like those provisionally used in science. It is the outgrowth of the functional finalities. It is a postulate. The specific moral laws, or expressions of the ethical principle indeed, are changeable, being the product of the principle with the varying empirical conditions of human society. The fundamental principle is unchangeable.

The consciousness of universal interrelation is not to be described as mystical consciousness. The identity of the self remains intact; it is never lost in the One or the All. The ethical consciousness includes indeed the consciousness of other selves related to our own, in a kind of superindividual consciousness. But this is reached along the sunlit path of action (So *act,* etc.), and not along the dreamy flux of emotionalism or in the silent depths of quietism.

perience.[5] Indeed, no amount of repetition would justify prediction. The problem in the case of causality is to determine the true antecedent and the true consequent. For at any moment there are innumerable phenomena that might possibly be antecedents of B. How obtain certainty that A is the causal antecedent? By the synthetic process. We assume a unity, say energy. We assume that there are differentiæ, say a certain mathematically determined quantum of mechanical energy in A, and a determined quantum of thermal energy in B. No sooner have these differentiae been mathematically determined, than in virtue of the assumed unity of energy underlying the differences, we pronounce the nexus to be necessary. We predict that B will always follow A.

Causality, therefore, is an example of a synthesis which over-arches sequences. The fact that the phenomena are sequent does not affect the principle involved. Whenever we contemplate an example of synthesis, that is, defined differentiae of some sort, and a defined underlying unity of some sort, the mind affirms that reality exists. There are degrees of reality. The degree of completeness with which the synthetic function is carried out in any instance determines the degree.

Ethical verification is likewise exemplification, though in another sense. When the ideal plan of ethical relations is presented, the ideal plan being a synthesis not of sequences but of all co-existent entities whatsoever, the mind assents to this ideal plan as representing the complete synthesis or the complete reality. The more explicitly and definitely the relation between

---

[5] The frequent recurrence gives us a sense of safety in expecting the consequent on the appearance of the antecedent. But the sense of safety should not be confounded with the sense of the certainty. We expect that day will follow night, because it has followed innumerable times. But no amount of repetition can warrant the assertion that it will and must do so. The Pragmatist view explains the sense of safety in expectation, but does not appear to account for the certainty in prediction, as for instance in the astronomer's prediction of an eclipse.

the ethical units is conceived, the greater the conviction of reality resulting. Now frustration after partial achievement has the effect of making more explicit the idea of the plan of relations as it ought to be carried out in human life. And in this sense I would have the reader understand the main practical argument of the book—that frustration is the condition of our intensified conviction as to the reality of the supersensible universe.

In virtue of the constitution of our minds we cannot help acknowledging as real that which is synthesized. Synthesized and real are synonymous terms. Hence the idea of the completed synthesis necessarily is the idea of the ultimate reality.

NOTE II

The three principal respects wherein Kant has failed to justify his affirmation that every human being is to be regarded as an end *per se,* and not to be used as a tool, are:

1. Out of the bare experience of oughtness, absolute constraint, he seeks to derive personality. Out of the empty categorical imperative he seeks to draw a substantive entity—a being possessed of worth.

2. The society of ends *per se* described by him is not a true society, but a collection of atomic individuals juxtaposed. The capital flaw in his ethics is here. He begins by detaching the individual. He studies the individual, and discovers, or believes himself to have discovered, that something happens in him (the consciousness of absolute constraint) which entitles him to be considered worth while on his own account.

Next, since the formula of university proposes instability by others as the test of a moral act, all others are called in as concomitants of the detached atom first considered. Each of the concomitants in turn is an atomic entity. It is in this mechanical way that the conception of a kingdom of ends, or a holy community, is supposed to be validated. Kant's mistake is to assume that an individual regarded as an isolated being can

137

be worth while, can be an end *per se.* The notion of end involves relation to others, not mechanical juxtaposition, but intrinsic connection. No one is worth while by himself. He has worth only as an organic member of a spiritual whole. The unique quality which lends him incomparable distinction is the creative life which emanates from him and quickens cognate but diversely modified life in his associates.

3. Kant's version of the ethical rule is strong on the side of interdiction, but quite inadequate on the positive side. He tells us that we are to look on others not merely as means to our own ends, but also ends *per se.* The vagueness is in the formula "not merely . . . but also." Where the dividing line is to be drawn he does not tell. I am at liberty to use the services of others in the prosecution of my own interests, as they may use mine, since we are social beings and dependent on one another. But how far may I go in this direction? On this point we are left wholly in the dark. Kant admits into his system the so-called natural ends,[7] such as wealth, culture and the like, gives them leave to abound, only with the proviso that they may not overpass a certain limit,—the limit beyond which they would interfere with the rights of fellowmen. An instrumental view of wealth, science, culture, as positively promoting the ethical end of man, he does not and cannot establish.[8] But the instrumental view is precisely that in which *modern* society has most at stake, on the working out of which the solution of our most pressing problems,—such as the labor problem, the problem of the family, the problem of patriotism and international relations—is entirely dependent. If Kant has failed at this point, as I believe he has, his usefulness as a guide in the reconstruction of modern life is seriously diminished. What he had set out to demonstrate, the inalienable worth of man, remains; but foundations other than his must

[7] A hybrid conception, since in nature there are only happenings, but no ends.

[8] His efforts in some measure to remedy this defect in the Doctrine of Virtue are artificial and unconvincing.

be found. For the formula "not merely as a means but also as an end" I would substitute: Treat every man as a spiritual means to thine own spiritual end and conversely . . . treat the extent and the manner in which we are to use one another as means being determined by the criterion that our exchange of services shall conduce to the attainment of each other's ends as ethical beings conjointly.

NOTE III

I would also ask the reader to consider well the effect upon the philosophy of life of the position taken throughout this volume that there is no intellectual bridge between the finite order and the infinite order. This involves dropping creation at the beginning and immortality in its usual sense at the end. Creation is an attempt to show how the world, including man, proceeded out of the infinite. Immortality is an attempt to express how man returns to the infinite. In this volume man's dealings with the finite order are represented as having for their purpose the achievement of the conviction that there verily is an infinite life, a supersensible universe. Creation systems, pantheistic systems, certain evolutionary systems, also the Hegelian system, are futile attempts to explain the How. But explanation is impossible; for to explain means to understand, and to understand means to trace an effect to its cause. And causality is not the kind of synthesis applicable to a coexistent totality.

Among practical consequences note the difference between the theistic attitude in fatal sickness and the spiritual attitude.[9] The theist presupposes that there is a God to whose will he must patiently submit. But theism is a principle of explanation, the God-idea being employed to account for the finite order. God is thus made responsible for the suffering of the sick as well as for all other evils in the world. Hence the very idea which is presupposed in order to produce patience

• See Book III for a fuller development of this point.

139

raises up doubts and perplexities, which imperil patience. If God made the world why does he permit pain and evil? The spiritual attitude, on the contrary, ethically interpreted, does not presuppose the idea of a divine order as a dogma, but offers it as the product of the experience of suffering itself. The conviction that there is in man an essential spiritual self, a holy thing, and a spiritual universe, a holy community, are not gifts to which we fall heir at birth, or by some sort of revelation borrow from the experience of ancient teachers; they are a supreme good to be arduously worked out by ourselves. And the interpretation given to the facts of suffering and frustration is that they can be used as the means of bringing to birth in us that supreme conviction.

In general it may be said that the purpose of existence, both of the individual and of the race, is so to work in the finite world as to become possessed with ever greater distinctness of the conviction of the reality of the wholly real world, the infinite supersensible universe.

The attitude of the Christian is other-worldly. He shuns intimacy with the finite world and turns his face toward his "true home." The attitude herein described is that of hearty attack upon the business of life, and close embrace of all the partial reality which finite experience contains, with a view of thus acquiring in some measure an appreciation of the utter reality of which these partial realities are hints and glimmerings.

NOTE IV

In the case of any new theory, it is true that one must live with it for a considerable time before acquiring the habit of thinking in accordance with it. The older habits constantly crop up and interfere with the correct understanding of any new point of view. This is especially so of a new attitude towards reality. The world seems topsy-turvy to one who learns for the first time that grass and the leaves of trees are not really green apart from the eye that sees them, that beings with different organs might interpret differently that which stimulates the human eye to its specific color reactions. The heliocentric theory, when first announced by Copernicus, outraged naive commonsense. It exacted a new habit of thinking in regard to the relation of the sun to the earth,—the real relation, apprehended by intercalated mental processes being the direct opposite of the apparent relation. The sun evidently revolves around the earth, nevertheless the truth is that the earth revolves around the sun.

Modern science reveals behind the palpable world around us unimaginable fluids, speeds, and physical units which are so sublimated in thought as to be barely distinguishable from metaphysical entities. The habit of penetrating with radium-like glance the concrete screen of things, and of seeing behind the screen the company of atoms, ions, etc., may be gradually acquired; but the older habit of regarding the palpable and visible *as* the truly real continues to assert itself in conflict with the new habit.

The ethical unit in an ethical manifold postulated in the text as the closest, though still symbolic, reading of the ultimate reality, makes a similar demand upon the reader, and requires of him in like manner the formation of a new habit of thinking, against which the older habits will doubtless continue to protest.

The most obstinate of the older habits that stand in the way has been dealt with in the note on causality, namely,—the unscientific habit of ignoring the boundaries of science, and of taking the method employed in the physical sciences as the sole method that leads to certainty. The prejudice of causality is probably ineradicable, just as the illusion that the sun revolves about the earth persists. But we can at least reach the point of realizing that it is a prejudice, and to this extent overcome it. If it be synthesis, or the employment in insepa-rable conjunction of the two functions mentioned, that for the human mind spells reality, then one kind of synthesis called causality, that of sequent phenomena, does not exclude the ampler, though ideal synthesis, which is carried out in the mental production of the ethical manifold. So much I wish to add to the statements contained in the text in regard to the theory.

But there is also a new habit to be acquired in regard to the practical ethical consequences of the theory. The chief of these is the prizing of distinctive difference above uniformity or sameness. The ethical quality is that quality in which a man is intrinsically unique. The ethical act is the most completely individualized act (I ought perhaps to say personalized, but the completely individualized act *is* that of a unique personality). In brief, the emphasis is here put on that in which a man differs from all others, and not on the common nature which he shares with the rest; or rather, since the common nature is not denied, the stress is put on the intrinsically different mode in which the common nature is expressed in him.[10]

The accentuation in current ethical discussion of the common nature of man, and the fallacious assumption that the common interests are the pre-eminently moral interests, that uniformity is the test of ethical quality, is easy to understand. It is the reaction of the modern world against feudalism, a social system not yet entirely outgrown, in which the empirical differences of rank and birth were made the basis of intolerably oppressive discriminations, and in which it was an accepted axiom that some men are baked of better clay than others. It is also a reaction against the capitalistic system that has taken the place of the feudal, in which wealth is to a considerable extent made the standard of social appraisement.

It is against these false discriminations that the voice of humanity is now indignantly raised, affirming the moral equality of all men. But equality is mistakenly taken to mean likeness in the sense of sameness, not in the sense of that fundamental like-

[10] Difference in the ethical meaning is not to be confounded with mere idiosyncrasy, or originality, not to say eccentricity. It is the kind of difference which elicits correlated difference in all spiritual associates.

ness on the background of which the desirable unlikenesses stand forth. And this notion of equality as identical with sameness leads to great practical aberrations. Thus, for instance, women are not only to be recognized as the equals of men, but are to be the same as men,—their education patterned on that of men, their specific functions, as far as possible, ignored. For unlikeness is supposed to connote inferiority, and inferiority is justly repelled as morally intolerable. But aside from this one example, the stressing of the common nature, or of the basis of likeness at the expense of the oustanding unlikenesses, leads to other leveling tendencies of which modern democracies furnish many unpleasing illustrations. Thus uniform popular opinion, encompassing the individual on every side, penetrates into his inmost thinking, so that he hardly ventures to hold to his own judgment against the judgments of the majority. And the impulses of the mass tend also to threaten his independence in action. There is indeed a certain intoxication in the very sense of being submerged in a large whole, a certain glad loss of self in great impersonal movements, a certain strain of democratic pantheism, as it were, that takes the place with some of mystic absorption in Deity. But whatever the value that may attach to these upswellings of feeling, it is counterbalanced by the circumstance that in proportion as indiscriminate devotion to society as a whole becomes the paramount motive, the suborganisms of society, the family, the vocation and the state, in which the ethical personality is ripened, are threatened with effacement. Instead of moral equality it were better to use the term "moral equivalence." The differences are to be stressed; they are the coruscating points in the spiritual life of mankind. That every man is the equal of his fellows means that he has the same right as each of the others to become unlike the others, to acquire a distinct personality, to contribute his one peculiar ray to the white light of the spiritual life.

144

BOOK III

APPLICATIONS: THE THREE SHADOWS, SICKNESS, SORROW AND SIN, AND THE RIGHT TO LIFE, PROPERTY AND REPUTATION

CHAPTER I

INTRODUCTION

THREE main thoughts should be kept clear: the end to be realized, the incongruity of the finite and the infinite order, and hence, thirdly, the indispensable ministry of frustration in the realization of the purpose of life.

In regard to the so-called moral end of life, there has been much variety and contrarity of teaching. I shall touch only upon that aspect of the doctrine expounded in the previous book wherein it seems to resemble other doctrines, and where a distinct statement of the difference is therefore imperative. "So act as to develop the faculties of thy fellow-man" is not the rule proposed. "So act as to develop the so-called good qualities in the man" is not the rule proposed. The rule reads, "Act so as to bring out the spiritual personality, the unique nature of the other." Now, in putting the matter in this way, we incurred the danger of seeming to concentrate attention on the individual as a detached being, we seemed to have him only in mind, though it is true, in respect to what is intrinsic in him, the irreducible ethical unit which he essentially is. We must, therefore, constantly remind ourselves that the ethical unit, while unique, is at the same time an inseparable member of a society of differentiated units; that its very distinctiveness consists in injecting, as it were, streams of dynamic energy into its fellow-beings. Or, as I have elsewhere figuratively put it, the distinctiveness of any ethical being consists, so to speak, in emitting a ray the color of which is nowhere else to be found, the miraculous quality of which consists in acquiring this color at the very instant in which it causes counter or complementary colors to appear in its fellow-being. (I am using the words "instant," "miraculous," "ray of light," etc., of course, in a wholly figurative sense.)

We have at last, this is my belief, achieved a positive definition of the spiritual nature. The spiritual nature is that which forever is social in a supra-social sense, as embracing not only human society, but a universal society of spirits. The spiritual nature is that of which the very life consists in starting up unlike but equally worthwhile life elsewhere, everywhere. The spiritual experience to get hold of, therefore, is the consciousness of this inter-relation.

The moral end to be realized, in accordance with the deductions of Book II, is "So to act upon another as to evoke in him, and conjointly in oneself, in the same movement and counter-movement the consciousness of the interlacedness of life with life, the reciprocal, universal, infinite interrelatedness.

Now, as a fact, we never realize this end. If we did we should possess what alone is properly called freedom,— freedom in the positive sense being the exercise of power peculiar to ourselves, welling up out of our veriest self, and executing the totality of its effects. Freedom is marked by these two signs: energy coming unborrowed out of self, and producing the totality of its effeets. I am free when the thing I do is verily my own, when the 'power released is the power of my essential self; and when that power is nowhere checked, inhibited or interrupted, so that it produces its due, that is, its universal effects.

An ethical being in an ethical universe would be free. The dynamic energy proceeding from it would be aboriginal. And since it would radiate upon every other member of the infinite society, it would also produce the unstinted plenitude of its effects. Each ethical unit, at its station, would be at once the *producer and the recipient of the totality of life.*[1]

It is apparent from what has been said that the superlative, sublime thing, freedom, is not realizable except in an infinite world. And hence that the supreme end to be realized by man as a finite being cannot be the full release of unique power in himself. But neither can the end be approximation. In so serious a business as a philosophy of life we ought not to play with words, nor delude ourselves with the implication of proximity seern-ingly contained in the word approximation. For it being admitted that we cannot reach the ideal, approximation seems to suggest that we come into its neighborhood. But the truth is that the more we advance the less do we arrive in the immediate neighborhood of the ideal, the distance at which it lies becoming ever more remote.

[1] Incidentally it may be remarked that in introducing the category of interrelation we remove the objection against freedom "which remains unmitigable so long as freedom is supposed to be a kind of causality, competing with natural causality. Causality is the unity of a temporal manifold of sequent phenomena. The concept of interrelation is the concept of the unity of co existent entities.

The moral end, therefore, for a finite nature, like that of man, is just to realize the unattainableness of the end. There must be no heaven-on-earth illusions, no resting in the development of our inadequate human faculties, and no illusions as to approximation. The unattainableness of the infinite end in the finite world by the finite nature is the Alpha and Omega of the doctrine, as I propound it. Only after this truth has been fully faced and recognized, shall we be in a position to take in the vast significance of the fact that we are nevertheless under a certain coercion to persist in our efforts to attain the unattainable, and in inquiring into the source from which this pressure comes, we shall be led to infer the influence in us of an infinite nature enshrined in this finite nature of ours. In other words, to admit the unattainableness of the end in a finite world by a finite being is the very condition of our acquiring the conviction that there is an infinite world, and that we, as possessing an infinite nature, are included in it.[2]

I have now covered the points mentioned: the end to be realized, the incongruity of the two orders, and the cardinal importance of frustration as a spiritual experience, as a means of spiritual education.

From this point of view the whole question of how to deal with the frustrations of life assumes a new aspect. Lessing published his well-known essay on the Education of the Race towards the close of the eighteenth century.[3] Interest in the subject has since been obscured by

[2] See some fine remarks on the unattainableness in Tyrrel's *Christianity at the Cross-roads.*
[3] *Die Erziehttng det Menschengeschlechts.*

150

the scientific movement, and especially by the evolutionary philosophy. The latter excludes the idea of education in the proper sense, and substitutes for it a natural process, a genetic unfolding. The education of the human race, and of the human individual from the spiritual point of view consists in a series of efforts never to be intermitted, but not necessarily following each other in an orderly series, aiming to embody the infinite in the finite.

Both partial success and failure in these efforts are instrumental to the achievement of the task of mankind. Both serve to make more explicit the character and extent of the ideal, while the ultimate inevitable failure painfully instructs man in the fact of the incongruity of the two orders. The only outcome of human history that we can view with satisfaction on a large scale, is the same as that which we should regard as the best outcome of an individual life, namely, the growing conviction and the clearer vision of the eternal spiritual universe as real. We might say that that man had lived best who on his death-bed could declare with perfect truth: "I have achieved the certainty, and in through the vicissitudes of my life, that there is a universe." I here emphasize again the distinction between universe and world. To say that the universe is "good" is equivocal. The term "good," as commonly used, describes the moral striving of a finite nature, and not the quality that belongs to the spiritual universe and its members, thinking of them as ideally we must, as freed from finite limitation. Of the spiritual universe, we might use the term "supra-good," only we should then be careful to add that the "beyond good" is to be conceived as lying in the direction of the good, while transcending it. Thereby we avoid the pitfall of Nietzsche and of others who speak in a totally different sense of the "beyond good and evil." We read of a man blessing his children on his death-bed. The highest type of man is the one who *in articulo mortis* can bless the universe.

The discrepancy of the finite and the infinite order appears on the physical and moral sides. On the physical side it thrusts itself upon our attention in the circumstance that juxtaposition and sequence are incapable of being unified, or totalized. Space and time and that which fills them, matter, are by nature incongruous with spirit. On the moral side the incongruity appears in the deflecting forces of appetite and passion which hinder us in the attainment of the spiritual end and, in the fact that our so-called higher faculties are in irreconcilable conflict with one another. The harmonious union of all of them in any individual is a fiction. It is impossible to be fully developed on all sides. And in addition the social substrata in which the spiritual relation has to be worked out, are themselves too deeply beset with internal contrarieties to serve their purpose adequately. The sex relation, for instance, is to a certain extent favorable to the achievement of spirituality, that is, of living in the life of another; yet on the other hand there are elements in it that defeat this very object.

I write, therefore, at the head of such words of counsel as I can hope to give in respect to the conduct of life, the word *Frustration.* It is understood that this word is not used in the pathetic sense. First because there is partial achievement, moments in life at which the rainbow actually seems to touch the earth. Love and marriage, the completing of a beautiful work of art, the discovery of a new law of nature, the emancipation of an oppressed class, are examples. But these partial successes are presently seen to be partial; they are followed, or even in the moment of triumph, permeated, with the sense of incompleteness and the foreboding of new obscurities and perplexities advancing upon the mind. Yet essentially the doctrine is not a melancholy doctrine, because frustration, though a painful instrument, is yet a necessary instrument of spiritual development. We are not open to the reproach of dampening the zest and relish for life of those who are setting out to try the hazard of their fortunes. They shall put forth their best effort to succeed, but let them be so guided herein that they may meet in the right attitude of mind the disillusionment which is the condition of the revelation. The shadows will and must descend before they can be parted, disclosing the landscape of the spiritual universe.

CHAPTER II

THE THREE GREAT SHADOWS: SICKNESS, SORROW,

SIN

HAVING concentrated attention upon the point that the end is not the development of any particular faculty or assemblage of faculties, but the awakening in man, in and through his development, of the consciousness of interrelation, of life in life, we shall now turn to the three great shadows: sickness, sorrow, sin. In the case of sickness the suffering, however acute, must be made to pass over into action. There is a certain work to be done, something to be accomplished on the sick bed. What is it? I shall briefly review a few of the answers that have been given.

First, the Stoic says: A man in pain is to resist the pain by an act of will, thereby demonstrating that his essential self is inaccessible to bodily suffering. "If there is a pain in thy limb, remember that the pain is in thy limb, and not in thyself." Now the fortitude of the Stoic is admirable as far as it goes; his counsels are bracing and manly. But, because he is a materialistic pantheist, the reason he gives for his defiance of pain is not convincing. In effect his appeal is rather to the empirical than to the spiritual nature of man. The spiritual nature is characterized by humility; the appeal of the Stoic is to pride. Fate with all its sledgehammer blows shall not crush him. Yet the Stoic's pride when put to the supreme test does not avail, and the proof of it is that at the last it breaks down in suicide.

We come to a second answer. There is business in hand for the sufferer on the sick bed. What is the business? To hide the expression of his suffering, so that the cloud which rests on him may not cast its shadow upon others, obscuring their sunshine. But, we are bound to ask, are others always worthy of such consideration? Is not our sympathetic regard for their pleasures, their sunshine, often misplaced? Are not their pleasures often selfish and frivolous? The Greeks believed that outcries in situations of great distress are perfectly legitimate, since they seem to afford a kind of relief. Is it not cruel to forbid such outcries? In our age the view prevails that it is a proof of moral grandeur to suppress the signs of suffering. But the cynical question obtrudes itself whether it may not be the collective selfishness of the multitude that imposes this rule. The common run of men desire to go on their way undisturbed by cries that emanate from the sick chamber, and perhaps it is on this account that they impose a rule of behavior based, not on the principle of human worth, but on its opposite. The individual forsooth is not to count; the unhappiness of one is not to interfere with the happiness of the greater number!

There is, however, another view of the matter possible. Everyone carries his own particular burden. When tortured by some painful malady, we are apt to think that others, because they wear a smiling exterior, are therefore free from pain. But often those who seem in sound health are in fact as great sufferers as we, or even greater. And physical pain is not the only kind of suffering. Why, then, should I, for one, add to the troubles of others by imposing my own upon them? Put in this way, it is plain that there is an ethical element in the kind of behavior that is expected of a manly person. But the reason assigned, sympathy with the pleasures of others, is unconvincing. Unless there be some good to which grievous suffering can be made instrumental, there is no warrant for enduring it. As for the Stoics, so for the philosopher of sympathy, the logical end would be suicide, at least when the pain is exceptionally intense.

There is a third answer. Something is to be worked out on the sick bed. What is it? To be purified in the furnace, to learn patience and humble submission to the inscrutable will of God. Patience is the supreme virtue. "Be patient, Oh, be patient," I once heard a dying man repeat with touching accents. But patience for the sake of what? There must be some object to be gained by the patience to make it commendable. I can be patient in a storm at sea if I may entertain the hope of reaching port. I can be patient in conducting a difficult scientific experiment if I may hope that it will issue in an important discovery, or prepare the way for such discovery by others. I can be patient in sickness if I have any reason to expect a return to health. But patience for mere patience's sake is absurd. Well, then, the third answer is,—patience for the sake of manifesting your faith and trust in a wise and beneficent Deity. Why he has sent this suffering, why he has so made

156

the world that it is replete with the agony of sentient creatures we do not know. We cannot know. But he knows. Trust him, have faith in him: "Though he slay me yet will I trust him."

Here a genuine characteristic of the spiritual attitude has been expressed, but the ground on which it is put is once more unconvincing. How do I know that there is such a being as this wise and loving Deity of whom you tell me? By the evidence of his works, by the testimony of the world he has created, by the life for which I am indebted to him. But the world is the playground of good and evil forces. There is a semblance of design; there is on the other hand apparently the wildest disorder. The stars in their courses travel with incredible celerity in every direction, but no astronomer has ever yet been able to discern a plan in their journeyings. Human life is full of sorrow as well as joy; and whether there be more sorrow or more joy in the lives of most persons, who will venture to say? There is kindness, but there is also cruelty. There is cooperation, and there is merciless competition. There is health and bloom, and there is miserable physical decay. At present, in my case, suffering and sorrow are in the ascendant. The picture of the Deity as fashioned from the evidence of experience is dark and bright, cruel and kind. If he be omnipotent, why did he introduce the elements of discord and trouble into his creation? Why, in particular, does he at present torture me so cruelly? In order that I may believe in him despite the evidence! But how can I believe, seeing that in my own case the evidence on the bad side preponderates ? Thus the mind

of the sufferer on his couch of pain gropes in the labyrinth of argument and counter-argument—for the intellectual processes are often preternaturally acute in
times of physical suffering—and there is no outlet. In
a fine spiritual nature there is something which pleads
that the counter-arguments ought not to prevail. Des-
perately, by an act of faith, a man lays hold on his
God. But presently his faith again relaxes, his state
of mind becomes confused, and unless supported by
strong impressions received in and retained from childhood on, the third answer will not avail him.

There is business in hand on the sick bed. What is
it? The fourth answer, the answer as it appeals to me,
depends on the very incongruity of the finite and the
infinite order. Every attempt to explain this incongruity breaks down, every theodicy is a fiction. To explain is to find the cause of effects. But the notion of
cause does not apply to the relation between the finite
and the infinite. And of the infinite order itself we
possess only the plan or scheme of relations. The members of this ideal world are related to one another in
such a manner that the essential uniqueness of the one
is to be provocative of the diverse distinctiveness of the
others. This, as I think, is a very fruitful formula, fur-
nishing a rule of conduct to be applied to our finite relations. But it sheds no light on the uniqueness itself,
which is forever ideal. What in its ultimate constitution our spiritual being may be, remains unknown.
Did we know, were we capable of comprehending the
infinite order, and seeing things in that supersolar light,
we might then be able to solve the insoluble riddle,

the coexistence side by side of the finite and the infinite. As it is, the problem of finiteness especially in its human aspect of suffering and evil is impenetrable, inexplicable. *But if we cannot explain suffering and evil, we can utilize them for a definite spiritual end.* And that end is to achieve through the ministry of frustration and the persistence of the effort toward the unattainable, the consciousness of the reality of the spiritual universe and of our membership in it.

The answer, therefore, which I should offer, is based on this pivotal distinction between explaining and using. And thus the business in hand, the end to be gained, is the intensified realization of our spiritual interconnectedness with others, the life in life. To this end we accept from the Stoic, though for a reason which he does not give, resistance to pain, and from the philosopher of sympathy the obligation of not clouding the life of others with our shadow, and from the theologian the law of patience—and we take a step beyond all three.

Let me carry this out somewhat more in detail. To gain the consciousness of interrelation, there must be an object outside of myself of supreme interest to me, enabling me to transcend the ego. Now, pain has the opposite effect, that of concentrating attention on the ego. Pain builds a prison around us, raises up high walls which shut us in. Anyone in great pain is incessantly reminded of his physical state. In order that the mind may pass out of the prison cell and over the encompassing wall, there needs to be some object beyond the wall appealing enough to solicit the outward movement. This object is the spiritual self of my fellowmen. It is my concern for their spiritual self which is their highest good, it is my eager wish to reinforce what is best in them that works the transcendence of the ego and of its pains. In such supreme moments the lesser values dwindle into relative insignificance. And what is best in others is the same consciousness on their part of the interrelation. It is this that I am to awaken in them, to strengthen in them by the intensity with which I myself realize it. In the case of loving kin and friends, they, too, suffer with me. In vain I try to hide my sufferings. They divine what I try to suppress; and the more I try to suppress it, the more they suffer with me. They suffer not only with the suffering, but with the attempt to conceal the suffering. I have seen this in the case of a mother at the bedside of her dying daughter. They go with me to the brink of life. They enter into the anxieties and forebodings that haunt my mind as I face death. There may be young children that still need fostering care. Dangers to the family may arise after I am gone. The more my life is implicated in the lives around me, the more as I stand on the edge of life will my thoughts be occupied, not with the obliteration of my empirical self, but with the future of those that survive—that best future of theirs which I long to assure. And they, in turn, if they are fine natures, will pass through this inward experience with me. Thus I descend into the darkness and the depths, and they descend with me; and I am also to rise out of the darkness and the depths, and am to gain the force to do this in order that I may lift them with me.

This is the business in hand. I am to draw myself

out of the depths, to overcome the centralizing, egotizing effects of physical and mental pain, in order by my effort to make those around me realize the intensity with which I feel my interrelatedness with them, and thereby to reveal to them the same spiritual power in themselves. Plans for the future education of the children, counsels of peace, by way of anticipation for the too lonely hours that await the most loving and the most beloved,—these things have value chiefly in so far as they are insignificant of the indissoluble interlacing of life with life.[1]

[1] I have spoken of the sick bed as surrounded by loving friends and near of kin. There are sick beds where the situation is quite different,—in the poor wards of hospitals for instance. Nevertheless, the loneliest person is never without certain human relations. It may be the pauper in the next bed, the nurse, or the physician, to whom his behavior will be of lasting meaning.

I would add a word as to the attitude of a person who is threatened with insanity, and who is aware that the disease is approaching. His last conscious act should be to honor the community to which he belongs by voluntarily putting himself out of the way of harming them. Not that the physical harm is itself the principal thing, but that the wish not to harm physically is the sign of his sense of the ethical relation in which he stands to his fellows. Also a person threatened in this way ought to be willing to put himself in the keeping of others, even of strangers, as being no longer himself competent to judge rightly of what shall be done to him. It is true that in accepting the judgment of strangers as a substitute for his own he is taking the risk of being treated with insufficient consideration, and possibly even mistreated. Yet the jeopardy in which he thus puts his future, the sacrificial act he performs, is evidence of mental nobility at the very moment when mental night is about to set in for him.

CHAPTER III

BEREAVEMENT

WHEN we reflect on what actually happens in cases of bereavement, we shall find great diversity in different situations. It may be that the deceased person has led a worthless life, and that the grave is allowed to close over him without much regret. Nevertheless, the honor due to worth that *never appeared in him* ought to be shown. In the worst cases we may not treat human beings like animals. Besides, there are generally one or more persons who seem to have an unreasoning natural affection for the wretched being, and so he does not go wholly without the tribute of tears. Others, like sufferers from cancer, pass through days, weeks, months of acute pain before they die. In their case it is said that death comes as a relief, and often the final relief from the suffering obscures the loss.

Again, in most men's lives there is an upper and an under side. Though the public career of statesmen, poets, artists may be dazzling, yet their faults or obliquities are probably well enough known to those who have seen them at close range. Obituaries are seldom truthful. Sometimes, however, the reverse happens; men whose names are held up to public obloquy are not always as black as they are painted. Their worst side

162

becomes known to the public, yet they sometimes possess wonderfully fine traits.

Very pathetic is the mourning for a baby, and its unfulfilled promise, or for a defective child, long a burden, yet strangely grieved for when its feeble little flame of life is extinguished.

The most poignant sorrow is that which cannot be communicated to others or shared by others, because the tie severed by bereavement, like that of husband and wife, is between two only. The loss by death of a beloved life companion is apt to lead to an inconsolable state of mind, because in this relation, when finely interpreted; the empirical and the spiritual appear almost to coincide. The ethical rule, Live in the life of another, live so as to enhance to the highest degree the possibilities of another, seems almost no longer a counsel of perfection but an actual experience. Hence the utter grief into which the sundering of the tie is apt to plunge the survivor. On the other hand, Jonathan Edwards said on his deathbed to his wife: "Our relation has been spiritual, and therefore is eternal." And there is indeed an element of eternality in marriage, only it is not the sex relation as such that is or can be conceived of as eternal. It is not man and woman in their empirical form to which this attribute belongs. Marriage is the sign; the spiritual relation that which is signified.[1]

[1] In the New Testament, despite the preference expressed for celibacy, the relation of the bridegroom to the bride is used metaphorically to represent that of Christ with the church, and among the mystics the same figure represents the union of Christ with the believing soul.

It may be objected that marriage being a tie strictly between two, one can hardly think without repugnance of an equally intimate, nay, far more intimate, relation with all spiritual beings whatsoever. Yet the spiritual relation is one in which the ethical being is conceived to be in touch with each of the infinite beings that comprise the spiritual universe, pouring its essential life into them, and receiving theirs in return. Is not then the sign incompatible with and contradictory to the thing signified? But it is not of the multitude of mortal men and women surrounding us that we think when we speak of the eternal hosts. From this surrounding swarm of mortals, we retreat, taking refuge in the inmost privacy which we share with one other only. Yet this very inmost intimacy, so far as it is pure, is the emblem of that pure intercourse of essential being with essential being in which we are related to all.[6]

Following up the subject of bereavement, we find the following consolations employed:

The first to be mentioned is, "Bow to the inevitable."

---

[6] I call attention to the difference between the view here expressed and that of Emerson in the last paragraphs of his *Essay on Love,* where he says: "Our affections are tents of a night. Our warm loves are clouds that pass over the firmament of mind with its overarching vault, its galaxies of immutable lights. In the personal relations we are put in training for impersonal submergence and absorption in God." In my own view the infinite community of spiritual beings that takes the place of God consists altogether of personalities. Godhead, if you choose to apply that name to this infinite society, is not a person but a community of personalities. Personality is not drowned in the impersonal. On the contrary, the individual becomes a personality through his relation to his associates in the eternal life.

164

I include this because frustration is inevitable, on account of the discrepancy between the finite and the infinite order, and because we are to use inevitable frustration for the purpose of experiencing the reality of the ideal. But without this use in mind, the inevitable presents itself as a mere blind necessity, in which we can see neither right nor reason, a hostile doom that simply crushes us. The psychological effect of the thought of an event as inevitable, it is true, is in any case calming, but the tranquillity thus induced is a heavy and hopeless one. And those who accept the inevitable in this stupefying manner often become meaner in their way of living. The light of life is for them extinguished. They put up perhaps with creature comforts, or with work that merely keeps the mind occupied, and prevents it from fretting the wound, thus allowing slow time to cicatrize it.

There is, however, a larger way in which a materialist may regard the inevitable. The world in his view being a vast machine, he may, as it were, identify himself with the machine, and thereby rise in thought superior to the injury it inflicts on him. But though we can imagine someone thus deadening his feelings when he himself is the victim, we cannot well conceive of the same remedy applying when a beloved person, say an only child, is being crushed under the Juggernaut car of the world-machine. *The great test of one's philosophy of life is whether it helps us in the case of those whom we love, rather than in the case of the sufferings we experience in our own person.*

A second consolation is: Remember the universality of sorrow. Look around you, behold the vast multitude who are suffering like you; remember the countless generations who have suffered in the past, think of the generations to come that will suffer in like manner. Such are some of the consolations of the choruses in the Greek tragedies. Latent perhaps in this mournful view of the facts of existence is another aspect of the matter, namely, the uprising from frustration toward ideal realization. And in so far as this other uplifting view is indeed latent or suggested, the thought of the universality of sorrow has an ennobling effect. On the other hand, without the explication of what may be regarded as implicit in them the consolations of the Greek choruses are inexpressibly saddening.

A third and active variant of the former consolation is: Seek to mitigate the sorrow and trouble of thy fellow-sufferers. Appease the passion of thine own grief by compassion and the works to which it leads. And by as much as activity of any kind is better than passivity, or mere feeling, by so much is this third kind of consolation better than the ones above mentioned. But at bottom the same criticism applies to it. It leaves still unanswered the question, To what end this suffering both of others and of oneself? Not Why? is the question, but To what end? How bereavement may be used so as to bring it into relation with the final end of life?

A fourth consolation is the popular belief in immortality. This is a resort to supernaturalism, and the supernatural should ever be distinguished from the supersensible. Immortality as popularly held involves the continued existence in some empirical form of the essential, central entity in man. For the suggestion that new organs may replace the wornout terrestrial body does not alter the empirical character of the conception. The new organs are still conceived in some vague fashion as similar to those with which we are acquainted.

Finally, my own interpretation of consolation may be set forth in contrast to all these. Again I say that for the bereaved, as for the sick, there is business in hand, there is a task to be performed, a work to be done. What is it? Let me endeavor to explain. The spiritual nature of man is incognizable, only the plan of the relations between spirit and spirit being given. Yet to think of a relation at all we must think of entities or objects between which it subsists. Of the spiritual part of our fellow-beings, therefore, we are bound to fashion mentally a symbolic image, one that shall stand for the real object, the spiritual nature, though we are well aware that it does not adequately express it.

When the beloved person is no longer visibly present, the work we do upon the symbolic image of him is not to cease. We are to review, to summarize the whole existence of a departed friend, as we have probably never done while he was with us. We are to get the total perspective of his life, to see the fine qualities standing out more distinctly; to seize the net result of his existence so far as those character traits are concerned which in him were most analogous to spiritual traits. This image we can now ideally contemplate with the advantage that none of the actual infirmities of his nature can mar it, and that no future events can henceforth alter our impression. The work of clarifying the image of our friend goes on unimpeded. And our own activity in the process of purifying his image of all that was merely fallible in him benefits us in return. The effect of this activity of ours on the datum of his life is our permanent gain. Thus both what he was and what he was not is stimulative. While he lived we performed the function of elimination and concentration with a view of producing progress in him and in ourselves jointly. Progress, induced by us, so far as he is concerned, for all we know is at an end. Progress so far as we are concerned is assured by the activity we continue to expend as long as we live on his memory. And the memory, or the image, stands for the beloved person. There is real mental intercourse wherever there is a movement of one mind towards the outgoings of another, even though the retroactive relation be suspended. The beloved person benefits me, though I no longer benefit him, except indirectly so far as in my own life I possibly expiate his short-comings and in so far as I bestow on other living persons the advantage I receive from my mental intercourse with him.[8]

What, then, is the business in hand? What is the work to be done? Plainly to tie anew the threads that were broken, to bring it about that the loss, infinitely painful though it be, shall lead to gain, to substitute for the mixed relation of touch and sight the purely spiritual relation.

One more remark must be made in connection with the above. There is at present a tendency to dishonor the

---

[8] I have real intercourse with Aristotle and Kant, as the outgoings of their minds are still effectual in me—more vital intercourse than with many of those who surround me.

past in comparison with the future. Interest seems to lie in what lies ahead. Hence a breathless, forward-urging mood. One consequence of this is that the dead are less honored than of old. Within a single generation, for instance, I have seen not a few eminent persons in the city of New York pass away who up to the time of their death and in their obituaries were greatly and justly praised. I have hardly ever seen their names publicly mentioned since. Already they seem practically forgotten. In our national history likewise only a few of the most eminent are remembered. In like manner in families, the names even of father and mother are seldom mentioned by their surviving adult children, and ancestors at second remove are barely remembered. Now excessive reverence for the past, as in China, is a mark of stationariness. A retrospective point of view is inconsistent with progress. Our face must necessarily be turned toward the future. And yet forgetfulness of those human beings whom we have known, and who represented to us while they lived much of the best that life had to give, seems inhuman and incredible. It is true that I have drawn a sharp distinction between the empirical selves and those spiritual selves which the former for a time enshrined. The empirical selves have now disappeared. The gleam of love in the eye, the luster of beauty, whether of form or of expression, that touched for a season the sacred features, have vanished. On the other hand, the spiritual self as a member of the spiritual universe is confessedly past knowing and past imagining. On what object then shall memory dwell? It may dwell on the empirical self in so far as it was the

169

sign of the thing signified, in so far as the being we knew and loved was to us convincing of the reality of that spiritual world which itself is incognizable by sense or mind. The greatest boon any human being can confer on another is to serve him in attaining the end for which he exists; and the supreme end for us all is the realization of our interrelation with the infinite community of spirits. The woman whom we say we loved, we loved precisely because she revealed to us that spiritual galaxy—because she was a Beatrice, ascending with us, and opening to our sight the eternal expanses.

CHAPTER IV

THE SHADOW OF SIN

IF any term in the moral vocabulary stands in need of strict redefinition, it is sin. Three elements combine to complete the idea of sin: first, that the deed was one that ought not to have been done, not so much because of its painful consequences to others or to self, or to both, or, by repercussion on society as a whole; but because it was opposed to what is intrinsically right: in other words, because it contravened the kind of inter-relation which would exist in its purity in the ethical manifold.

Secondly, the idea of sin implies that the sinner himself is the doer of the deed, or that there is to this extent freedom of the will. I do not say that he is the cause of which the deed is the effect. Causality appertains to sequent phenomena. As regards freedom of the will, the distinction between the category of interdependence and that of causality is vital. A long series of causes, such as bad heredity, bad environment, etc., may have led A to determine to murder B.[1]

[1] The category of interdependence implies that the lines of energy between A and B cross, so that A is subject to B's influence, B subject to A's influence, simultaneously. The simultaneity of the relation distinguishes the category of interdependence from that of causality.

171

The notion of the freedom of the will as here viewed signifies that no matter what the causal series may have been which leads up to the act, when the act itself is about to be performed, when B is about to experience the effect of A as cause, in that moment the relation of interdependence between A and B ought to arise before the mind of A and withhold him from completing his evil purpose.

Thirdly, it is characteristic of sin that the fuller knowledge that the harmful deed is sinful *comes after the act,*—that it is the Fruit of the Tree, the enlightenment of the eyes. As the serpent said: "If ye eat of the fruit ye shall be as gods."

Many a man has done what is called evil, and done it most deliberately, knowing evil as evil. Remember the career of a Caesar Borgia, the extermination of the Caribbean Indians by the Spaniards, the outrages on women perpetrated during the present war, the exploitation of human labor practiced on a large scale among the civilized nations. That the blackest crimes may be committed with a full knowledge of the horrible consequences to the victims seems hardly to admit of doubt. Evil is known as evil.

But evil in its character as sin cannot be fully recognized prior to the act. In this respect the Greeks had a certain prescience of the truth when they asserted that no one can knowingly commit evil; only they failed to distinguish between evil and sin. A man *can* knowingly commit evil, but cannot with full consciousness commit sin. The knowledge of the sin is the divine elixir which may be distilled from the evil deed ("Ye shall be as gods"), and the object of every kind of punishment should be to extract that pain-giving but ultimately peace-giving elixir.

Above I mentioned the criminal as the extreme type. But evils in less formidable guise, though not on that account less evil, refined invasions of the personality of others, spiritual oppressions, sometimes deliberate, often unwitting, are included in everyone's experience. And the process of expiation, by which evil is transcended through the recognition of sin (with its prostrating effect at first, its strangely elevating effect later on) is alike applicable to all. The best of men have to go through this ordeal as well as the worst. Especially is unwitting transgression inevitable. Sophocles makes it the text of his philosophy in the *(Edipus,* though the solution offered is that of Greek enlightenment and not that of the more profound ethical consciousness.

We have next, in close connection with sin, to consider the tremendous question of responsibility, interpreted from the point of view of our ethical principle. Responsible means answerable. Answerable to whom, and in what sense? As commonly understood, it means answerable to God the Law-giver, to God regarded as the Author of the moral law. God is likened to a sovereign. Any infraction of his law is an offense against the sovereign. Answerable means subject to the pains and penalties which it suits the sovereign to annex to moral offences. There is no intrinsic connection implied between pain and redemption. The pain is supposed to break the will of the offender, or to mellow him, so that he will in future obey the mandates of the sovereign without a murmur.

Again, responsibility may mean responsibility to society. Crime is infectious. A fissure opening at any one point in the dykes erected against crime may let in a flood. The social order as a whole is threatened in every single violation of law. The offender must answer for his defiance of the public will by being subjected to the pains or penalties which society annexes to his crime. The object is the same as before, to break him into submission, to fit or force him into the social mould, to make him harmless, or if possible what is called a "useful citizen." No internal redemptive change in the nature of the evildoer is contemplated, except as it may be necessary to lead him to a useful or at least a harmless life. The antisocial attitude is to be replaced by the social attitude. Appeals to enlightened self-interest, and to the sympathies are commonly thought sufficient for this purpose.

Thirdly, responsibility means responsible to oneself. There is an inner forum, a tribunal in which the spiritual self sits in judgment on the empirical self. Conscience, the voice of this spiritual self, pronounces the verdict. (Cf. the passages in Kant in which this figure of speech is used.) These are metaphorical expressions.

To grasp the meaning of responsibility from the ethical standpoint, we must lift into view the concept of *the task of mankind as a whole,* and of the individual as a factor in the fulfilment of that task. This introduces a momentous turn into the discussion of the subject.

The task of mankind is to arrive through its commerce with the finite world, through its unremitting efforts to incorporate the infinite plan within the sphere of human relations, at an increasingly explicit conception of the ideal of the infinite universe; and through partial success and frustration to seize the reality of that universe. Responsibility means *participation in this task,* sharing its doom, and attaining in oneself, in part, its sublime compensation. The evildoer is to achieve the knowledge that his evil deed is sin, that is to say, that it not only carries with it harm to others and indirectly to himself, but that it is *the defeat in him* of the task which is set for the human race as a whole on earth. Instead of doing his share in fulfilling this task, in gaining a footing in the finite world for the spiritual relation of living so as to enhance the life of others and thereby his own, he has miserably sought to enhance his life at the expense of other life. The knowledge that he has so acted sears his awakened soul like fire, but it is also the beginning of healing. The transgressor, now sees what he did not see before. He sees by way of contrast the holy pattern of relations which in his act he has travestied, the holy laws which he has infringed, and in imputing sin to himself for transgressing them, he at the same time proclaims himself in his essential being holy, that is, capable of executing them, or at least of striving unceasingly to do so. It is thus that he opens within himself the sources of redemption, unseals the deeper fountains of spiritual energy.

That man is responsible means that he is answerable to do his share in discharging the task of mankind. And when he is inwardly transformed by the consciousness of the holy laws, and of himself as intrinsically committed to holiness, he does thereby advance the business of his kind on earth. In him humanity does take a step forward on the spiritual road. In him one other member of our race has been lifted out of evil, becoming perhaps, from the spiritual point of view, a more advanced member of the forward-pressing host than those who have never passed through an experience like his, who have not been overtly tempted, who have remained conventionally moral, who have not realized the evil that remains unexpurgated within them, and have not passed through the cleansing process of self-condemnation and rebirth.

The incongruity between the finite and the infinite order is the basis of this doctrine of responsibility. Mankind is responsible for seeking to embody the infinite in the finite. It fails to do so, but gains its compensation. The individual shares this responsibility, but both mankind and the individual jointly take a step forward whenever an evil deed is recognized, branded and expiated as sinful. The object of punishment, whether inflicted by society or self-inflicted, is to promote this regeneration which is the expiation.[2]

[2] This implies that the evil deed shall not be lost sight of, simply forgotten. Compare the inadequate account of repentance as given by Goethe in *Faust* and elsewhere.

Evil in its ethical meaning presupposes worth as attaching to human beings. To do evil is to offend against worth. To assert the worth of man is to view him as one of an infinite number of beings, united in an infinite universe, each induplicable in its kind. Of this spiritual multitude ideally projected by us as enveloping human society only our fellow human beings are known to us. *The moral law is the law which reigns throughout the infinite spiritual universe applied within the narrow confines of human society. It is applied within those confines, it is spiritual, universal in its jurisdiction.*

The task of humanity as a whole is to embody more and more the universal spiritual law in human relationships, and thus to transform and transfigure human society. In the New Testament we read the expression: "the light of God reflected in the face of Christ." The ideal here indicated may be expressed in the phrase, The spiritual universe with its endless lights reflected on the face of human society! The task of humanity is one which can never be completed, one from which mankind may never desist. To see evil as sin is to see it as contravening the collective task of mankind, the task of weaving the human groups more and more into, the fabric of the spiritual relations.

To see evil as sin is to see any single act or series of acts ideally in their infinite connections. This is what I mean when I say that the knowledge of sin comes after the act. I do not mean that there may not be before the act a vague consciousness of the ramified consequences of evil, but that the fuller knowledge of it as sin is the fruit of the act. Nor do I mean that evil in its deeper significance is revealed to every guilty person. The opposite is obviously true. What I mean is that it is possible after having eaten of the Fruit of the Tree to gain the enlightenment, in other words, to become aware of the intrinsic holiness of our nature in consequence of our offense against the holy laws. If anyone should ask "Must I then do evil in order to gain the enlightenment?" the answer is that this question is an idle one. No one can escape doing evil. If not in its grosser forms, then in ways subtler and more complex, but not therefore less evil, every one is bound to make acquaintance with guilt. He need not go out of his way to seek occasion, let him see to it that he improves the occasion when it comes, as inevitably it will, to his spiritual advantage.

CHAPTER V

The Right to Life

THE thoughts presented above on the subject of sin naturally lead over to the next topic, the obligations we are under regarding the life, the property and the reputation of others. The ancient moral laws unquestionably remain: "Thou shalt not kill"; "Thou shalt not steal"; "Thou shalt not bear false witness." But their application is extended and their significance intensified by the positive definition which has been given to the term *Spiritual.*

So long as the mere inviolateness of the human personality is emphasized, without any defined conception of what it is that is inviolate (the inviolateness without the infinite preciousness), there is danger that the physical part of man will be invested with the sacred character that belongs to the spiritual, that the two, the spiritual and the physical parts, will be identified.

The result will be mischievous in two ways: First, while the act of killing will be reprobated, a kind of tabu being attached to bloodshed, the taking of the life of fellow beings in more indirect ways, or what may be called constructive murder, will be lightly regarded. The following case is mentioned by a recent writer. The directors of a railroad refused to vote the sum of five thousand dollars to provide a certain safety appliance for their cars. Soon after an accident occurred, in which a number of men were killed. The accident might have been prevented had the five thousand dollars required for the installation of the safety appliance been voted. Now the men were undoubtedly killed by the directors of the company. As to the difference in the degree of guilt in the case of direct and indirect murder, there is room for casuistical debate. The consequences it is true were not present to the directors' minds. But are they not responsible for the very fact that the consequences were excluded from their view? They were intent on their dividends, and ignored the endangered lives. But is not this the substance of their guilt? Does not moral progress lie in the direction of extending the sense of responsibility so as to cover the indirect taking of life? Similarly the use of poisonous substances in industry, bad sanitation, inadequate fire protection, must be stigmatized as indirect murder. The Commandment "Thou shalt not kill" must extend over a far wider area than it has covered in the past.[1]

Secondly, the positive definition of the spiritual nature enables us to perceive more distinctly that the physical part is the means and the spiritual part the end, and to draw the necessary consequences. That which is means is not to be cherished if to do so would defeat

[1] *Vide* note at the end of the Chapter.

180

the end itself; hence the physical life is *not* to be preserved if by preserving it we deny or defeat the very purpose which the physical part is to serve. So long as men have the tabu feeling about bloodshed, the fact that life ought of right to be taken in certain instances will seem a hopeless contradiction of the general rule against killing. Keeping in mind the spiritual end of existence on the other hand, we affirm unhesitatingly that it is better that a man should die than commit a heinous crime. It was better for the young girl mentioned in a well-known tale, threatened with outrage, and seeing no other possible way of escape, to strangle herself with her own hair rather than submit. According to the opinion of certain scholastic writers on ethics, dishonor resides solely in the consent of the soul, and where this is absent the mere physical infringement cannot leave a moral stain. This is a helpful point of view in regard to the victims of the atrocities of war, the inmates of certain Belgian nunneries, and the hapless objects of unspeakable brutality in certain Polish villages. The anguish of a pure-minded woman who becomes a mother under such circumstances is hardly conceivable. And to discriminate between the infamy done to her and her own unpolluted soul is a plain duty, as well as to relieve the innocent off spring of outrage from any participation in the guilt to which it owes its existence. But the case to which I refer is different. It is one in which the choice remains between voluntary death and submission to intended violation. Submission in such a situation argues a kind of consent, or at least the absence of a sufficient revulsion.

It is right to kill an intending murderer supposing

that there is no other way of preventing him from committing his crime, whether the intended victim be oneself or someone else. It is not only the life thus protected from attack that is saved, but the murderer in a sense is saved as well, so far as he can be saved, by the intervention. Also the members of his family are saved, humanity is saved from moral disgrace in his person. The same reasoning applies to the position of the extreme non-resistants. They will not, they tell us, do a wrong to prevent a wrong. In their eyes to take the physical life of another is in every possible instance an absolute wrong. They fail to take account of the instrumental relation between the physical and the spiritual parts. And on the same grounds, a defensive war, a war to ward off aggression, may be theoretically justified. But here the application of the theory is dubious as well as dangerous. Exceptional cases of high-handed aggression that ought to be resisted occur, but aggression is rarely, if ever, one-sided. As a rule, there is more or less wrong on both sides, and the tangle of accusations and mutual recriminations is almost impossible to unravel. Very rarely, indeed, if ever, is right altogether on one side, and wrong on the other, though predominant right may be on one side and predominant wrong on the other. And aside from this, the instruments of destruction in modern warfare have become so monstrous, the efficiency notion applied to war has led to such ruthlessness, the attempt to distinguish between the civilian population and the armed forces has so nearly broken down, that right-thinking persons everywhere are now eagerly intent on how to prevent aggression before it can take effect, rather than to resist it after it has occurred.

NOTE

The casuistical question may be raised whether from this point of view we are not all murderers. The amount I spend on my house, food, recreation, might if divided prolong the life of many a child in the slums. Am I not then actually a parasite, that is, a murderer? It is this shocking scruple that has led fine people to live among the poor, and to try to equal- ize their mode of living with that prevailing in the environment. The motive is noble, though as a matter of fact they may never succeed in doing what they set out to do because they never actually touch bottom. There are always depths of poverty to which they can not descend. They may spend comparatively little, yet that little is far in excess of the spending of the most indigent. And had they stripped themselves of everything they would have been face to face with the *reductio ad absurdvm* of their method, for they would have abandoned civilization and degraded their human life to the level of the wayside tramp.

What is inspiring in their example is just the immense compassion, the willingness to give up so much. But the method itself is not a solution.

Are we then murderers, all of us ? Perhaps a distinction may be drawn between acts which in themselves are hostile to the life of fellowmen, like overtaxing the worker, and acts which tend positively to maintain the higher values of life,—such as the providing of decent shelter, support and education, for the members of one's family. It is true that, as Tolstoy warns us, we easily slip into indefensible luxury under the pretence of maintaining the higher values. But this does not affect the validity of the distinction itself.

And yet the distinction does not relieve us of what may be called our share of the social or collective guilt. The exploiter

183

is chargeable with individual guilt. I who am trying to keep up the standard of civilized living within my little sphere am nevertheless conscious of participating in the social guilt, the guilt of a society that has permitted and still permits such misery to exist. Well, it does exist, and I can do but a very little to change it. Can I then endure the contrast between my own lot and that of the greater number. Is it not true after all that if I give up the comforts, or let me say the helps to the maintenance of the higher values, I should be saving the lives of many children? Those children are dying because I am not dividing my possessions among the poor. Can I stand up and look at that fact, at those deaths?

The only answer which it is possible to give at the point we have thus far reached in our exposition is: push on, perfect civilization, a way will eventually be found to uplift the masses and make them partakers of the future civilization. The other alternative, that of Tolstoy, is stagnation. Yet I cannot disguise from myself the fact that in the meanwhile, while we are trying to push on, millions are perishing. This is the true "burden of world pain," not the sentimental world pain due to the fact that one is not having oneself the best kind of a time in the world, but the pain caused by the fact that while we are reaching *forward to* help the suffering masses, those masses, though composed of individuals morally as worth while as ourselves, and many of them doubtless better, if we only knew it, are perishing before our very eyes, and that we stand by and cannot save them. I have said that in the meanwhile while we are trying to push on, millions are perishing. The actual moral problem so often overlooked is underlined in the words "in the meanwhile."

There is one pathetic consolation. Envy is not the widespread vice which it is sometimes represented to be. Those who are in trouble take the will very largely for the deed. People in the worst conditions are grateful to anyone who shows a real desire to help, even if his actual performance does not go very far. And there is a still finer trait in ordinary human nature, namely, the tendency to find a certain vicarious relief in the joy of the few, provided that their joy be pure.

The Right to Property[2]

"Property," according to Blackstone, "is the sole and despotic dominion which one man claims and exercises over the external things of the world in total exclusion of the right of any other individual in the universe."

Orthodox jurisprudence, like orthodox religion, is characterized by the absoluteness of its formula. It ignores the genesis of its concepts in the long line of antecedent historical development, and it disdains to entertain the demand for modification, though the circumstances of the time loudly call for it.

"The sole and despotic dominion which one man claims and exercises," etc., may be a fact, but it is not a right. Property can only be regarded as a right if shown to be subservient to the ethical end,—the maintenance and development of personality. Orthodox jurisprudence effaces the end, and treats that which is or has been at one time a means as if it possessed a sanctity of its own. On the other hand, the empirical treatment of jurisprudence, in dismissing the supposedly absolute means, tends to leave out of sight the ethical end, and to treat the social institutions as subservient to mere convenience.

The following propositions will indicate the changes

[2] A right is a claim of one person upon another or others, and the justification consists in its relation to personality. Rights exist between persons for the sake of the maintenance and development of personality.

in the conception of the right of property required by our ethical theory.

1. Property is a relation between a person or persons and things. There can be no property right in persons, but only in things.[3]

2. The right of property faces in two directions: Toward outside nature and toward fellow human beings. We have a right over the external things of nature. We have a right to the services, though not to the personality, of fellow human beings. These two aspects of the right of property must be kept apart and defined.

It is sometimes held that the human race as a whole, as over against nature, has the right of dominion. Nature, it is said, is our quarry, we can take out of it the stones we need to construct the edifice of civilization. Nature is our tool. The laws of nature, as science discovers them, become our servants. Nature offers the raw material which we consume. Nature has no rights as against man. But I hold that neither has man rights as against nature, except in so far as he rightly defines the end in the interest of which he makes use of nature—the maintenance and development of personality.

To suppose that the right of property as the extension of personality over things is tenable without re-

[8] Animals, for the purpose now in hand, may be regarded as things, being devoid of personality, though certain modifications in the treatment of animals are prescribed by the fact that they are sentient creatures. But there is no moral interdiction of the involuntary servitude of animals.

gard to its instrumental use, to suppose that bare appropriation of nature as of "treasure trove" is a prerogative of man, is to lend countenance to the false notion of occupation, or first appropriation, which has confused the ethics of the subject in the literature of jurisprudence, and prevented a right understanding of it. If bare appropriation be the foundation, then the first comer has a right against his successors, since the extension of personality over the thing has been actually accomplished by him, and that is all there is to be said about it. Again, on this view, a case may be made out for vested interests, that is to say, for those who have successfully appropriated the earth, yes, and the fullness thereof, and who having thus effectually extended their personality over things without regard to the uses they make of their possessions, are then to be entitled to remain indefinitely in secure ownership of them.

Without an ethical standard, without the notion of an end to be subserved, stubborn possession will always be able to resist modification, and on the other hand attempts at modification will be haphazard. Neither the human species collectively nor the individual has a right simply to appropriate the things of the external world. Neither the first occupier nor the last is entitled to his goods unless he can make out a greater good in the interest of which he should be allowed to possess them.

But the case of primary occupation is academic. It occurs on Robinson Crusoe's island and in legal fiction. Even when the white race invades Africa, it does not commonly take possession of unoccupied land, but dispossesses the natives. On what ground does it dispossess them? Is there an ethical standard by which the dealings of the civilized nations with the populations of Africa can be measured? Is the introduction of the appliances of modern civilization, the opening up to trade, a sufficient ground for the subjection or the extermination of the inhabitants? In this connection it becomes clear how urgent a more clarified conception of property rights is. False ideas of this so-called right are to no small extent responsible for the massacre of the inferior races, and the mutual slaughter of those who covet their lands. A proclamation of the Queen of England or of the Emperor of Germany, or the signature of an irresponsible chief to a treaty the meaning of which he scarcely understands, transfers millions of subjects and their territory to one or other of the European powers. What right of property have these European powers in the territory and the peoples acquired by them in this fashion?

The last example shows that the right of ownership; except in very rare instances, is not in question in respect to the dealings of man with nature, but comes into play chiefly in the relation of man to his fellows. There are competitors to be outstripped, thwarted. There are weaker fellow-beings to be subdued. The use of force and cunning in acquiring property is well nigh the general rule. Are there any ethical ideals which, if they could be realized, might disclose a better way, might bring order into this frightful chaos, and abate the conflicts? From the ethical ideal as outlined in previous chapters this follows:

The extension of personality over things is a right in so far as things are employed to maintain and develop potential personality. The use of the services of a fellowman is a right in so far as his services are used in such a manner as to preserve and develop his personality as well as that of the user.

In speaking of the use of the services of others we touch upon the social aspect of the property relation, and here is the crux of the whole matter. It is coming to be affirmed more and more that property is a "social" concept, that it cannot be explained either as implying a relation of the individual to outside nature, save exceptionally, nor as a relation of the individual considered atomistically to other atomic individuals. The social tie, it is held, is intrinsic. The nature of man as such is social, but the word "social" in current discussion is very ill-defined, and is commonly understood to denote merely the fact of the interdependence of men upon one another, without conveying the idea of a rule or standard by which the system of interdependence may be regulated. Vague notions, such as that of social happiness, are believed sufficient to take the place of such a standard.

Let me then consider first the bare fact of interdependence, and see what follows from it, and how far it will take us.

Every man has manifold wants for the satisfaction of which he depends on others. His wants are legion; his ability and opportunity to satisfy them exceedingly limited. It is this cross relation that expresses the so-called social nature of man. But the reciprocal dependence of men upon one another for the satisfaction of their wants by no means constitutes an ethical tie. The tie between the Greek master and the Greek slave, as described by Aristotle, was social, but not ethical. The same is true of the tie that united the Southern planter to his negro slaves. The relation was indeed far more social than that between the modern mill-owner and the operatives in his factory, but still it was not ethical. The reason is clearly stated by Aristotle himself. According to him the slave is a living tool: the purpose of his existence is not realized in himself but in his master. He fulfils the end of his being by setting free the higher functions exercised by his master. But from the ethical point of view no man may be regarded as the tool of another. Each human being is an end *per se,* and the highest object of his existence is to be fulfilled, not in others, but jointly in them and in himself.

I have just said that the social and the ethical views are not synonymous or coincident, as the loose use of language in current literature would imply. I go farther and say that the social and the ethical point of view are even on their face contradictory. It cannot be denied that the natural system of interdependence resembles that of the body and its members. A hierarchy of organs and of functions is apparent in the human body, and likewise in the social body. Some men do the lowest kind of work. Their function appears to be to produce food, clothing and shelter, to satisfy the mere physical wants. Some are the hands, so to speak, of society, while only a very few effectually represent the brain.

The simile has been carried out in detail by well-known writers, in both ancient and modern times. It is quite true that the artist and the scientist are dependent on the manual laborer, just as he in turn is dependent on them. But then, consider the difference in the dignity of the services they render one another. Was not the Greek, who saw things dispassionately as they are, right in asserting that, taking society in the large, the purpose of human life is fulfilled in the few, and that the greater number exist in order that by their inferior services they may enable these few to express humanity in its highest terms?

It seems to me that the kind of social arrangement contemplated by the great Greek philosophers, and by some of the mediaeval publicists, as well as by certain modern thinkers, is unquestionably social. The fact of interdependence is stressed by them. The ethical note of equality, or, as I should prefer to put it, equivalence, is left out.

I have endeavored in a recent book to indicate how the ethical system may be superinduced over the social system.[4] Here I am concerned chiefly to mark as strictly as possible the distinction between the two terms social and ethical. And I must, therefore, at once amend my previous statement that property is a social concept by saying that it is the concept of a social relation considered as the substratum in which is to be worked out the ethical relation.

[4] See Chapter VII on "An Ethical Programme of Social Reform" in *The World Crisis,* published by D. Appleton and Company, 1915.

The general consequences of the property conoept as defined are these:

1. He who will not work, neither shall he eat; or better, he who will not work if able-bodied shall be disciplined and trained in such a manner that he will work. The fruits of nature do not fall into the lap of mankind. We are not living in a state of Paradise. The human race is engaged in the arduous labor of constantly renewing the capital on which it subsists. As a member of the race, everyone is bound to do his part.

2. No one has a property right in harmful or superfluous luxuries, since property is the control of external things for the maintenance and development of personality; and luxury, so far from maintaining, undermines personality, and hinders its development.

No one has ethically a right of property in great fortunes like those accumulated under the modern system of industry. Whatever is in excess of one's needs, rightly estimated, is not appropriate to one, not proper to one, not his property. Since the present system of ownership cannot be changed abruptly, the idea of the stewardship of wealth has been suggested to quiet the consciences of those who have come to realize that they have no moral right to excessive wealth. But the idea of stewardship should be held with fear and trembling. It is at best a makeshift, a bridge leading over to something more sound. It may be so taught and received as to seem to justify by philanthropic use the possession of great fortunes. But the power to dispose of vast funds for philanthropic uses may come to be itself a badge of superiority. And even if this be not so, if surplus wealth be used modestly, and with a sincere intention to apply it in the best possible way, there is yet no surety that any individual owner will have the breadth of vision, the experience, the insight, to discharge adequately the function of distributor. The defects of his early education, habits ingrained in him in the course of his business career, may lead him to bestow lavishly in one direction while turning a deaf ear to the appeal of other needs even more urgent and fundamental. Nothing short of the collective wisdom of the community, the collaboration of the best, can safely direct the surplus wealth available for social benefaction.

3. Everyone is ethically entitled to a share of the products furnished by nature and worked up into usable shape by his fellows, and also to the direct services of fellow human beings, in so far as that share and those services are necessary in order to enable him to perform in the best possible way the specific service which he in turn is capable of rendering. Our ethical theory here supplies us with a principle which takes the place of remuneration. There is no such thing as a just remuneration of labor, there is no such thing as a fair wage, if the wage be considered as the equivalent of, or the reward for the work done. It is not possible by any process of calculation to construct an equation between labor and reward. The laborer is assuredly not entitled to the product of his labor, as the current formula awkwardly puts it, for it is an entirely hopeless undertaking to try to ascertain what the product of any man's labor is. In the modern forms of industry, the contributions of the different factors engaged in pro-

duction are intimately intermingled, play into one another, and are inseparable. Neither the so-called workers alone are the producers of wealth, nor the employers and capitalists, nor yet both together irrespective of the labors of past generations of which they enjoy the usufruct. The question, what is a fair wage, or a fair profit, is badly posed. There is no such thing as a fair wage or profit in the sense of a fair compensation for the work performed.

The proper payment of the human factors engaged in production is unascertainable genetically, *i.e.,* if one goes back to the origin of the product. It can only be approximately determined by fixing attention on the end to be served. And the end in each case is the maintenance and development of personality. In other words, that is a fair wage which suffices to enable the different functionaries cooperating in production each to perform his function, or render his service, in the most efficient possible manner. The solution of the labor question must be along teleological not genetic lines. Adequate nourishment as to quantity and quality, suitable dwellings, educational opportunities, etc., are all indispensable to the rendering of service, even by "common laborers." Specific requirements come up for consideration with respect to the different special functions, and those who perform them.

My intention in this chapter is to indicate the bearings of the ethical theory on living questions of the day. Nothing is more emphatic in the programmes of the Working-class than this demand for social justice. Nothing is more discouraging than to see the futile efforts made to define social justice by extemporizing a notion of fair adjustment which goes to pieces in every serious labor controversy.

One more remark should be made in regard to what is meant by property as a relation between persons and things considered as a means of developing personality. A convenient illustration is the use of a block of stone by a sculptor. The sculptor's attempt at self-expression is an effort to combine two things in themselves uncongenial, an ideal image, and an external tangible thing, the block of stone. The mental image does not leap from the mind upon the stone and transform it magically into its own likeness. The external thing, the stone, offers resistance, and the resistance limits the artist's effort. But the limitation itself becomes in time an indispensable aid. For the ideal image as at first it started up in the artist's mind was vague, and the limitations imposed by the intractable nature of the material compel him to articulate the image, to grasp more firmly its complex details, and thus to become more surely possessed of it. The same is true of the mental thing which we call the relation of cause and effect in the mind of the scientist, and of his endeavor to impose this mental relation on the sequence of phenomena observed by him. And the same is again true of that supreme thing which we call the ethical ideal, and of the effort to embody it in the social relations. The attempt to express the ethical ideal in human society inevitably hits on limitations, and leads to frustrations. We have in our heads fine schemes of universal regeneration. We find elements in human nature that resent and resist our Socialisms, our communisms. We desire to enlarge men's moral horizon, the field of their moral interest, to lead out from the family to the nation, to fraternity in general. We presently discover that we are losing the benefit of the closer ties. In the very process of building we seem to be in danger of destroying the foundations, and to be building in the air. In this way our formulations of the ethical ideal are tested. We are compelled to recast them, and the frustrations which we meet with become the means of clarifying and articulating the ideal itself, and of enabling us to experience more vividly the coercive impulses that go out from it.

The Right to Reputation

The ethical rule is to show a sacred respect for the reputation of others. In the present discussion intellectual and moral reputation may be considered separately.

Under the first head of intellectual reputation, certain points suggest themselves, one of them in regard to controversies concerning priority of scientific discovery. What is the sense of such controversies? What difference does it make whether the law of the conservation of energy was first enunciated by Helmholtz or by Robert Mayer, or whether the method of fluxions was invented by Newton or Leibnitz,—not to mention lesser contrarieties of claims? Would it not argue, on the part of the scientists and their friends, a more entire devotion to objective truth if they showed[1] themselves indifferent to personal credit? The discovery, the invention, it may be said, is important, not the reputation of the discoverer or the inventor. Nevertheless, such controversies are carried on in a lively spirit. And it is usually felt that something more than vanity is at stake, that a man is entitled to be named in connection with the productions of his mind.

Such controversies resemble a suit at law undertaken to determine a disputed title to some valuable property. Plagiarism is different. It is barefaced intellectual theft. The title to the property in this case is not disputed. The plagiarist just steals an idea or a form of words in which an idea has been happily expressed, and palms it off as his own, hoping to escape with his stolen goods undetected. In this case too, it seems, one might say the idea is important, not the authorship. Nevertheless, a profound resentment is felt, not only by the author, but by the general public, against a plagiarist.

A rule is ethical when the conduct prescribed is instrumental to the development of personality. Respect for reputation is ethical because reputation is a help to the development of personality. A man projects his mind outward, so to speak, into the productions of his mind. As a thinking being he anchors himself in outside reality. He transfers himself, as it were, into an external thing,—a discovery, an invention, the expression of an idea in apt language,—each a thing that goes on existing independently of himself. To deny his connection with it is to infringe upon his personality, to efface his personality in so far as his personality is enshrined in his mental product.

Again, a man's reputation as a scientist or scholar is

a prop to his personality as a thinker. A man can never be quite certain of the validity of his thinking until it is approved by the consensus of the competent. To win that approbation is to know that as far as he has gone he is on sure ground. He can thence proceed, can turn toward new problems with a sense of power and a measure of self-confidence not previously attained. To rob him of his reputation is to deprive him of this invaluable aid to further mental development.[5]

Coming next to moral reputation, we find that the ethical rule requiring respect for the moral character of others is even more exacting, and that any contravention of it deserves an even more strenuous reprobation. The Decalogue prohibits the bearing of false witness and this rule is extensible from courts of law to ordinary conversation, since the principle involved is the same. The Sermon on the Mount menacingly

[5] A remark may here be in place regarding the erudition expended in determining which of the writings attributed to some great philosopher like Plato are spurious, and which genuine. Is the time and labor spent on such researches worth while? The object in this case is not so much to clear or vindicate the reputation of the philosopher, or to give him his due, as to rescue for posterity, free from corruptions, a living and quickening thing to which he has given birth, and which the world cannot afford to lose. For the work of a great philosopher like Plato is alive, and is valuable because it is still quickening. And it is quickening, not because of any positive formulation of truth (like a scientific law), but because of the élan of the human spirit with which it is vibrant in attacking the eternal problems of life and destiny. The same applies to the industry of modern critics in collecting material wherewith to facilitate the deeper understanding of some great poet like Dante or Goethe.

warns against judging others: "Judge not that ye be not judged." Buddha enjoins his followers to refrain from malicious gossip, and includes a prohibition to this effect among the principal pronouncements of his religion. All the great teachers of ethics and religion insist on this point, perhaps because the natural propensities of men constantly tend in the opposite direction, and are so hard to restrain. To stab one's neighbor in the back, morally speaking, to insinuate base motives, to spread damaging reports about him, to suggest as possibly and then as probably true rumors which one does not positively know to be untrue, to allow private repugnance to take the place of evidence, —are infringements of the moral reputation of others with some of which notoriously many even of the so-called best people are chargeable. I do not here speak of the grosser attacks, attacks on character inspired by envy, rivalry, and greed. The soundness of the rule is generally admitted, though its violations are past belief and without number.

But is the rule itself as to moral reputation tenable? There is a difference between intellectual and moral reputation at which we must at least cast a glance. Intellectual reputation is a fairly safe index of merit; moral reputation is not. A man's mind is reflected in his intellectual performances. Is the same true of his moral character? Is not the moral character an interior, elusive thing? The real character escapes the eye of the outside spectator and judge; and if this be so, why should it be so important a matter to safeguard a man's moral reputation, seeing that the reputation he deserves is past finding out? A public official, for instance, is accused of corrupt practices. He is innocent, and his friends and he are indignant at the damaging accusations brought against him. But if not guilty of the palpable derelictions with which he is charged, yet, in view of his opportunities and education, he may not be less blameworthy for other acts with which he has not been charged, and in his heart of hearts he knows that this is so. Why then, this outcry?

Other examples might be adduced. The honor of a young woman is attacked by the circulation of atrocious rumors, and the reaction at this most sensitive point is certain to be extreme when the falseness of the accusation is exposed. But is outward decorum, correct behavior, always a sure sign of inward purity?

There is this difference then between the intellectual and the moral character. The one can be measured, the other cannot. But the reply to these sophistical objections is still the same as before. The purpose of the ethical rule is to furnish aids in the development of personality. The aim in view is not genetic, but teleological, not to determine how far in analyzing a man's character down to the bottom he may be found to be already admirable, but to help him in attaining excellence, by progressively advancing toward strength and virtue. And moral reputation is a great help to this end. It is a prop on which he can lean. He who does right acts and has the credit for them, is thereby encouraged to do other right acts. And if the inner voice whispers, as it is sure to do in the finer natures, that the good opinion of his fellows, founded on his correct deportment, is undeserved, the shame of it may lead him to more determined efforts to merit the character which, on however insufficient evidence, is attributed to him.

Reputation is sacred because it is an almost indispensable means to further mental and moral progress.

CHAPTER VI

IN the last chapter we treated the imputation of evil to the innocent. We must now consider the right attitude toward actual evildoers.

In discussing sin, one of the points emphasized was that of the moral solidarity between the individual and society. The moral interest of the individual is always identical with the moral interest of society; and, on the other hand, the failure of the individual is a social failure. The human race sags morally at the point of some particular member of it.

Again, we defined the task of humanity as the incessant endeavor to embody the ideal spiritual order in the finite sphere of human relations. This effort meets both with partial success and with failure. The gain derived by the human race from its experiences, its labors, its sufferings, is that the spiritual universe in its unattainable elevation and sublimity is more and more revealed to the inner eye; in other words, that by way of effort and recoil, and renewed effort and renewed recoil from the finite, the infiniteness of the infinite world is realized. The essential point is that the boon of realization must be gained both through partial success and failure. Now sin is failure; everyone fails, everyone is convicted of sin. There is no exception. In insisting on this point the Christian account is exact. Only it should be remembered that sin or failure itself is one of the instrumentalities by which the end of human existence is achieved. These preliminaries being understood, certain propositions may be brought forward as to the treatment of sin, and in particular as to repentance, punishment and forgiveness.

Repentance is recoil, recoil not from the bad act and its painful consequences, but from the principle underlying the act. Every kind of sin is an attempt in some fashion to live at the expense of other life. The spiritual principle is: live in the life of others, in the energy expended to promote the essential life in others. Moral badness is self-isolation, detachment. Spirituality is consciousness of infinite interrelatedness.

Punishment, rightly regarded, is a name for the steps taken to lead the unrepentant up to the point of repentance, i.e., up to the recoil. Punishment is itself criminal when undertaken for any other object. Punishment on the vindictive *lex talioms* theory, or on the bare deterrent theory, is excluded. Reformatory punishment as commonly understood is no less inadequate, because it restricts the idea of reformation as a rule to the externals of conduct.[1]

[11]   mean that it is usually considered sufficient, for purposes of reformation, to bring the wrongdoer up to the average standard of law-abiding citizenship, to restore him to the bosom of society as a safe and industrious member. Whereas a person who has had the searching experience of deep guilt is a candidate for a higher station in the moral scale. Humanity having fallen in him, he should be helped to rise to a higher than the average altitude. This at

The steps taken to lead the evildoer up to the point of repentance are to be criticised from this point of view. Transient or prolonged separation from ordinary society may be necessary. Severe discipline may be indispensable. Capital punishment, however, is wholly out of the question, since the prevention of the crime now being impossible, the achievement of the spiritual gain is the point to be aimed at. But the most effectual aid in promoting repentance is faith in the better nature of the wrongdoer, in that spiritual principle resident within him which no crime committed by him can wholly crush, and which in the most apparently hopeless cases is still to be presumed. But faith in the good that persists in those whom we call bad must go hand in hand with the acknowledgment of the bad that remains unexpurgated in those whom we call good. The prison reformer who poses as impeccable and righteous himself can never win the confidence of the poor human derelicts with whom he has to deal nor effect in them the desired change. He must share with them the conviction of sin if he would impart to them the power of the resilience which he experiences within himself.

Faith in the potential power of goodness resident in the evildoer is often confounded with forgiveness. The distinction between the two, however, should not be obliterated. Faith is help proffered from the outside to effectuate the inner change. Forgiveness is a record of the fact that the change has actually taken place, and belief

least should be the aim. Consider the fact that Jesus selected some of his most spiritual companions from among publicans and harlots.

that it is likely to be permanent. Forgiveness, in the mind of spiritually-minded persons, takes place almost automatically when the conditions on which it depends are fulfilled. So long as he remains unrepentant a man cannot be forgiven, although we may have the conviction that it is in his power to repent and the earnest desire to bring about the change in him. Jesus on the Cross says: "Forgive them, for they know not what they do." Perhaps "open their eyes so that they may see the Light" may be the more just interpretation of the meaning—not "forgive" in the strict sense, for forgiveness is not feasible while the heart of the offender remains closed. [2]

Both faith and forgiveness are factors in regeneration: the one to assist in accomplishing the change, the other to assist in making it permanent. But both the faith and the forgiveness are exceptionally difficult in the case of our personal enemies. *Enemies in the spiritual sense there are and can be none.* Every human being, even one who has done me the most cruel harm, is yet, from another point of view, a fellow member of the spiritual society. But to discriminate between the two relations in which the man stands to me—that in which he is my foe, and the other in which he is my fellow—to be able to put aside as less important the harm he has done, the suffering he has forced me to endure, and to desire with perfect sincerity that the recoil, the

[2] Compare the words addressed by Sir Thomas More to his judges when sentence of death had been pronounced upon him— "For though you have been my judges to condemnation, may we meet merrily hereafter in everlasting salvation."

transformation, may take place in him, that is the most searching test of one's own ethical character.[3]

The forgiveness of personal foes, when complete, establishes a strangely tender spiritual fellowship between the pardoner and the pardoned. Both have transcended their normal empirical selves, both have become partners in a sublime transaction: the one delivered from the clinging of his baser desires, the other released from his first crude reaction against evil. They will never forget what they thus owe to one another. They will continue to walk hand in hand, the one still leaning, the other supporting and himself unspeakably strengthened by the support he gives.

Finally, to forgive is not to forget—quite the contrary. To forgive is to remember the past action, but to remember it as belonging to the past, as the act of one who has since undergone the great change. The miracle of the change of water into wine at the feast of Cana would not have seemed so wonderful to the guests had they not remembered that what was turned into wine had before been water. To forgive is to remember that what was water has become wine.

[3] Everyone admires a disinterested prison reformer, one who is able to see and to call out the good in a so-called bad man; but it is one thing to be disinterested and generous towards men who have acted bad*ly* towards others, and quite another thing to take the ethical attitude towards those who have acted wickedly towards oneself. Hence the touch-stone of the character of the prison-reformer is to be found in the way in which he behaves and feels towards his personal enemies, for instance, towards those who malignantly attack him and interfere with the business of prison reform on which he has set his heart.

And he, too, who has been forgiven may not forget. The remembrance of the past he will need as a warning and a safeguard.[4] Not to see the essentially divine nature in others, and thus also in one's self is the essence of the wrong. To teach the guilty to see it is the object of punishment. To forgive is to declare that what before was ignored is now seen and known.

*Perhaps I may add a word as to the forgiveness of those who, by an extension of meaning, may be called our intellectual enemies. By intellectual enemies I understand those whose point of view is radically opposed to our own, whose principles and premises, if accepted, would render the entire theory of life on which we act, and on which we found our convictions, untenable. We are apt to be exasperated in listening to them, or in reading the works in which they express their opinions. We are apt to feel that there is no room in the world in which we live for such ideas as theirs, that we and they cannot exist side by side. The bitter feuds of rival religious factions, the notorious *odium theologicum,* and in more recent times the thinly veiled animus shown in the controversies of philosophical schools are all alike traceable to this source. Racial antagonisms, too, are partly to be accounted for on the same ground. There are certain primary attitudes of mind, modes of feeling and directions of impulse, the correctness of which we cannot demonstrate just because they are primary, and which we all the more vehemently assert when we find them disputed. Love your intellectual enemies, may usefully be added to the stock of moral commandments ; keep an open and hospitable mind to opinions and ways of acting, thinking and feeling which naturally repel you. And it will help us to discipline ourselves in this difficult behavior if we reflect that the views most contrary to our own are nevertheless sure to contain some element of truth which we cannot afford to disregard, and which will serve the purpose of correcting and supplementing such truth as we may ourselves possess.

CHAPTER VII

THE SUPREME ETHICAL RULE: ACT SO AS TO ELICIT

THE BEST IN OTHERS AND THEREBY IN THY-

SELF[1]

IT is difficult to see the potentially divine nature in men when masked by the forbidding traits which human beings so often exhibit.

A number of vital considerations will now have to be emphasized as pertinent to the subject we are dealing with.

The first point is that the character of every person contains contrary elements.[2] Let the two kinds of qualities be called the fair and foul, or more simply still the plus and minus traits. The bright qualities, the plus traits, are undoubtedly more predominant in some, the dark or minus traits in others. But potential plus qualities exist in the worst characters, and potential minus traits may be surmised, and on scrutiny will be found, in those whom the world most admires.

---

[1] Or more exactly act so as to elicit the sense of unique distinctive selfhood, as interconnected with all other distinctive spiritual beings in the infinite universe.

[2] The conception underlying Robert L. Stevenson's sketch of Jekyl and Hyde is to be taken seriously, and applied without exception *mutatis mutandis* to every human being whatsoever (but see footnote p. 76). It is not original with Stevenson. The French, who are perhaps the keenest psychologists, long ago invented the *apercu* that everyone has the defects of his qualities.

A second point is mentioned as an hypothesis not indeed as yet verified, but I believe verifiable, namely, that certain defined minus traits will be found to go with certain plus traits. Wherever bright qualities stand out we are likely to meet with *corresponding* dark qualities or dispositions, and conversely. There are, I am persuaded, uniformities of correspondence between the plus and minus traits, and it would be of greatest practical help in judging others and ourselves if these uniformities could be worked out. A kind of chart might then be made, a description of the principal types of human character, with the salient defects and qualities that belong to each. Extensive statistical treatment of a multitude of biographies would lay the foundation for such an undertaking; also sketches of the prominent characteristics of nations, like those furnished by Fouillee, would be utilized. Also the study of the character traits of primitive races as partially carried out by Waitz in his *Anthropology* and the character types of animals, so far as accessible to observation, might be used for comparison. Instructed in this manner, we should, on coming into contact with others, either on their attractive or repellent side, be prepared to expect and to allow for the opposite traits. And we should learn to see ourselves in the same manner; we should see our empirical character as it really is, the dark traits side by side with the bright. The courage to wish to know the truth about one's self is rare, and when the revelation comes or is forced upon us, it often breeds a kind of sick self-disgust and despair. The saint at such times in moral agony declares himself to be the worst of sinners. He has striven to attain a higher than the average moral level, and behold he has slipped into only deeper depths. The minister of religion, the revered teacher, the political and social leader, when abruptly shocked into self-examination by some evidence of grossness or deviousness in themselves, no longer to be glossed over or explained away, are fated to go through the same ordeal. A profound despondency is the consequence. It is not only the badness now exposed, but the previous state of hypocrisy that seems in the retrospect intolerable. Some persons live what is called a double life in the face of the world. But who is quite free from living a double life in his own estimate? Achilles said of himself ("cumberer of the ground"). Many a man has echoed that cry with a bitterness of soul more poignant than that which Achilles felt when he uttered the words.

Now the principle of the duality[3] of character traits, or as we may also designate it, the principle of the polarity of character, applies to our natural or empirical character, and our empirical character is not our moral character. The distinction between the two will serve, as we shall presently see, to rescue us from the state of moral dejection just described. But first it is indispensable to fix attention on the natural character, to recognize that we are composite, each and every one of us, and that the all-important thing to know is which of our plus qualities go with which of the minus. Here

[3] The use of the term duality is not intended to exclude the possibility of multiplicity, but only to call attention to one striking bifurcation of human character.

the psychologist can help us. Here a great field is open for a practical science of ethology. This would give us a more adequate knowledge of the empirical character, the substratum in which ethical character is to be worked out.

Point three opens up a great enlightenment in regard to the whole subject. It is that the distinction must be drawn, and ever be kept in mind, between the bright and dark qualities and the virtues and vices. The bright qualities are not of themselves virtues. The dark qualities are not of themselves vices. To suppose that they are, to confuse the bright with virtue and the dark with viciousness, is the most prevalent of moral fallacies.[4]

A person is found to be kind, sympathetic, gentle, and on this score is said to be virtuous or good. But gentleness, kindness, a sympathetic disposition, while they lend themselves to the! process of being transformed into virtues, are not of themselves moral qualities at all, but gifts of nature, happy endowments for which the possessor can claim no merit. And sullenness, irascibility, the hot, fierce cravings and passions with which some men are cursed, are not vices, though it is obvious how readily they turn into vices as soon as the will consents to them.

The question becomes urgent: What then is a virtue? The fair qualities are the basis, the natural substratum of the virtues, the material susceptible of trans-

*Stevenson falls into this error. He confounds Jekyl with the virtuous and Hyde with the vicious side of character. In reality the one should stand for the empirical plus traits, the other for the empirical minus traits.

formation into virtues. In what does the transformation consist? When does it take place? The answer is, when the plus quality has been raised to the Nth degree, and in consequence the minus qualities are expelled. This result, of course, is never actually achieved. The concept here presented is a concept of limits. But in the direction defined lies growth and continuous development not of but toward ethical personality. In public addresses I have often said: Look to your virtues, and your vices will take care of themselves. I can put this thought more exactly by saying: Change your so-called virtues into real virtues: raise your plus qualities to the Nth degree. And the degree to which you succeed in so doing you can judge of by the extent to which the minus qualities are in process of disappearing.

One or two examples will illustrate the pivotal thought thus reached in the exposition of our ethical system with respect to its practical consequences. To raise to the Nth degree is to infinitize a finite quality, or to enhance it in the direction of infinity. I shall take two examples, one *self-sacrifice*, the other *justice*, both viewed in their finite aspect as plus traits requiring to be subjected to the process of transformation.

The empirical motive of self-sacrifice may be egocentric or altruistic. In egocentric self-sacrifice, doing for others is a means of exalting the idea of self to the mind of the doer. He uses others, not as sacred personalities, worth while on their own account, but subtly exploits them by benefiting them. He uses them as objects by means of which to achieve a finer self-aggrandizement. He may indeed go to the utmost lengths of devotion for his friends. He may perform for them the most repulsive offices. He may give freely of his means, denying himself meanwhile comforts and even necessaries in order perhaps to extricate them from pecuniary difficulties. He may contribute in refined ways to their pleasure. As a physician he may watch night after night at the bedside of the sick, foregoing sleep though fatigued to the point of exhaustion in order to be at hand to mitigate the pains of the sufferer, jeopardizing his own health in order to assist others in recovering theirs. Yes, he may even give of his own blood to renew their ebbing life. In all this he will look for no material compensation. Gratitude, especially gratitude expressed in words, is repugnant to him. The lofty image of self which he strives to create would be marred if any such coarsely selfish motive were allowed to intrude. All that he requires, but this he does inexorably require, is that his beneficiaries shall silently confess their dependence on him, that he shall see the exalted image of himself mirrored in their attitude, and that they shall move in their orbits as satellites around his sun. The egocentrism is veiled and easily confounded with the purest moral disposition. But it is there all the same, and the proof of it is that the very same person who is thus friendly to his friends, and an unstinting benefactor to those who pay him the kind of homage he exacts, is capable of behaving with almost inconceivable hardness and even cruelty toward others who will not stand in this subordinate relation to him, or who in any way wound his self-esteem. Sister Dora, serving enthusiastically in a small-pox hospital, while neglecting the nearer duties at home, intent on dramatic, histrionic self-representation, is likewise a palpable instance of egocentric self-sacrifice.

The self is precious on its own account. The nonself, the other, equally so. A virtuous act is one in which the ends of self and of the other are respected and promoted jointly. It is an act which has for its result the more vivid consciousness of this very jointness. Egocentric self-sacrifice errs on the one side, the personality of another being made tributary to the empirical self, despite the actual benefits conferred. Altruistic self-sacrifice errs in the opposite way. In it the personality of the self is effaced or made servile to the interests or supposed interests of another. Not, let pie add, to the real interests, for the spiritual interests are never achievable at the expense of other spiritual natures. The wife or mother is an instance, who slaves for husband or children, obliterating herself, never requiring the services due to her in return and the respect for her which such services imply, degrading herself and thereby injuring the moral character of those whom she pampers. An historic instance of the altruistic error on a larger scale is afforded by the Platonic scheme of scientific breeding under state supervision, a suggestion revived in modern times, in which freedom of choice between the sexes, and the integrity of the personality of those concerned, is sacrificed to the supposed interests of the community. Nietzsche's doctrine may possibly be regarded as a compound of the two errors described, the Superman representing the egocentrism, while altruistic self-sacrifice, entire annulment of their personalities is expected of the multitude.

It is easy to distinguish the plus and minus qualities in the characters of the egocentrist and the altruist: in the one case, beneficence combined with hardness; in the other, service of others combined with absence of self-respect.

The second example to be briefly considered is the finite trait commonly mistaken for justice. A typical illustration of this is presented by the merchant who ascribes to himself a just character on the ground that he is punctual in the payment of his debts, that his word is as good as his bond ; or by the manufacturer who entertains the same opinion of himself because he pays scrupulously the wages on which he has agreed with his employees. [8] One wonders that so great and pro-

---

[6] Contract-keeping is peculiarly the moral rule applicable to mercantile transactions. To apply it without modification to the dealings of employers and wage-earners is to intrude the mercantile standard into the industrial sphere. This is what we are now witnessing. The industrial standard is only in process of development and clarification, and the accepted mercantile standard is really in conflict with it. Among merchants it is of the very essence of their transactions that a contract shall not be invalidated, despite the injurious consequences to one or the other party which it may turn out later on to involve. The security of commercial transactions would be gone if revision of the contract should be permitted whenever consequent loss appears. Again, and this is particularly important, merchants are assumed to be on a footing of equality in dealing with one another, equally free in accepting or rejecting a proposed contract, equally competent to take care of their respective interests. The relation of employers to wage-earners however is not that of economic equals^ but of the economically stronger with the economically weaker. And this difference is of cardinal importance it)

found a notion as that of justice should be understood so superficially, restricted to such narrow limits, and that rational human beings should claim to possess so lofty a virtue on the score of credentials so inadequate. The reason is that the empirical substratum of justice is mistaken for the ethical virtue itself. This substratum may be described as an inborn propensity toward order in things and in relations, a natural impatience of loose fringes, a certain mental neatness. Hence insistence on explicitly defined arrangements and on simple, over-simple formulas. These are favored because they keep out of sight the complex elements which if considered might introduce uncertainty and possibly disorder into the situation. Thus a manufacturer, impatient of looseness, over-rating explicitness, will be led to grasp at a formula of justice which reduces it to the bare literal performance of a fixed agreement, no matter with what unfreedom, owing to the pressure of want, it was entered into by the wage-earners, and no matter

determining the rule of justice as it should obtain in the industrial sphere. I do not of course intend to imply that an agreement between employer and wage-earners once made should not as a rule be kept as scrupulously as that between merchant and merchant. What I affirm is that in view of the greatness of the injury possibly inflicted upon the weaker, the economically stronger party is bound at least to share the responsibility with the weaker for the essential fairness of the terms of the agreement before it is finally completed. Nay, I would go a step farther, and say that despite the indispensable condemnation of contract-breaking, provision should be made for possible revision in cases where it can be shown that exceptional hardships have appeared, unforeseen and unforeseeable at the time when the agreement was made.

how deteriorating the effect of the insufficient wage may prove to be on their standard of living.

But it is a far cry from this empirical predisposition to the sublime ethical idea itself. The idea of "the just" as exemplified in any act performed by me includes the totality of all those conditions which make for the development of the ethical personality of others in so far as it can be affected by my action. To do a just act is to act with the totality of these conditions in view, in order to promote the end in view, which is the liberation of personality or at least the idea of personality in others and in myself.

It is thus evident that a just act—an ideally, perfectly just act,—can be performed by no man. First because the right conditions of human development are but very imperfectly known, and are only brought to light by slow degrees. Secondly because even as to the known conditions of justice, for instance the abolition of the evils of the present industrial wage system, a single employer, or even a group of well-intentioned employers can bring about the desired changes only to a very limited extent.

Raising the finite quality underlying justice to the Nth degree therefore means opening an illimitable prospect. The ethical effort in this, as in all other instances, is destined to be thwarted. It is an effort in the direction of the finitely unattainable; the effort itself, with the conviction it fosters as to the reality of that which is finitely unattainable, being the ethically valuable outcome. The just man, therefore, in any proper sense of the word, is one who is convinced of the fact that he is *essentially not a just man,* and a deep humility as to both his actual and possible achievements will distinguish him from the "just man" so-called, who arrogates to himself that sublime attribute on the ground of the scrupulous payment of debts, or the fulfilment of contracts. Humility in fact will be found to be the characteristic mark of those who have attained ethical enlightenment in any direction. It is the outward sign from which we may infer that the finite quality in them is in process of being raised to the Nth degree.

I have given these few specific illustrations of my meaning, but what has been said applies equally to any of the plus qualities. The plus qualities are the ones which are favorable for transformation into the infinitized ethical quality. The ethical principle itself is one and indivisible. Any one of the plus qualities, when ethicized, will conduce to the same result. From whatever point of the periphery of the ethical sphere we advance toward the center we shall meet with the same experience. Thus self-affirmation or egoism when in idea raised to the Nth degree will reveal that the highest selfhood can be achieved only when the unique power of a spiritual being is deployed in such a way as to challenge the unique, distinctive power that is lodged in each of the infinite multitude of spiritual beings that are partners with us in the eternal life.

And altruism, or care for others, at its spiritual climax, will conversely involve the recognition that true service to others can only be perfectly performed when the power that is resident in ourselves is exercised in its most vigorous, most spontaneous, and most self-affirming mode. And as the diverse empirical qualities which we observe in one another all appear to be modes of or cognate with these two principal tendencies—the self-affirming and the altruistic—the method of transfiguring empirical qualities which has been set forth may be found to apply in every instance.

CHAPTER VIII

THE SUPREME ETHICAL RULE (*CONTINUED*)

WHATEVER the steps that have thus far been taken, they are preliminary to the final step. And the *method* of "salvation," the distinctive feature wherein this ethical system differs from others, may now be briefly stated. So act as to elicit the unique personality in others, and *thereby* in thyself. Salvation is found in the effort to save others! The difference in method consists in the joint pursuit of the two ends, that of the other and that of the self. The controlling idea is that the *numen* in the self is raised out of potentiality into actuality by the energy put forth to raise the *numen* in the other,—the two divinities greeting each other as simultaneously they rise into the light.

It is thus that both egoism and altruism are transcended. To be egoistic is to assert one's empirical self at the expense of other empirical selves. To be altruistic is to prefer the empirical selves of others to one's own. It is not true that self-realization, keeping to the empirical signification of self, leads insensibly to altruistic conduct. The life of the great "self-realizer," Goethe, may be cited in evidence of this. Nor is it true that preference for the empirical self of another necessarily involves maintaining the integrity of one's own empirical self. In the empirical field egoism and altruism are conflicting and mutually contradictory. It is in the spiritual field that they cease to be so, because both disappear in an object of the will which includes them both and transcends them both. If this be so, it may be asked why does, the formula we have adopted read: So act as to elicit the unique personality in others, and thereby in thyself? Why not conversely:—So act as to realize the unique personality in thyself, and thereby in others ?—since in any case the ends in view are to be achieved conjointly. The answer is that in the pure spiritual field, in the world of ideal ethical units, it would make no difference from which point of view the relation were regarded. But when the spiritual formula is applied as a regulative rule to the mutual relations of empirical beings there is a difference. Thus applied, it must necessarily be couched in such terms as will make the spiritual birth of the other the prime object, and the spiritual birth of the self its incidental though inseparable concomitant. This is so because ethics is a science of energetics, which has to do with the potencies of our nature in their most affirmative efferent expression. All our higher faculties are active, and touch for good or ill the lives of those who surround us. Even the secret thoughts which seem only to affect our own individuality, inevitably project their influence upon our associates.

Now ethics is a science of *right* energizing. And since as a matter of fact we do inevitably energize in such a manner as to affect others, the fundamental question in ethics is: how are we to regulate the incidences of our natures that fall upon other lives so that they shall be right? Since we cannot help acting upon them and influencing them, how can we act rightly toward them and rightly influence them? And the rule supplied by the ethical principle is: Act upon their empirical selves in such a manner as to draw from their empirical natures the hidden personality, or at least the consciousness of it. And the repercussion of the rule is: in the attempt to do so you will convert your own empirical self into a spiritual personality, or at least evoke in yourself the idea of yourself as a spiritual personality.

Incontestably, in the attempt to change others we are compelled to try to change ourselves. The transformation undergone by a parent, in the attempt to educate his child is an obvious instance. No parent is a true parent at the outset. As his perception deepens of the real needs of the child, which is so entirely dependent on his self-control, on his wisdom as well as his love, he will realize more and more his own deficiencies, and seek to remedy them. The same is true of the professor in relation to his students, of a leader and his followers, of a religious teacher and those who look to him for advice and help. In all such relations when rightly understood there is simultaneous growth on both sides. In the ethical sphere there is a law of levitation, the contrary of the law of gravitation that obtains in the realm of matter. We actually tend to rise from a lower to a higher level in proportion as we bend downward to lift those still lower than ourselves.

CHAPTER IX

WE now have to consider how to acquire the faculty of seeing the light that in our fellowmen is often so deeply hidden. We can love only that which is lovable. If we could see holiness, beauty concealed within our fellow-beings, we should be drawn towards them by the most powerful attraction, willingly living in their life, and permitting them to live in ours. We should then love all men, for we should see in all what is unspeakably lovable. But the empirical man stands between us and the spiritual man, and the empirical woman between us and the spiritual woman; and very often the former are most repulsive, even when their ugly traits do not affect us personally, even when as spectators merely we observe how they behave.

Much more is it well-nigh insuperably difficult to worship, in the sense of holding worthy, those whose characteristic traits directly offend us, or are perpetual thorns in our side. We must somehow learn to regard the empirical traits, odious, harmful or merely common-place and vulgar as they may be, as the mask, the screen interposed between our eyes and the real self of others. We must acquire the faculty of second sight, of seeing the lovable self as the true self. And how without self-

223

deception we can possibly succeed in doing so is the question.

In the first place, it is my own craving for resurrection out of that death in life to which I seem doomed that must impel me to penetrate to the essential life in others. My own spiritual nature is in fetters, and to burst the fetters, to escape from the prison, there is but one way. The unique personality, which is the real life in me, I cannot gain, nor even approximate to, unless I search and go on searching for the spiritual *numen* in others.[1] The force which incites me to penetrate beyond the em-

[1] In a previous chapter I remarked that the cheap estimate of others and of oneself is due to the habit of regarding human beings from the point of view of the use they can be put to, ignoring the wonderful and mysterious energies and potencies which are exhibited day by day in every human being. If the force stored in an infinitesimal particle of radium is calculated to excite admiration, how much more the forces exhibited in man, looking at him merely as the stage on which the spectacle of these forces is displayed. Consider the occurrence of such a thing as thought, the sheer miracle of mentality, the working of the constructive imagination in the artist, etc. If we sufficiently dwell on these inward facts about men, instead of merely emphasizing their external utility to one another, we shall thereby be put in tune, as it were, for the higher spiritual view of man. The difference I have said is like that between understanding the theory of electricity and merely turning on electric power in the workshop or the home. And yet the scientific contemplation of the miracles of human nature as seen from within, while it serves as a propaedeutic, cannot actually bring us up to the ethical point of view. For this sort of contemplation reveals only the working of impersonal forces or powers, thought, feeling, impulse in their endless actions and reactions, similar, in so far as they are impersonal, to the forces observed in nature. The ethical point of view alone discloses a centrality, an underivative, irreducible core, a substantive being, personality.

pirical traits of others, to surmount the walls which surround the shrine in them, is the consciousness that unless I do so I am myself spiritually lost, I remain myself spiritually dead. For it is only face to face with the god enthroned in the innermost shrine of the other that the god hidden in me will consent to appear.

The expression "death in life" means living, even living passionately and in a way efficiently, with a sense, nevertheless, underneath of the hollowness, the futility of the objects of pursuit. The death in life is the state of discontent that slowly gathers and augments in a man's mind as he pursues his customary ends, as he reviews his intellectual achievement, the books he has written, the pictures he has painted, the meager outcome of his schemes of social reform, the uncertain result of his efforts at moral self-development. It is the ensuing distaste for what he has actually accomplished, the disallowance of it as in any way ultimately satisfying. And yet this death in life is itself the well-spring of resurrection, out of which is engendered an irrepressible yearning of the mind to attach itself to something greater than all ephemeral interests, to something that has eternal worth, and is of such a kind as to communicate of its eternal nature to him who touches it. The god in the other, the eternal personality in the inner sanctuary of the other, is that object which must be sought and touched. The cry of my own soul for salvation is the impulse that leads me on to search for that object. Without the previous discontent, I shall not seek; without the appraisement of the temporal ends and interests of man as in the last analysis unsatisfying, I shall not set out on my quest. Enmeshed in the jungle of the empirical world, I shall find no exit. I shall remain the victim of the illusion that the peace I need can be found in the realm of temporal desire. I shall commit what the theologians called Original Sin, that is, the preferring of "the works of the Creator to the Creator himself."

But there is a second force that must act in conjunction with this keen desire for personal liberation or highest personal self-affirmation. It is the sense of the *dependence of others* upon what I can do for them. Notoriously it is the dependence of the child that evokes in the parent the noblest qualities of which he is capable, the self-denial, the incessant willingness to labor for the good of the offspring. It is the dependence of the student on the teacher, of the disciple on the master that elicits the latter's best thought. It is the dependence of the multitude on the religious teacher that puts him on his mettle. But if the dependence of others upon oneself is to produce its appropriate results, that dependence will have to be interpreted in a spiritual sense. We shall have to think of others as dependent on us not only for the necessary empirical services we are bound to render them, but those empirical services themselves will have to be regarded as instruments by means of which we may render them the highest spiritual service.

This leads to a more *rigorous scrutiny of the notion of service* than has hitherto been customary.

The question we must answer, and it is one that has never been adequately met, is: What is it in the other that we are to serve, what is the true object of our service? Man is worth while on his own account.

Now no one can pretend that the welfare of the animal, part of man is an object worth while on its own account. To satisfy the hunger or the thirst of another, or to promote his health is to serve his body. But the body is the servant of a master. And I am not bound to serve a servant. If I am to serve the servant at all it must be for the sake of the master. Who then is the master ?

The same argument applies also to the intellect. Human science is after all but a narrow littoral along the illimitable continent of nescience. No one who compares the intellectual achievements of mankind with the problems that remain unsolved will pretend that the accomplishments of the intellect are worth while on their own account. The mental no less than the physical part of us has a master. There is an object higher than the acquisition of knowledge to be attained in the course of the mind's endeavors to acquire knowledge, namely the growth of the scientist towards unique personality, as will be shown in the chapter on the Vocations in the last Book. Analogous considerations apply to art and its achievements.

And if someone should say that neither the satisfaction of the body alone, nor of the intellect, nor of the aesthetic sense, nor of the affections, but of all of them taken together, is to be the object of our service, the answer is that this would be merely serving a whole household of servants, and still not serving the master. This quite aside from the fact that the ideal of happiness as consisting in the harmonious gratification of the various elements enumerated is chimerical. Since some of the most indispensable elements of happiness, such as freedom from disease and from bereavement, are beyond our control. While even the higher faculties are far from harmoniously cooperating, the one-sidedness of human nature being such that a marked development in one direction is actually incompatible with complete development in other directions.

Unless, then, there be some master end in everyone's life, one paramount to all others, to which all others are subordinate (the subordination and the renunciation involved being themselves means of spiritualizing one's nature) there is no point to the notion of service. That master end I have defined as the attainment of the conviction of one's infinite interrelatedness, the consciousness of oneself as a member of the spiritual universe, a απαξ λεγομενον [2] in the eternal life, a source of energy
induplicable in its kind, which radiates out and touches at the center each one of the infinite multitude of spiritual associates, and receives from them the effect of their aboriginally diverse modes of energizing in return.

[1] have mentioned two motives that impel me to search for the *numen* in others. The one, the craving for my own liberation from the death in life, my own desperate outreaching toward salvation; the other, the sense of the dependence of others upon me. Yes, but this dependence of theirs I must now interpret as spiritual dependence. I must look for them also beyond the death in life to life itself. I must have the courage and the truthfulness to look upon neighbor, friend, wife, husband, son, daughter *sub specie (etcrnitatis*, that is, as primarily spiritual beings, and estimate any physical, intellectual

[2] An expression occurring once only.

228

or emotional help I can give them by the consideration whether it does or does not advance them toward the master end of their being.

Courage of this sort is rare, because precisely the physical, mental and emotional wants of those who depend on us are the most obvious and clamorous. I do not of course mean that we should not attend effectually to their immediate wants. How could we avoid doing so? How could we neglect the health, the education, etc., of our children? What I say is that we should acquire the habit of looking upon the immediate ends as instrumental, and keep in view the supreme end which they in turn are to serve, and that we should beware of what I have called the fallacy of provisionalism—that of supposing that we are at liberty to provide for the lower immediate necessities first, leaving the higher and the highest needs to be attended to later on.

The manner in which parents commonly plan for the future of their sons and daughters is perhaps the fittest illustration of the idea I am here seeking to exclude. During the period of infancy they pilot the child through the dangers that beset its physical existence. Later on, what is called education, the preliminary mental training required to fit the young for the business of life, is felt to be imperative. Then comes the selection of a vocation with a view of assuring the material basis of subsistence. Still later, the advancement of the sons or daughters in their chosen vocations, or their social success occupies perhaps the parent's mind. Thoughts of a happy marriage flatter the parent's imagination. If the moral side receives attention, the utmost that as a rule is demanded is that the young person shall not fall below the average moral standard that happens to prevail in the community. And it is in such ways as these that we are apt to respond to the claims of those spiritual beings for whose essential future welfare we are to so large an extent responsible.

To widen this all too narrow conception of our responsibilities, the following reflections may be found useful. A father in the last decade of his life realizes acutely the brevity of his own past existence. The curve of his life is now rapidly descending. Supposing him to be nearing seventy, his adult sons and daughters may by this time have reached the age of thirty or forty. Looking back on the thirty or more years that separate him from them, and remembering how like a dream the intervening years have glided by, it may come home to him with sudden force how soon these, his sons and daughters too, though now in their prime, will reach the point at which he has arrived. The error of parents is to think of their grown sons and daughters only as moving on the upward curve of life. They stop short in imagination there. They look forward to marriage, vocational success and the like, as finalities for those who are still young. We ought to remember that the upward curve in the lives of our children will presently descend just as ours has descended, that the few decades which separate them from old age will pass as quickly for them as they have passed for us,—almost in the twinkling of an eye,—and we ought to ask on their behalf as we must on ours,—What is to be the result of it all? What does it all profit? And it is this thought that will turn our attention for them as for ourselves to the spiritual end which should be dominant at all times,—in the morning, at noon, and in the evening twilight of a human existence.

All that has been said has to do with the arousing in us of the desire to see in others the god, the *numen,* the master end. The wish to escape from our own death in life, the sense of the dependence of others on us as interpreted,—these two are the means of stirring us up to go forth upon the quest, and the seeking is already more than half the journey. Seek, and ye shall find. But what exactly is it that we are to seek? What are we to see in the other ?—The spiritual nature. But what is the spiritual nature? I have frequently urged that the lack of a definite description of the spiritual nature is the chief defect in ethics up to the present time. This defect I endeavor to supply. The spiritual nature is the unique nature conceived as interrelated with an infinity of natures unique like itself. The spiritual nature in another is the fair quality distinctive of the other raised toward the Nth degree. We are to paint ideal portraits of our spiritual associates. We are to see them in the light of what is better in them as it would be if it were transfigured into the best. We are to go on as long as we live painting these ideal portraits of them. We are to retouch their portraits constantly. We are not indeed to obtrude or impose upon others these sketches, these mental creations of ours, but to propose them diffidently, reverently, to hold them up as glasses in which our associates may possibly see themselves mirrored. It is for them to accept in whole or in part our rendering of their inner selves or to reject it. But we are not to desist from our labor in creating the ideal portraits, for in this consists the spiritual artistry of human intercourse.

Our friends we are to see in the light of these glorified sketches,—our friends and our enemies too. For only thus can we win them, and be essentially their benefactors. There is no power so irresistible, it has been said, as love. I do not quite accept the word Love. It signifies the feeling that goes with the ideal appreciation of others; and mere feeling supplies no directive rule of conduct. But it is true that the power of ideally appreciating others, of seeing them in the light of their possible best, and the feeling of love consequent on this vision, is the mightiest lever for transforming evil into good, and for sweetening the embittered lives of men. No greater boon can anyone receive from another than to be helped to think well of himself. Flattery is the base counterfeit of appreciation. Spiritual appreciation, appreciation of the inner self despite the mask, is the greatest of gifts, to manifest it is the greatest of arts. In its supreme form it is the art of going down to the lowest of human beings—the man in the ditch, the woman on the street—and making them think well of themselves because of possibilities in their nature they themselves hardly surmise. It is also the art of making the most developed and advanced human beings realize in themselves something still higher and better than they have ever reached. It is this art by which the supreme human benefactors have worked their spiritual miracles, and it is an art which to the extent of our ability we must each acquire and practice, if human society is to be redeemed.

There are specially two points to be remembered: the one, that of seeing the unattained excellence in those who are already in the way of excellence; the other, where there is or seems to be a complete absence of fine qualities or of the promise of development, as in the case of backward children, that we should still not abate one jot of hope or effort, seeking to win even the smallest improvement, in the conviction that the best possible under the circumstances is incalculably worth while. For, compared with the infinite ideal even the achievements of the most advanced and most developed fall infinitely short, and what are they more than the best possible under the circumstances. The best possible under the circumstances represents for us the absolute best.

Now a word in regard to those who resist the better influence which we may seek to exercise over them, for instance, the so-called black sheep in families. Our chief concern should here be to prevent the resistance from infecting ourselves and provoking unethical reactions. Ethics is a system of relations. The ethical point of view consists in seeing the relation between the offending person and ourselves as it ought to be, in seeing with perfect objectivity the kind of conduct ideally required by the relation on both sides, seeing it and thereby assisting the other to see it. But we shall never succeed in doing this until we purge from our thoughts and speech every trace of private irritation. If we can point out to the one who has gone wrong how he has hurt another, and has spiritually hurt himself; if while we do this we see the fineness that is possible to him and make him realize that we see it, we shall not utterly fail. I am aware that other methods should accompany the spiritual appeal. In some cases, a temporary separation is indicated, in other cases, a prolonged change of environment, or the gradual formation of new habits of industry and application, the awakening of interest in some pursuit that leads the mind away from egocentric preoccupation. Psychology and experience crystallized into commonsense have valuable counsels to give. But, along with the technical aids, the spiritual influence should never be lost sight of or relegated to the second place.

And finally two ideas should be mentioned which are pertinent to broken relations, as for instance to the unhappy marriage relation and to interrupted friendships: One that the break is never complete. There remain certain threads unsundered, which should be most sedulously preserved intact. They may serve as points of attachment to weave the tie anew. Again, and this is still more important, thought that the break would never have occurred if the relation had been as finely conceived as it ought to have been on my side as well as on the others. Take friendship as an example. A friendship of many years' standing is suddenly wrecked. Why? What were the terms on which the friendship had been based? What had friendship meant to me?—A certain personal attraction, mutual aid and comfort, taking counsel together, sympathy in joy and sorrow. These are valuable elements of friendship, but they do not even touch the essential point. They do not describe the principal function which a friend has to fulfil. The friend ideally is one who stands alongside another as the spectator of his spiritual development, as one who appraises his friend's advance toward the master end of life disinterestedly, and yet with deepest personal concern. He is the mirror in which his friend may see the stages of his spiritual progress reflected. Now I have lost my friend. Why have I lost him? Because he was never a true friend to me, and, I must add, because I was never a real friend to him. I have not really lost him, because I never really possessed him. And on making this discovery I shall have a new light shed on what friendship might mean. I may never be so fortunate as to find the actual friend, but I shall know what he ought to be, and what it is in me to be to him. And when I say, "what it is in me to be to him," I think of resources of my inner being which have never been called out; I think of the worth that belongs to me as a spiritual being capable of giving forth and receiving highest spiritual influence, and I am thereby immeasurably aggrandized in my own esteem, the self in me is lifted nearer as it were to its infinite counterpart in the eternal life. I walk henceforth on a higher level, I dwell amid serener presences. And this aggrandizement of the self, not on the ground of what I am but what I may be, and of others too, not on the ground of what they are, but what they may be, is the compensation derived from the bitter experience of broken relations. And what has been said of friendship by way of example is true of frustration in marriage as well, and of frustrations of every kind.

NOTE TO BOOK III

I may mention a certain test case for trying out the proposed rule, namely, to idealize the fair quality in others, and thereby achieve the concomitant transformation of the self. I mean the case of the victims of a cruel race prejudice, such as is entertained against the colored people of the South by the more brutal whites. I remember a long evening which I once spent in the company of a leader among the colored people, and one of the best men I have ever known. I looked that night deep into a suffering, sensitive human soul, and I tried to put myself in his place. I realized the hardships of his lot, the anguish that I myself should suffer if I were in his position. But would there be the spiritual equivalent? Would the way I had found in trials less poignant be the way of release? To make the situation clear, I selected two points in which the white man, my supposed oppressor, has the advantage, two fair qualities of which he can boast. His family life is purer on the average than that of a large number of the colored people. And he has also learned in the case of white men to distinguish between the criminal and the innocent. He will protect the latter, and give up the former to justice. Now my own people, putting myself in the place of the colored man, are backward in both these respects. In consequence of the long centuries of slavery their family relations are often unstable, while they are apt to shield the colored criminal from the arm of the law. In both respects I want to represent to myself the white man as he ought to act. He ought to help me lift up my race, first, by making their family life purer and more stable. But instead, many of the whites debauch the women of my race, while perhaps respecting those of their own race; moreover, by refusing decent accommodation on railroads they compel educated and refined colored women to travel in cars in which the coarsest men are herded together.

Again, how can I, as a leader among my people, teach them

236

to distinguish between the criminal and the innocent of their race so long as mobs of white men indiscriminately lynch the innocent and the criminal of my race alike on the barest suspicion? Against their actual behavior I set up in my mind a picture of how the superior race, superior in point of civilization, but still morally backward, ought to act. I can but suggest this picture, keep it in view as a constant protest, or still better as an imperative model.

But I can do more. I can turn upon myself, and upon others of my own people who are in advance of the majority of them, and presently I shall be compelled to admit that amongst ourselves something of the same pride of superiority exists, something of the same prejudice against those who are lower in the scale. For there is also a stratification and a hierarchy of higher and lower among the oppressed. And the relatively higher are apt to behave toward the lower in the same fashion as their common oppressors behave toward them all. We find the same tendency among other oppressed races, as for instance in the attitude of certain of the Spanish and the German Jews toward the Polish and the Russian. Purge thyself, therefore, is the incisive monition; purify thine own nature of that pride which hurts so cruelly when it is directed upon thee from without. Let the sin committed against thee be the means of purifying thee from the like sin. This is the spiritual compensation, this the thought that leads to inward peace!

BOOK IV

APPLICATIONS: THE ETHICS OF THE FAMILY, THE
STATE, THE INTERNATIONAL RELATIONS, ETC.

CHAPTER I

THE COLLECTIVE TASK OF MANKIND AND THE

THREEFOLD REVERENCE

THE social institutions, the family, the organs of education, the vocation, the political organization, the organization of mankind, the ideal religious society are to be treated as a progressive series. The individual is to pass successively through them, advancing from station to station toward ethical personality.

In designating the social institutions as an ethical series, care must be taken not to confound the terms of the series as now existent with the terms as they would be did they conform to their ethical functions. For instance, even the monogamic family is as yet only in part ethically organized. School and university are adrift as to their ethical purpose. The majority of mankind are engaged in occupations which it would be absurd to call vocations, and the international group exists as yet barely in embryo. Hence when we speak of the social institutions as a progressive series through which the individual is to advance towards personality, we are describing the aim of social reconstruction, not the present state of things. The spiritual nature of man must create for itself appropriate social organs. It has been painfully engaged in the attempt to do so since the existence of our race on earth.

In each of the social institutions we are to distinguish between the empirical substratum and the spiritual imprint which it is to receive. We find in each ready to hand some natural non-moral motive or set of motives of which we are to avail ourselves in the endeavor to evoke the spiritual result. Thus in the family the non-moral motive is affection due to consanguinity; in the school sociality, the school society being the first society into which the child enters ; in the vocation there is the craving for mental self-expression, in the state, patriotism, or the feeling we have for the larger whole in which we are included on the basis of similarity of language, historic tradition, etc. The natural basis of the international group of society is the empirical, and as yet in no way ethical, fact of the commercial and industrial interdependence of the different countries, a fact used by M. Bloch and his more recent followers as an argument against war.

In popular literature the empirical substratum and the spiritual relation to be produced by means of it are constantly confused. In any genuinely ethical system they must be carefully discriminated.[1]

In each of the social institutions, or, as we may now call them, the phases of life experience through which the individual must pass on the way toward personality, the winning of the ethical result depends on observance of *the threefold reverence.* What I mean by the three?fold reverence must be explained in some detail, es-

[1] Thus the interdependence of nations in respect to their material interests is often erroneously expatiated on as if it constituted an actually ethical bond between them.

pecially as the reader might otherwise be led into identifying my view with that expressed by Goethe in *Wilhelm Meister*. The three modes of reverence mentioned by Goethe in his sketch of the "pedagogical province" have for their background the poet's pantheism. The view here set forth is based on ethical idealism.

In order to introduce my thought let me go back to the phrase repeatedly used in Book III—"the task of humanity." Mankind as a whole, the generations past, present and to come, have a certain work to do, a task to accomplish. A collective obligation rests on our race, spanning the generations.

The spiritual conception of the collective task is the basis of the threefold reverence. The spiritual result, as was said above, is in every instance to be superinduced upon an empirical substratum. The empirical substratum in this case is mankind considered as a developing entity, which partially reproduces in the present the mental and moral acquisitions of ancestors, partially increases the heritage and passes it on to the newcomers.

I, as an individual, am also inextricably linked up backward and forward with those who come before and those who are to come after. I cannot take myself out of this web. The task laid upon human society as a whole is also laid upon me. I am a conscious thread in the fabric that is weaving, conscious in a general way of the pattern to be woven.

But viewed empirically the development of humanity is haphazard. Much is preserved from the past that ought to be cast aside. Many traces of past error remain unexpunged in the life of the present. A mixed stream, compounded of good and evil, passes through our veins into our successors'. The empirical fact is simply the fact of partial reproduction, partial augmentation and partial transmission. The ethical conception of progress depends on the view that there is an ideal pattern of the spiritual relation in the mind of man, destined to become more explicit as it is tested out and that the present generation ought to appraise the heritage of the past according to this pattern, preserving and rejecting and adding its own quota in such a way as to enable the succeeding generations to sift the worthful from the worthless more successfully, and to see the ideal pattern more explicitly.

The threefold reverence has been described as reverence towards superiors, equals and inferiors. For this inadequate description I would substitute the following: In place of reverence towards superiors, reverence for the valid work of ethicizing human relations already accomplished in the past, reverence for the precious permanent achievements and for those who achieved them,— the "Old Masters." The human race has gained a certain ethical footing in the empirical sphere. The general task has not to be begun *ab initio.* In the act of separating what is worth while from what is worthless, in the very process of revision and reinterpretation, we manifest our reverence for the past. It is thus that true historicity is distinguished from blind conservatism. And besides, by studying the old masters, we acquire a certain standard of excellence. Since those who have contributed epoch-making advances ill philosophy, in religion, in science, inspire us by the grandeur of their attack on the great problems ; and the spirit of their attack, is unspeakably stimulating to us, even when we reject their solutions. We cannot too humbly sit as disciples at the feet of the great masters if discipleship has this meaning.

Reverence of the first type prescribes the same attitude towards preeminent personalities among our contemporaries. They rank with the great predecessors inasmuch as they are in a way for us predecessors. They are in advance of us. To revere them is to endeavor to come abreast of them, to obtain the advantage of the forward movement which their superior capacity enabled them to initiate, and to start where they leave off, adding our small quota.

The second kind of reverence is directed toward those who are, in respect to their gifts and opportunities, approximately on the same level with us, but whose gifts differ from and are supplementary to ours. In our relation to them we may learn the great lesson of appreciating unlikeness, and working out our own correlative unlikeness by way of reaction.

The third kind of reverence is directed toward the undeveloped, among whom I include the young, the backward groups among civilized peoples, arid the uncivilized peoples. We are to reverence that which is potential in all of these individuals and groups, and we do so by fitting ourselves to help them actualize their spiritual possibilities. Reverence of the third kind takes the highest rank among the three. The spiritual life of the world is a deep mine as yet explored only near the surface. The unrealized possibilities of mankind are the chief asset.

But in order to effectuate our purpose with respect to the undeveloped, we must have reverence toward the great Old Masters, to gain a certain standard of excellence ; and reverence towards unlikeness in others to become ourselves differentiated individualities, and in order to respect the unlikeness which we shall presently likewise find in the backward and the young. So that the three reverences play into one another and are inseparable from one another, the first two being indispensable to the third. They are in truth a "trinity in unity." But the third reverence is the supreme one. The chief objective must be the undeveloped, because our face must be turned toward the future, because the task of mankind is as yet in its early stages. The third reverence is supreme. Now it is only when we have grasped the meaning of the triple reverence that we can fully appreciate the significance of the family as the first matrix in which the reverential attitudes are to be acquired. It is only then that we can rightly conceive of the organs of education, and of the end upon which the activities of school and university should converge. And similarly we shall find our interpretation of the vocation, the state, and the international society illuminated by this conception of the three-fold reverence.

In popular religious teaching the individual is thrust into the foreground. His salvation as a detached entity is the principal object. In positivism and evolutionalism society in its empirical aspect is exalted, and the individual tends to be regarded as a stepping-stone. In the spiritual interpretation of the collective task as outlined, the individual remains integral and sacrosanct. The spiritual society of which the image is to be imprinted on human society is a society of indefeasible ethical personalities. [2] The individual even now at his station in the present attributes to himself this lofty character and the various obligations which he already recognizes, and which he endeavors to fulfil, afford him ample opportunity to vindicate his spiritual selfhood. If in addition he looks forward longingly to the future, and to the greater spiritual fulfilment that may be expected among posterity, this expectation is founded on the belief that what he already possesses in germ will then be more unfolded, that the ideal of the indefeasible worth of man of which he is already conscious in himself will then be more completely recognized and its infinite implications be more fully understood. [3]

[2] While at the same time the ethical personality, unlike the "windowless monads" of Leibnitz is effectuated only in the cross-relations which subsist between each one and his spiritual associates.

[3] I may here point out the bearings of this general point of view on the much-mooted and confused question of the value of the study of history. Ranke holds that the aim of the historian should be to reproduce factually the occurrences of the past. Robinson insists on the uses of history. But uses to what end? The history of the past is fragmentary and full of gaps. The data with respect to some of the most important periods are irrecoverable. The attitude of the human race towards its own history, I take it, should be like that of an individual towards his past. I cannot really resuscitate my past. Memory is treacherous. Much has been forgotten. The events of my youth are discolored when seen in the perspective of later years. I should try to know myself as far as I can, but with a view of pressing on and realizing with such light upon myself as I have, the ethical aim. The same applies to mankind. And the important point is in the review to disengage the ideas that controlled the principal social institutions in the past, and to appraise these

ideas from the standpoint of our present ethical insight. Thus, in treating the history of the family, we should single out the ideas that controlled the family relation, the idea of the *patria potestas,* the feudal idea, or the connection of the family with landed property. In writing the history of the organs of education, we should bring into view priestly education as among the Brahmins, musical or aesthetic education as among the Greeks, the idea of princely education, the idea of preparation for the government of an empire, which accounts for the system of the English universities, the controlling idea of the German universities. And then at the end of our survey we shall be in a better position to discern what is to be the ideal of school and university education in an ethical democracy. The same applies to the controlling ideas of the state, and of the remaining social institutions.

CHAPTER II

THE FAMILY

THE family is in process of change. We should fix attention on the kind of change that is desirable. The change desirable is the more perfect expression of the ethical ideal in the life of the family. One striking fact is that in the past the family was never supposed to exist merely for the "benefit" of its individual members. The latter view is an individualistic novelty of our age, and, as commonly understood, it is radically false.

Under the caste system the family subordinates the welfare of its members to the function of the caste. Society being stationary and stratified, the family is the organ for the reproduction of a stratified social system.

A similar view prevails under feudalism. We of to-day resent the idea underlying primogeniture. From the modern point of view we ask why the eldest born should be preferred to his brothers. Primogeniture appears to us to assert the inequality of individual men; but from the feudal point of view the eldest born was preferred, not as an individual, but as the steward of the family property. The family had a fixed place in the social hierarchy, and to maintain this place the estate was to remain undivided in the hands of one person.

Now what is amiss with the modern family? This is profoundly amiss—that the idea of the family as serving a larger purpose is disappearing, and that the family is supposed to exist for the benefit of its individual members, benefit meaning happiness. Frequent divorce and disintegration are the natural consequences of this view, for if the tie exists solely for the happiness of those bound by it, then it ought indeed to be dissolved when the relation entails suffering.

Society has passed from status to contract, and many seem to hold that contract is the last word, the true expression of freedom. We have passed from status to contract, we must pass on from contract to organization, and thus to true freedom.

Status is based on the analogy of the animal organism. The caste society and the feudal society, ethically regarded, are spurious organisms. This spurious type of organization is no longer viable,, and now bald individualism is taking its place. The malady with which the family is afflicted is individualism. The desirable change is genuine organization on the basis of the spiritual equivalence of all functions.[1] The relation of the family to the general social task of organization is twofold. The family is the seminary in which shall be implanted the germinal principle of organization, that principle which is destined to transform all the subsequent terms of the social series, the instrumentality to be employed being the three-fold reverence. Again, the family will reach its more perfect form in proportion as the succeeding social institutions, the school, vocation, state,

[1] Spurious or bastard organization was based on the empirical preeminence of some function like that of the priest or the warrior.

250

shall themselves be essentially organized, the influence of the later terms retroacting on the first term.

The family, in the spiritual view of it which I am sketching, differs from the family of other days, and also from the modern family, in two particulars. It does not recruit some one social class or stratum. It does not direct the offspring into a single specific vocation. It is the vestibule that leads into all the different professions and vocations. And secondly, the family does not prepare the young to enter into a vocation for the purpose of securing happiness. It does not regard the vocation as servile to the empirical ends of the individual, but as a phase through which he is to pass on the road toward ethical personality, the fulfilment of the objective aims of the vocation being the means of acquiring the ethical development which the vocation is competent to furnish. Thus we regain, but on a much higher plane, what the family possessed before it began to break down under the influence of modern individualism, namely, an ulterior greater purpose imbedded within itself and yet extending beyond itself.

When we have grasped this relation of the family to the subsequent terms of the social series, and bear constantly in mind as we should that the three-fold reverence is the instrument by which *organization* is to be effected, we shall then be able to give adequate reasons why the monogamic ideal alone is the true ethical ideal, why the marriage relation, if it is to be ethical, must be permanent between two and exclusive of all others.

Let me briefly point out the relation of the monogamic family to the three types of reverence. The

third type ranks highest. The tie of consanguinity between parents and offspring supplies the empirical substratum. To be interested in the undeveloped, to surmise possibilities as yet wholly unapparent, to go to infinite pains to nurture and educate an immature being
like a child, for all this natural affection is almost indispensable. As a rule no one can so love a child as its own
parents do. The plan of state education for infants to
replace home education is advocated by some on the
ground that professional kindergartners and teachers
are more competent to train the budding human mind
than unpedagogical fathers and mothers. The function to be performed by the scientific educator in cooperation with the home is doubtless not to be
missed; but taking children away from under the care
of their parents, assembling them in what would be
equivalent to state orphan asylums, is a procedure
which precisely for pedagogical reasons would be preposterous. For the parent supplies that concentrated
love for the individual child, that intimate cherishing
which the most generous teacher, whose affections are
necessarily distributed over many, can never give. And
the child needs this selective affection. The love of the
parent is the warm nest for the fledgling spirit of the
child. To be at home in this strange world the young
being with no claims as yet on the score of usefulness to
society or of merit of any kind, must find somewhere a
place where it is welcomed without regard to usefulness
or merit. And it is the love of the parents that makes
the home, and it is his own home that makes the child
at home in the world.

It does not follow that parents in general do reverence the spiritual possibilities latent in their children.

The natural affection is there, but the empirical substratum and the spiritual relation are not to be confounded. The kind of reverence of which I speak is an ideal thing to be worked towards, not something that as yet actually exists, save in exceptional cases. In the caste family and the feudal family the father incarnated, as it were, the social system so far as that stratum or class was concerned to which he belonged. He inspired awe. He demanded implicit obedience. It was the existing social system that spoke from his lips. But this system itself had an arbitrary character, and the worship of the father was hardly ethical. The modern family goes to the opposite extreme. In it the relations between parents and children are loose, and tend to become more and more so. Reverence is scarcely looked for by the parent, and is not likely to be accorded. On the individualistic theory the child at a very early age is treated as an equal, and whether encouraged to do so or not is apt to assert its independence. The members of the family are not joined in an organic connection, but resemble a collection of atomic units that easily -fall apart. The ethical relation, the real reverence must spring from the service the parent renders in bringing to light the specific individuality of the child with an eye to the transmutation which it is to receive in the later terms of the social series. Not only highest gratitude but genuine reverence are due to the parent who performs this office. "You have given me physical birth, you are now giving me spiritual birth," will be the child's response to the parent's efforts.

Thus much may be said as to the reason why the marriage relation should be exclusive. The principal reason why it should be life-long, is that the office of the parent in furthering the spiritual development of the children does not end when they reach the threshold of manhood or womanhood. On the contrary, the finest touches are often added to the work of education when the sons and daughters have become established in a business or profession, and have founded families of their own. The wisdom gathered from the experience of their elders, the disinterested counsel inspired by love, will then be of the greatest use to them. The young mother, especially, confronted with the problems of child-rearing, will naturally turn to her own mother for advice. The son, who comes to close quarters with the difficulties of life, will find in the father, who is detached from life and has the tranquil vision of old age, his best friend.

In speaking of the third type of reverence I have already included all that need here be said of the first type. The reverential relation is mutual. The child will truly reverence the parent who on his side reverences the child's spiritual possibilities. The child does not understand the word Spiritual, but is unconsciously affected by the thing itself which I am here describing. A person who has the vision, who has the gift of divining what is as yet unmanifested, will convey to others the illumination of his vision. The child will realize in his parent the presence of something higher, and will revere it, worship it. Certain looks, certain expressions of the countenance, certain gestures, though not understood in their meaning at the time, will be imprinted on memory to be recalled in later life and then understood. But it is essential, in order to evoke reverence in the young, to have it oneself. He who does not steadfastly revere something, yes, someone greater than himself, will never elicit reverence in others.

The second type of reverence, towards those who are unlike ourselves but none the less our equals, can be inculcated in an elementary way in the family through the relations of brothers and sisters. Fraternal feeling is an empirical means whereby to produce or at least prepare the way for a very notable spiritual result—the willingness not only to respect difference in others, but to welcome it. In current teaching the emphasis in fraternity is placed on likeness. It should rather be placed on the unlikeness. These exist, and are sometimes very marked between brothers, and often cause discord and separation. The novices in life should therefore be taught betimes to overcome their repugnance to those who are unlike themselves, and the common relation of the brothers to their parents will be helpful to this end. Naturally we dislike the unlike. Alienness is ever productive of disharmony. The fact, however, that the unlike person in the case of a brother is the child of the same parents draws us powerfully toward him despite the tendency to recoil.

I must not omit to mention that the triple reverence is most naturally and easily learned in the family, because of the simplicity of the relations, and the limited number of persons involved.

The question may be raised whether the single family should remain the primary social unit, or whether a group of families united in close cooperation would better fulfil the purposes for which the family exists. The privacy and separateness of each family would not need to be disturbed, cooperation might be limited to specific objects, such as simplifying the work of the household, providing kindergarten education for the young children, better play facilities, separate study rooms for adolescents, common entertainments for all, and a service of song at the beginning or close of the day. One obvious difficulty in constituting such a group would be: the diversities of tastes and opinions, particularly such as are not perceived at the outset, but emerge on nearer acquaintance, and as the younger members grow up and develop their idiosyncrasies. One great advantage, however, would result if care were taken to include in the group persons belonging to different vocations—scientist, scholar, architect, lawyer, artist. Young persons as they mature would then have the benefit of contact with those who are intimately familiar with different lines of vocational activity, and would be helped to know their own mind as to their future career better than they commonly do now. Personal contact with one who is engaged in a certain line of work is a far better instruction as to the nature of the work than reading about it or observation from a distance.

The ethical theory of marriage has been developed in

my published addresses.[2] But certain topics not there treated I would at least allude to here in passing, and among them the need of a more careful study of the causes that lead to infelicity in marriage. Kant mentions, as an instance of the discrepancy between the natural and the moral order, the fact that the sex passion is often at its height before the period when marriage may be wisely entered into. There are other seemingly radical incongruities, for instance, that between the face, the features of a person and his real character. The one may be borrowed so to speak from some ancestor, while the real nature is quite at variance with the impression created by the face, so that one who thinks he marries A really marries B. There are diversities also between partners in marriage that only show themselves in the latter part of life, when the outlines of character are apt to stand forth bare. Besides, there is assumed to be, by some modern writers, a certain fundamental sex antagonism.

The whole question of the characteristics of sex requires to be far more carefully investigated than it has been. And here let me take the opportunity to express my positive appreciation of empirical science in connection with ethical theory. The chief object of this volume is to work out the general plan of the ethical relations, or the regulative principle in ethics, and this I am deeply convinced is supersensible and non-empirical. Applied ethics, however, is dependent not only on the regulative principle but on empirical science, that is, on an extended and ever-increasing knowledge of

[2] See *Marriage and Divorce,* D. Appleton & Co.

physiology, psychology, and of the environmental conditions that influence human beings, and I am keenly desirous to ward off the possible misunderstanding that the ethical theory here proposed is intended to replace the empirical science of man, individual or social.

> Without the way there is no going.
> Without the truth there is no knowing;

says Thomas a Kempis. The way is the empirical knowledge, the truth is the regulative principle. The way itself, as we proceed along it, will shed additional light on the truth. Nevertheless, without the outlines of the truth, without a goal in view, we should but be wandering blindly.

It is likely that the relations between persons in marriage will in future become more complex, and the difficulties of adjustment more serious, in proportion as under the influence of the new education the individualities of men and women become more developed. Problems hardly as yet envisaged will then become pressing. But whatever the difficulties, they can be overcome if the ideal purpose of marriage be kept in view, namely, that two beings of opposite sexes shall spend their lives in the spiritual reproduction of offspring. The relation is triangular. Husband and wife are each to elicit the distinctive best in the other, incited, impelled to do so in order jointly to evoke the distinctive best in the young. And the young represent posterity. What the parents do for their own children they do for posterity, since children are that portion of posterity which! comes under their immediate influence. And in this sense it may be said that marriage is an organ for the spiritual reproduction and advancement of the human race.

CHAPTER III

THE VOCATIONS

THE next term in the series of social institutions is the school, inclusive of its higher departments. But for reasons which will sufficiently appear to anyone who carefully reads this chapter, it is advisable to treat the vocations first.

A more ludicrous mistake cannot be conceived than that of taking the ideal for the fact, the wish for the deed, in matters touching the social institutions. Thus the term "vocational guidance" is often used, as if the occupations of the majority of men already answered to what is implied in the idea of a vocation as if, for instance, industrial labor in a factory were a "vocation" into which the young only needed to be guided, whereas guidance means, in this case, being directed into some mechanical *occupation* not already overcrowded, or turned into other unvocational occupations when they happen not to be over-filled. But what is true of monotonous, mechanical labor in factories is true in a greater or less degree of all human occupations. None of them at least are as yet vocations in the highest sense.

I dwell on this because, in describing the vocation as the third term in the series, I would not have the reader imagine that this third term exists in any adequate manner. Rather is it to be the task of what is often loosely called "social reform" *to create the ethical series,*—not only the third term (the vocation), but the whole series from beginning to end, the family, the school, the state, the international society, the ideal religious society. The phrase "social reform" is strictly correct only when used comprehensively in this way. To confine its usage to the more equable repartition of wealth, or to changes in economic conditions is unwarrantably to narrow its signification. Social reform is the *reformation of all the social institutions in such a way that they may become successive phases through which the individual shall advance towards the acquisition of an ethical personality.*

In sketching the ideals of the different vocations, I have to consider in what way each contributes to the formation of an ethical personality. There is an empirical side to each vocation. Every vocation satisfies some one or more of the empirical human needs; but in the very act or process of doing so, it ought, in order to deserve the name of a vocation, to satisfy also a spiritual need, to contribute in a specific way toward the formation of a spiritual personality.[1] Agriculture furnishes food. The different trades minister to a great variety of wants. The scientist extends our knowledge of nature. With this empirical aspect of the vocations, however, I am not here concerned. A scientific classification of the vocations is not a task to which I need address myself. *My task is an ethical classification of the voca-*

---

[1] Just as the family is the organ of physical reproduction, but in that very capacity is ethically required to bring to birth the spiritual nature of its members.

tions. As this has never been undertaken, the first attempt is difficult and perforce provisional.

I outline my topics as follows:

1. The theoretical physical sciences (including mathematics) considered from the point of view of the specific way in which the ethical personality may be developed by those who pursue them.

2. The practical counterparts of the theoretical sciences, *e. g.,* engineering, and the industrial arts in so far as they depend on and illustrate and use principles and methods furnished by science. Work in factories, mines, and also in the fields, is to be regarded as the executive side of theoretical science.

3. The historical sciences, those which have to do with mentally reproducing the life of the human race in the past, including history proper, philology, archaeology, etc.

4. The vocation of the artist.

5. The vocation of the lawyer and the judge.

The vocation of the statesman.

The vocation of the religious teacher.

The three last mentioned are classed together as educational vocations, that is, as vocations which, in respect to their highest significance, are branches of the *pedagogy of mankind,* having for their object to educate the human race; the ethical object of the lawyer being to educate society in the idea of justice; of the statesman to educate society in the idea of the state; of the religious teacher to educate society in the idea of the spiritual universe.

This conception of the lawyer, the politician, etc., as

primarily educators, is a point to which particular attention is directed. The significance of it will appear further on. I shall now indicate in bare outline what I conceive to be the specific contribution of the vocations mentioned to the formation of a spiritual personality.

Science

Conspicuously important in this connection is the question whether and by what means the pursuit of the physical sciences can be linked up to the supreme spiritual end of man. The scientist may develop into a great thinker in the course of comprehensive and intricate investigations, but he does not thereby necessarily develop into a personality. His mind will become in this way a mirror of the orderly procession of nature's phenomena. He will be the accurate recorder of what happens, the knowing spectator of the play, whose eye recognizes the actors, the forces, beneath their disguises. The pursuit of knowledge of this kind for the sake of knowledge, or it may be for the sake of exercising the faculty of cognition, represents the purely scientific conception of the aim of science. Whatever moral qualities are exacted of the scientist, such as accuracy or intellectual veracity, self-abnegation, scorn of mere vulgar pecuniary reward or celebrity, and at least a provisional disregard of the practical benefits to be derived by mankind from scientific discovery—all these fine traits of character are prized as subordinate to the strictly scientific object. The ethical character of the man himself is not regarded as the supreme end to be fostered by his scientific occupation, but as instrumental to his occupation the aims of which are said to be purely *impersonal.*

There is thus a scientific conception of the aim of science; on the other hand, there is an ethical conception of it. The former points in the direction of the indefinite extension of knowledge which never embraces a totality of the knowable, never reaches a limit, even in idea. The latter points to the *infinite,* not to the *indefinite,* sets up an ideal of the infinite as the goal, takes the man out of the flux, centralizes his individuality into a personality by relating him to the infinite, not as the mere spectator and scribe of nature, but through his action or other potential spiritual beings like himself.

The scientist, in brief, like every one else, becomes a personality by eliciting the potential spiritual nature in other human beings. But be it noted that he is to perform this task *as a scientist.* His particular occupation is to be the means of producing a particular spiritual result in others as well as in himself, and by this means his' occupation is to be converted into a vocation.

How? Through partial success and frustration. Partial success in the case of a scientist means for one thing, increased mental grasp, the power to hold before the mind ever more and more complex relations, —a faculty supremely serviceable in mastering complexities of relation in the economic, in the political spheres, in the sphere of international intercourse, in the sphere of the social relations in general, and wherever the ethical principle has to be applied. The scientific occupation trains powers which are to be exercised so as to illuminate obscurities in the ethical field.

The frustration which the scientist meets with when he reflects in thoroughgoing fashion on the business he has in hand is the inevitable realization that *Alles Vergangliche ist nur ein Gleichniss,* that the sphere of the finite in which he labors, though capable of indefinite extension, is forever incapable of being rounded out to a true infinity, and hence that the complete unification of the manifold (in which alone the reality-producing functions of the mind can find repose and ultimate satisfaction), can never be carried out in the manifold of juxtaposition and sequence with which, as a physical scientist, he deals. He will thus be led to face in thought the limits of what is finitely attainable, not only by him as an individual scientist, but by physical science in general. And in proportion as his spiritual nature is energetic it will then assert itself all the more resiliency after this defeat, and turn in a new direction, and towards another kind of truth, the truth which is discovered in the realm of *will,* in the sphere of intercourse with fellow human beings. The propaedeutic result of science with respect to ethical personality is the training of the more complex mental faculties. The positive result following the frustration is the new turn toward the spiritual, the escape from the spell wherewith the physical world enchains the mind, the dissipating of the widespread illusion that the truths of physical science are the only kind of truth, the more determined setting of the face towards a different kind of truth. The scientist, in brief, is to travel along the paths of the finite in order to arrive and stand at the gate of the infinite.

I have said that the boon of personality is gained in

intercourse with others, through the influence which we exert on others. How does the scientist as a scientist spiritually affect others? The great specific service, as I have just said, which he is to render is to destroy the illusion that the material world is a finality. And it is just he, the scientist, who works most successfully in the field of physical truth who must assist the rest of us in escaping from the spell to which we are all subject. He is the one, he who more than others succeeds in unifying the manifold of juxtaposition and sequence, to whom we look to liberate others as well as himself from the deceptive belief that the reality-producing functions of the human mind can be satisfied in the temporal and spatial manifold. Not from the tyro, not from the purveyor of "popular science" can we hope to learn the profoundest lessons as to the incapacity of physical nature to appease the spirit of man. It is from the familiar friend of nature, from one more deeply read than we are in her secrets, that we are to obtain this great instruction, to receive this boon.

Ethics is a science of reactions. Each vocation reacts upon the others. The general reaction of science I have mentioned. In addition the work of the scientist reacts upon agriculture, industry, etc. The industrial arts, as has been stated, are to be regarded as the executive auxiliaries of science, receiving from it the knowledge of the uniformities of nature, and in turn setting for science new problems by attention to which scientific theory is advanced.

The relations of science to art also need to be considered at greater length than is possible here. I have in mind inquiries into the scientific basis of music like those of Helmholtz, the scientific theory of color and the like, and also detailed studies of the return gift which art confers on science, especially the value to the scientist of that cultivation of the imagination which is gained by the contemplation and study of works of art. There are different kinds of imagination: the purely artistic, the scientific, the mechanical imagination, the ethical imagination. The function of the imagination in advancing science has been discussed by Tyndall and others, but the subject is far indeed from being exhausted.

The scientist then may be defined as one who stands in reciprocal relations to all other departments of human interest and activity, who gives to each from his specific standpoint as a scientist, and receives from each, from religion,[1] from art, from the practical vocations, etc. Ideally speaking, every man participates in all the principal interests and activities of the human mind. Every man is something of an artist, something of a practical or executive worker, scientist, religious being. But in each individual the different interests are colored by his special pursuit, and the influence he wields in return is modified in the same fashion.[2]

[1] All that I have said in the beginning as to the relation of the finite and the infinite belongs under this head.

[2] There is one point too obvious to be overlooked, but perhaps it had better be expressly mentioned. The scientist helps us to build our world, the physical nest in which we live, first by mastering nature's procedures, then by making possible inventions, which increase the security of our footing in the physical world; dispense us from the brute task of pitting our merely physical strength against the forces of nature; render communication between distant

There are three great tasks that occupy human life:

1. To build our finite world (science and its adjuncts).

2. To create in the finite the semblance of the infinite, or spiritual relation (art).

3. To strive to realize the spiritual relation in human intercourse (ethics and religion).

This discussion of science affords me the opportunity to give an exact definition of the word "instrumental" as I use it. And the word "instrumental" is of decisive importance as to the entire ethical conception of life. Instrumental in what sense? The finite ends of man are to be the means used in the pursuit of the infinite end. But in what manner are they to be the means? To be a *cheerful world-builder*, to take an active and whole-hearted interest in the improvement of material conditions, in political reforms, in the embellishment of earthly life—how is it possible to do this and at the same time keep the spiritual end in view as the supreme end?

Christianity in its pristine form,[3] abandons the task in dismay. Instead of seeking action in the finite world as a means, it counsels renunciation and withdrawal. Modern social reform movements, on the other hand, are devoted to finite ends, more or less ignoring the spiritual. How is it possible to work in the world, in the finite sphere, for an end beyond the finite? The answer, as I have shown in the case of science and the

peoples feasible, and thereby lay the first foundation for an international society.

* *Vide* Introduction to the First Book.

same applies to all other vocations), is to be found in the words "partial success and frustration." The finite, lesser ends, are means to the highest end in so far as we are partially able to embody the spiritual relation in the finite world, and in so far as the inevitable defeat of our effort to do so serves to implant in us the conviction of the reality of the infinite ethical ideal.

The points contained in this chapter may be briefly summarized as follows:

What is the relation of science to the ethical end? We are seeking to link up the world to spirit. Along what line can the connection be marked out in the case of science? Science is instrumental in founding more securely the empirical basis of self-respect, inasmuch as it gives to man to a certain extent a sense of mastery over nature. With the help of science he feels himself no longer the helpless sport of nature's forces.

The training in complex thinking afforded by science is favorable to the ethical reformer. Science also incidentally encourages the virtues of veracity, and the like.

Knowledge for knowledge's sake cannot be the final end of the pursuit of science, since the world of space and time with which science deals is not only not as yet rationalized but is not ultimately rationalizable.

While in all the respects just mentioned the pursuit of science is indirectly instrumental to the spiritual end —instrumental to the instrument—it is directly instrumental to it in so far as, at the hand of the supreme scientist, man is conducted through the finite as far as the gate of the infinite.

269

CHAPTER IV

THE PRACTICAL VOCATIONS

MEDICINE is the executive of the science of physiology, and the others, on which it depends. The physician has a certain work to do, a certain need to satisfy—the need of health, the alleviation of pain. In endeavoring to satisfy this need he uses the sciences that underlie his vocation and in turn promotes those sciences.

On the lower levels of agriculture and the industrial arts the same holds true. Our physical necessities vociferously demand satisfaction. They cannot wait. Men must have food or they perish. The agriculturist supplies the food they need. But the spiritual view of life declares that man, *while* engaged in satisfying his material wants, shall in so doing assert his spiritual nature. He is to hammer out his personality on the anvil of his empirical necessities. Even as human beings do not partake of food like animals, but indicate by the manner in which they take it the superior worth of the being who is dependent on food, so the agriculturist who raises the food should testify to his spiritual character. He does so in part at least by his reaction on the sciences which he applies, biology, chemistry, etc. The same holds good of the industrial occupations. The work a man does should be the means of promoting the development of his mental and aesthetic nature, and of his will. The mental and aesthetic development is acquired by mastering and reacting on the science and the art that enter into the trade. The development of the will, the most important of all, depends on the organic relations of the industrial workers among themselves and to their chiefs.

This raises the problem of the right organization of "industrial vocationalists" from the ethical point of view, and the following questions present themselves: Shall the present division into the two hostile camps of trade-unionists and employers continue? Or is it to be regarded as a makeshift, perhaps necessary during the present period of transition, but certainly untenable in the long run? Is the uniform arrangement contemplated by Socialism desirable, the government of every industry and indeed of every vocation by the representatives of the community as a whole? Shall what is called cooperation be adopted, that is, the formation of independent groups of workers on the voluntary principle, associated for the purpose of equably dividing the profits?

The three alternatives mentioned may be examined from various points of view. Here we consider them from the ethical point of view. Assuming that the ethical end of life is to be supreme, what kind of industrial re-organization of society will be most in harmony with it? All three plans are open to the ethical objection that they concentrate attention on the material gain to be derived from the industry instead of on the specific service which those who follow the industry as a voca-^ tion are to render. Collective bargaining between unions and employers is after all just bargaining. Socialism differs from trade-unionism not in the object so much as in the means. Instead of securing for the workers a larger share it would secure for them at once an approximately equal share. Cooperation aims at the same result as Socialism by voluntary association instead of by collective compulsion.

None of the three plans is ethically satisfying, and a fourth arrangement should be contemplated. Its characteristics are the following:

1. The idea of service to be pre-eminent instead of the gain, the wage or salary to be apportioned as the means of sustaining the worker in the best possible performance of the service.

2. The work done by the workers to be the means of developing them mentally, aesthetically and volitionally, the educational features therefore to be pre-eminent.

3. The industrial group to be transformed into a social sub-organism (in the ethical sense a sub-organ of the larger organism of the nation). By this is meant that the employers cease to be employers and become functionaries, while each worker in his place and in his degree likewise becomes a functionary. A common social service group will thus be formed embracing the chiefs and the humbler workers. The chiefs will be the executive and administrative functionaries, and will be safeguarded in the due discharge of their proper functions. The workers will riot attempt to wrest from their chiefs as they do at present the directive functions which properly belong to the latter (subject, however, to due control). To each of the lesser functionaries in turn

will be assigned a sphere within which a relative independence would be his.

The industry as a whole will be an *organ* of the *corpus sociale*, and this its character will be expressed in its government. The workers, not required to render implicit obedience to rules imposed upon them by masters and superintendents, will have a voice in the legislation of the industry, in framing the policy of the industry, in electing the chiefs, and in this way the development of the will, upon which I lay the greatest stress, will be attained. The will of the worker, at present fettered, will be liberated by the opportunity given it to become enlightened and effectual.

I am not here describing a scheme which is to be immediately launched in its completeness. I am illustrating the ethical principle as I see it as applied to this particular vocation. I am endeavoring to show how an occupation can be changed into a vocation. The constitutional government of industries would be an intermediate stage between the present autocratic form, in which more or less absolute power is vested in the employer, and that organic constitution of industry which is ethically desirable.

Thus far the following plans have been before the minds of social reformers:

A. Competition, or life and death struggle.

B. Modified competition, or raising the plane of competition, as it is called, that is, doing away with the more ferocious and unscrupulous methods of competition.

C. Socialism.

D. Cooperation.

I propose to add (E) organization in the ethical sense. The word "organization" is deplorably misused at present. It is commonly employed as a synonym for aggregation, which is the very reverse of organization. Thus "organized labor" really means aggregate labor, labor acting *en masse.*

A further remark on the difference between industrial vocationalism as outlined and Socialism may be of use in clarifying the main idea. The relative independence of the social sub-organism is the salient point. This kind of independence is based on the general conception underlying my entire ethical philosophy, that the ethical quality resides in uniqueness in distinctiveness, that ethical progress consists in driving towards individualization in the sense of personalization. This as opposed to those philosophies of life that see the ethical quality in uniformity. Socialism is on the side of uniformity. It is indeed an extreme expression of it. If sometimes it is urged that the relative independence of the vocational groups might be recognized in the socialistic state, the answer is that the tendency would be in the opposite direction. And besides, the all-important question is to what end the relative independence is to be used. Under socialism it would be used for the purpose of increasing the quantity of valuable products at the disposal of the community as a whole. From the ethical point of view, the independence of the organic group would be used to insure reciprocal relations, and by means of these the development mentally, aesthetically and volitionally of *the producers.* The distinction certainly is clear enough to its members, whichever way the reader may incline.[1]

The Historical Sciences

I refer now briefly to historical science. The ethical aim of history and its adjunct sciences is to redeem from oblivion as far as is possible the past of the human race, its documents, its monuments, the knowledge of its political adventures, its customs, laws and institutions, its religious beliefs. In view of the lacunae in our knowledge a complete revival of the past is impossible. We must therefore principally seek to understand the ruling ideas that have governed our ancestors, in the family, in the state, etc. The task of the historian is to present these ideas as seen in the light of their consequences, so as to help us revalue them from the point of view of present experience and insight. The

---

[1] The vocational group must be independent because the expert familiar with the conditions under which a service is performed is specially competent to decide on the improvements required to render the conditions more favorable to the development of human nature, the service more adequate. The representatives of the collective community, that is of the inexpert, outside mass (inexpert in respect to this particular service) can never perform the same office.

With regard to the present state of industry the gigantic obstacle in the way of improvement is obviously the subjection of the man to the machine. The great hardship which the millions of factory operatives suffer is not only the insufficient wage, it is the depersonalizing effect produced by the substitution of the machine for the hand and the blind subjection of adult workers to the arbitrary will of superiors. (Compare what I have said on this subject in the chapter on "An Ethical Programme of Social Reform" in *The World Crisis*.)

historian will thus enable us to carry over from the past what is truly valuable, for the business we have in hand.

There is just now a strong reaction against the kind of historical science which deals principally with wars and the actions of princes or of great leaders. Detailed attention is being given to the more obscure life of the people. But it must be remembered that mere penetration into the lower strata of bygone societies, the mere heaping up of facts concerning mass movements, is as unprofitable as the more picturesque recitals with which works on history were formerly adorned. The mass movements and *the ideas* which gave rise to them should be set clear as far as possible; but without the evaluation and the revaluation, or the ethical appraisement, the voluminous knowledge of details is merely stupefying, and leaves us as much at sea as ever.[2]

Many men have read many books on history, and filled their minds with information on subjects like the Protestant Reformation or the French Revolution, without being in the least wiser themselves, or more fitted to enlighten others in respect to the religious and ethical problems which were involved in these great movements, and which still touch us so closely today. As to the ordinary high school or college student, what as a rule does he carry away from his study of past "history"?

[2] Think of Mommsen, the author of a thousand treatises, whose knowledge of the facts of Roman history was unsurpassed and probably unequalled. Yet is his judgment on Cesar or Caesarism helpful as an ethical appraisement?

CHAPTER V

THE VOCATION OF THE ARTIST: OUTLINE OF A THEORY OF THE RELATION OF ART TO ETHICS

THE three great directions of effort are: to work in the finite; to create in the finite the semblance of the infinite; to realize through effort the reality of the infinite. The vocation of the artist is to create the semblance of the spiritual relation between the parts of an empirical object. The object may be a vase or a lamp; it may be a human figure, it may be a group of *dramatis personae*. By introducing into the discussion of art the idea that a semblance of the spiritual relation is to be produced by the artist, we get rid at the outset of the barren formula of unity in variety.

Let me endeavor to elucidate the main ideas that flow from this definition of the spiritual aim of art.

1. The two points to be discussed are: What is meant by semblance? and What is meant by the quasi-spiritual relation as subsisting between the parts of a work of Art?

First, then, there is the semblance of *totality*. The spiritual relation is characterized by the totality of the parts related. That totality is realized only in the universal manifold. But a semblance of totality is furnished in the case of colors by the circumstance that the chromatic scale is cut off at the bottom and top in consequence of our inability to perceive the colors below and above; the musical scale likewise presents a quasi-totality, and the human figure in its contours presents a thing cut off from its surroundings, and in so far relatively complete in itself.

Because the spiritual relation involves the idea of the perfect totality, a relative totality, due to the accidental limitations of our sensory organs and power of attention, may become a semblance of the spiritual totality. I say, *may become*. A certain relation must be established between the parts of the relative totality in order that the semblance shall result.

One thing is clear; the subject of the work of art must possess relative completeness, and be capable of being contemplated as circumscribed and separated off. It must stand out like a tree, or like an oasis encircled by the desert, or like an island. The subject of art cannot be a mere length of cloth cut off from the fabric of things as they reel unceasingly from the loom of time—the mistake of Realism.

The point, emphasized in our third Book, namely, that an empirical substratum is to be spiritualized, and that ethics consists in spiritualizing this physical and psychical substratum, applies to art, but with the difference, that in the case of art the physical or psychical substratum cannot be spiritualized, but is to be made to take on the semblance of spirituality.

Now what is meant by this kind of transformation? I can perhaps explain by using as an illustration the color scheme of a picture. The transformation appears in the difference between the colors on the palette and the colors on the canvas. The colors on the palette represent the empirical substratum, the natural colors; the colors seen on the canvas show the same natural tints after they have taken on a new or second nature.

The second nature,—in what does it consist? In the circumstance that each color on the canvas, by its juxtaposition and its relation to the rest, is altered in tone and value, and that all the rest are altered by it. The spiritual relation is a give and take relation actually carried out. The semblance produced in art is the illusive appearance of such a relation as seen by the beholder.

We have thus set down two points—the apparent totality, and the apparent give and take relation between the parts (the second nature assumed by the parts, the illusory transformation of the substratum).

A third point involved in the second is that each part of a work of art shall remain invincibly individualized, despite the closeness of the relation which connects it with the rest. The individual member of a work of art may never be submerged in the whole, may never merely convey the abstract idea of unity amid variation. The "unity in variety" formula is not only empty but misleading, based on the same misconception which we have noted in dealing with Kant and with the Pantheists. The unity of a work of art consists in the reciprocal effect produced by the members on each other. Hence the more accentuated, the more distinctive the members are, always provided that the reciprocal relation is maintained, the more artistically satisfying will be the resuit. In this manner the work of art will be true to its essential character as a semblance of the spiritual relation.

I have thus far spoken of the form. In regard to content I have only remarked that it must be capable of relative detachment. It must also be capable of interior articulation. The idea that an empirical substratum is to be transformed will here be found helpful in determining what is and what is not a fit subject for art. A vase or a pitcher is a utensil. As such it is a detached thing. Is it capable of articulation *without destroying* its utility? If it is, as the beautiful vases show, it is a fit subject for art to treat. The embellishment of utensils, of tables, chairs, etc., that is to say, the giving of artistic form to objects with which we bodily come into contact, is a means of casting the appearance of the spiritual relation over these objects, and thus in a fine sense making them congenial to ourselves as spiritual personalities. This justifies the time spent by artist artisans on their handiwork, and also justifies our availing ourselves of their products (provided that the store set by these symbolic reminders of the spiritual relation do not divert us from the main business of life, which is to attempt to *recdize* that relation in human intercourse). The war song sung by a primitive tribe is a detachable, empirical thing, and possesses natural articulation. It has its slow beginning, its gradual rise, its paroxysmic culminations, its wild ecstasy, its final dying down.

The love passion expressed in lyric form has for its

basis the natural ups and downs, dejections and trans-ports characteristic of that passion.

The theme of a tragedy, as Aristotle says, must have a beginning, a middle, and an end. Repetition (always with a difference), contrast, apparent triumph, defeat, and somehow a triumph in defeat—whatever may be the elements with which the tragic poet deals, the crude substance of them is furnished by the theme itself. And the result becomes artistic when the articulation is such that each part becomes a member of an organized whole, that is, when each part exchanges its first nature for the second nature mentioned above in connection with paint-ing. [1]

The next point of interest to consider is whether beauty is to be regarded as the invariable object of art. Relative detachment and susceptibility to articulation in the manner described are indispensable. But if tragedy is to be included, beauty cannot be the exclusive ob-

[1] Aristotle regards the *Oedipus Rex* as the most perfect exam-ple of tragedy; let it serve the purpose of illustrating the idea here proposed. Read the play and get the total impression of it. An-alyze it into its parts. Synthesize after the analysis. You will not fail to realize how every character, every speech and act, contrib-utes to the total effect, and how in turn every single factor in the play receives a new significance from its relation to the rest, while still retaining its obvious meaning (the meaning it would have when taken out of the context of the play). Take the first speech of Œdipus as an example. He is the king solicitous for the welfare of his subjects, to whom they look up with admiration and gratitude. He is the father of his people. Read this speech again after you have taken in the entire play, and note how its color is changed. How the firmness, the fatherly, protective attitude is now seen to be the outward mask of a fugitive soul, unsure of itself, haunted by hideous fears.

ject. Lear, on the heath, the harpy daughters, Lear and Cordelia perishing together, are not beautiful objects. The task of the artist is to produce the semblance of the spiritual relation in any material which is capable of bearing that imprint. In the great tragedies we are lifted into an exalted mood by the form of the work even though the subject treated evokes horror—perhaps because of the very contrast between the form and the subject-matter. Beauty, on the other hand, is produced when both subject-matter and form are satisfying to our needs or aspirations. A vase is beautiful when perfectly adapted to its use and at the same time perfect in form. For this reason any kind of embellishment, for instance, in architecture not structurally in place is offensive, while on the other hand mere structural utility without the formal touch is mechanical. It is not true that utility itself inevitably flowers into beauty.

It should be added, however, that the artistic expression even of unsatisfied desires may come within the scope of beauty. The "Lycidas" is beautiful, Wordsworth's "Laodamia" is beautiful, the Gothic form of architecture is beautiful, and so is Keats' "Ode to the Nightingale," and Shelley's "Ode to the West Wind." In such productions the adequate expression of the need itself affords relief and induces tranquillity. The mind ceases to strive toward a beyond longed for, and rests tranquillized in the longing itself. That it should thus aspire and long, in consequence of its higher nature, and the assurance of the existence of this higher nature, as evidenced by the longing, is peacegiving.

But it is hardly possible to discuss even in the most

cursory manner the subject matter or content of a work of art without drawing attention to the ideals which at various times have been expressed in art, and to the function of art in respect to these ideals. For here the *grandeur* of the great art as connected with the ultimate aim and purpose of life appears.

Art in its fictions has endeavored to present to men the solution of the problem of life, the things most worth striving for. The ideals, of course, have varied. In the Greek epic the heroes contend around the walls of wind-swept Ilion. They themselves are wind-swept apparitions. Life is short; presently they too will pass out of sight, yet their names and deeds will live after them. Fate is inscrutable. There is no ulterior meaning in things. To glitter for a time in shining armor, and then to be remembered in the song of the rhapsodists is alone worth while. It is this ideal of life that Homer records.

The romantic ideal of feudalism is reflected in the poems of chivalry. The ideal of the English Renascence is found in Shakespeare. The religious ideals are expressed in the Hindu temples, in the Parthenon, in the mediaeval cathedrals, and in the poems of Dante and Milton. The ideals of the oriental monarchs are visibly embodied in the Assyrian and Babylonian palaces; the ideal of the merchant class in the stones of Venice, in the architecture of the German and Flemish cities, etc. The plastic arts especially owe their rise and prosperity to the princely and religious ideals—to the demand for temples, churches and palaces suitable for monarchs or merchant princes to dwell and worship in. The aim of the artificer is to furnish a splendid setting for princes and divinities.

Mankind at different periods is in labor to give birth to ideals representing the purpose for which man exists, or the things that make life worth while, and art *assists in bringing to the birth these ideals.* It seeks to express them, and in the effort to do so it helps to develop and clarify them. This, and not merely to give pleasure, is its *grand* function.

In an age like the present, in which a new ideal is in the early stages of formation, art is likely to become, as in fact it has become, uncertain of its function, and hence apt to lose its direction, either turning back to the servile reproduction of past art forms, or seeking to achieve progress in the perfection of technical detail, or in the ways of subjective impressionism.[2]

The efforts of a serious artist today, in so far as he undertakes to assist in bringing to the birth a new ideal by his endeavor to express it, must necessarily be tentative, if not crude. But such as they are their worth, if wholly sincere, can hardly be overestimated.

In the vocation of the artist, as everywhere, the threefold reverence is the capital point. Reverence for the great masters, as shown not in slavishly copying them, but in understanding the qualities that made them great, and in delivering from past are the things that are to be

[2] The use made of pageantry, the revival of English and other folk-songs, the morris-dances and the like, the attempt to ennoble the leisure of the industrial workers by leading them back to forms of art which sprang up centuries ago in foreign countries, is evidence of the keen desire for art rather than a step in a new direction.

reincorporated and to live on; reverence for those who in different fields are intent on the problem of art to-day—all this to prepare the way for future artists, for the greater art that is to come.

The relation of art to ethics, or to the spiritual life, is now sufficiently clear. In general it is to produce the semblance of the spiritual relation, and thereby to rejuvenate the world's workers, to give them the joy of relative perfection, and thus to stimulate them to persevere in the real business of life, which is to approximate toward actual perfection. The specific task of the artist *at its height* is to enshrine in his creation the ideals of the age with respect to the ultimate purpose of human existence, and in the endeavor so to incorporate them as to assist in defining them.

The dangers of pre-occupation with art, however, must not be passed over. Just because it creates the illusion of perfection it is apt to encourage the indolence of our nature, which ever prefers to content itself with illusion, and to desist from effort. It is on this account that periods in which art greatly flourishes are apt to, lead to the halting of progress and eventually to decay. A second danger is that the artist, in applying the ideal of present perfection, is in danger of selfishly subordinating other persons to himself (cf. Goethe as a notable example), or of setting up a special kind of morality for artists.[3]

[8] Art, like science, is to be subordinate. The relation between persons and persons is mankind's supreme concern. The views above expressed differ radically from those of Schiller. See his *JEsthetic Education of Man.*

In a full account of the matter, the different so-called fine arts should be specifically treated from the point of view of this chapter. The particular contribution of each to the general purpose of art should be noted, the distinctions marked between painting, sculpture, poetry, etc., and in each case the kind of art which is favorable to the spiritual development of man be discriminated from that which is hostile to it. Plato attempted to do this in the case of music.

To summarize: What has been attempted in this chapter is a theory not of art but of the relation of art to ethics. The dominating thought is this: in a work of art each line, color, sound, word, must be irreplaceable, and on that account convincing. Each member must be indispensable in its place and the connection with the rest inevitable. Substitute for line, color, sound, etc., a life—an ethical being,—conceive the members to be not a few but in number infinite, and you have the spiritual ideal, which is the reality whereof the art work is a semblance. This is the relation of art to ethics —the quality which we call in art "convincing," in ethics we call "worth."

NOTES

As one example architecture may be mentioned. Architecture furnishes *the envelope for the social life,* the dwelling, the nest of the family, the workshops that house the vocational life, the public buildings that provide a habitation for the political life, the temples, the churches that enshrine the religious life. The relation of the enshrining dwelling to the inner social life should be the same as that of the body to the soul in sculpture. That which goes on within should be significantly indicated externally. The progress of architecture will depend on its holding fast to this idea, and changing the outside as the inner life changes. Thus, we have, or are beginning to have, a conception of the family very different from that which prevailed at the time when the princely mansions of the Renaissance were built. To reproduce these princely mansions because they beautifully expressed the princely idea is a mistake. To provide a proper dwelling-place for the modern family the architect should clearly apprehend what functions go on in the family, what the distribution of functions should be, and the rank to be assigned to the different functions. There is to be, for instance, in addition to the ordinary requirements, provision for separate study rooms, places of retirement, refuges of intellectual solitude for the adult members; a playroom for children, a place of reunion for the household religion. The formation of a number of families into a larger group {vid. supra) would help in the solution of this problem.

In like manner the conception of what a religious society should be is changing. The church-building, the Mosque, the Synagogue, certainly no longer declare the spirit and the purpose that animate the new religious fellowships that are forming among us today. The progress of architecture will thus depend, not on the out of hand invention of new styles, but on a thorough understanding of *the new kind of life which is to be domiciled within buildings*, accepting this as the empirical substratum, and articulating it in accordance with the spiritual relation of give and take between the parts; and the architect will assist in clarifying the ideal of the new kind of life that is to be lived within the buildings by endeavoring to give it outward expression.

One more remark: The limitations opposed to the artist, for instance to the sculptor, by the material in which he works, are a helpful illustration of one of the most important ethical truths. The material is found to be intractable to the idea. The hardness of the stone, the veins that run through the marble, the unpropitious qualities of the wood, are so many hin-

287

drances to execution. The value of these hindrances is that they compel the artist to achieve a more definite grasp of the ideal itself. Before the attempt to carry it out into stone, the idea is apt to be vague in the mind of the artist. The same is true of every ideal conception—that of the author before he writes a book, that of the social reformer before he attempts to carry his scheme into practice. And it applies no less to the ethical ideal of life in general. The empirical analogue or substratum is ductile to a certain degree, else we could never achieve even partial success. But it is also hostile and mutinous in many ways, and the fact that it is so compels us to adapt our ideal to existing empirical requirements, and to make it more explicit in the process of adapting it.

CHAPTER VI

EVERY vocation on its ethical side is educational. The reason for accentuating the educational aspect of the vocations connected with the state is that this educational significance is generally overlooked. The vocations referred to are those of the lawyer, the judge, the statesman, the teacher in the narrower sense of the word (the teacher in schools and universities).

The Vocation of the Lawyer

Vocation, as I use the term, invariably means related to the spiritual end of life. A profession or occupation becomes a vocation when he who follows it seeks to respond to the *call* of the latent spiritual possibilities in his fellowmen. If this be not the common definition of calling or vocation, yet I think it will bear scrutiny. It is the vocation of the lawyer to be the *teacher of justice* to his clients,—I mean of justice in so far as it is already embodied in law,—and at the same time to promote a desire for and a preliminary understanding of the justice which is not yet embodied in law.

The lawyer is commonly regarded as the learned *alter ego* of his client. The lawyer is the client as he would be if he were versed in the law, and skilled to employ it in his interest. The client is supposed to be an egotist, intent solely on securing his advantage to the fullest extent possible under the existing system of social regulations. The lawyer is his expert substitute. The judge appears on the scene as the impartial representative of the law.

From the vocational point of view the lawyer is an assistant to the judge, the agent not so much of his client as of justice. He is as much interested in the just issue of the suit as is his legal opponent. His educational function is to teach his client to take the same point of view. Another point, no less important, is the following: Law is a system of general rules, at best a rude social mechanics. And even as such it is constantly deflected from its ostensible purpose by selfishness and prejudice. The discriminations against women, the conspiracy laws against combinations of laborers, the laws enacted in the interests of landed aristocracies, are ample evidence in point. In every country the law as it stands is still largely infected with unfair discriminations, and it is the special duty of those who follow the legal vocation to open the eyes of their clients and of the public to these defects and to suggest remedies.

Every vocation has its special vice, that is, a kind of behavior the very opposite of that prescribed by the particular ethical function with which it is charged. The vice of the lawyer is *blind* conservatism (unless he is at the same time progressive and conservative he fails to fulfil his ethical function).

The judge, too, is a teacher, especially in criminal cases. The voice of the judges when he pronounces sentence on a criminal, should reverberate throughout the whole of society, awakening all men to the fact that society as such shares the guilt.

The Vocation of the Statesman

What I have to say on this subject will find its proper setting in the next chapter. In general, it is the vocation of the statesman to teach the citizens a sublime conception of the state. He is neither to be the obedient tool of the mass—the docile "public servant" in that sense—nor yet to impose his arbitrary will upon the people, consulting only his own genius. **The** one type is seen in the average American politician, who is or affects to be a mere instrument executing the public will; the other type is exemplified by the supermen statesmen of ancient and modern times. The ethically-minded statesman is to evoke the spiritual conception of the State in the minds of his constituents, and in the process of doing so to become more essentially a citizen himself.

The Vocation of the Educator

It was unavoidable to discuss the vocations and their aims before considering the school, college and university; for these institutions are orientated towards the vocations, are preparatory to the latter, and the true aim of school and university cannot possibly be defined unless the vocational outlook be first distinctly spread before our eyes.

In dealing with the vocation of the teacher, I shall

necessarily be led to define the purpose of the social institution in which he labors and I shall for the sake of brevity use the word school to designate the social organs of education, which cover the period of childhood, adolescence and the beginning of manhood and womanhood.

The school is like the hundred-gated Thebes. It leads out into a hundred vocational avenues. But note the following: its aim is far greater than merely to prepare the student for that future vocation to which he is best suited. It should no less supply the incentive for creating new vocations, and for changing what are at present still occupations into vocations. The school searches out the individuality of its pupils. It undertakes to differentiate and to personalize individualities. But when it has done its part, it sends the pupils into a world where little account is taken of the finer differences of aptitude, where occupations predominate and vocations are few, and where most things, ethically speaking, are still in the rough. The school cannot indeed transform society by merely raising its indignant voice and asking society to pay heed to the finer things which it has fostered, and which often are subsequently crushed. But it can at least contribute to the vocational evolution of society by reiterating its unsatisfied demands.

Taking the three-fold reverence for my guide, I lay it down in the first place that the school is an organ of tradition. True conservatism has its place in the school. In it are preserved the knowledges and the skills of the past. The heir of today comes to his own by appropriating the products of past thinking and past labor, and the school superintends the process of appropriation and assimilation. At the same time it sifts in tradition what is clean from what is unclean, what is true from what is false, what is usable from what is dead. Reverence is shown in this very sifting process. To revere the past is to make the past live again; but only what is vital can go on living.

The teaching should be reverential in spirit. The business spirit, the drive towards mere efficiency, cannot in the long run satisfy. Efficiency as commonly understood has in view the utilities of the moment. It merely exploits the past for the sake of present interests, and as a rule is unmindful of the future. Industrial efficiency, in particular, reverses the right ethical relation between work and personality; instead of work being so contrived as to liberate personality, it is mechanized so as to sacrifice personality.

The teacher should be reverent towards the great masters of his own craft, his own art. No one is reverenced by others who does not himself habitually revere someone. The teachers should be acquainted at first hand with the master educators, such as Plato, Comenius, Pestalozzi and the others.

I pass on to speak of the second type of reverence. This involves cordial reciprocally stimulating relations between the members of the teaching staff. It is generally agreed that no other factor counts for more in shaping the character of the young than personal influence. The best personal influence, however, is not unilateral, like that which radiates from a single teacher upon his class. The best is that which proceeds from cross-relations between a number of teachers. Just as in the home it is not the father singly, nor the mother singly, but the reciprocal relations between the two that touch child life to finer issues and create a spiritual atmosphere in the learner, so also in the school the best spirit is created by the relations of reciprocal furtherance between the teachers, each doing his work in such a way as to make easier and more successful the work of his colleagues, with a strong sense of partnership in the common work of man-building.

The teachers as an organized body should also relate themselves to an organized body of parents. Home and school should not merely cooperate but interpenetrate. The interests and efforts of both are centered on the same young lives. The home is supremely concerned in what goes on in the school, and the school in the kind of influence that prevails in the home. An organized conference of parents is in a position to render signal service to a school by appraising its ideals, by keeping tally on the extent to which acknowledged standards are carried out, and by joining in the unceasing endeavor to advance the standards. Schools must be backed by the interest and appreciation of the community. Parents whose children are pupils of a school are for that particular school the best representatives of the community.

The school is to prepare its charges, not only for vocational life, but for citizenship. Teachers must be good citizens. They cannot give what they do not possess. They must keep in living contact with the civic and social movements of the time.

The first and second types are instrumental to the third. Now here, if anywhere, a new departure in educational philosophy is called for. For when we discuss this third kind of reverence, the question of all questions is raised: To what end do we educate? What is to be the aim and outcome of all our effort? And our answer to this question will depend on our philosophy, and if our philosophy is ethical our answer must be distinctively ethical. Froebel was a pantheist, and his pantheism colored his conception of the educational end. Pestalozzi was an eighteenth century humanitarian. Many modern writers on education are biological evolutionists. Others even expressly disclaim any general outlook, and appear to be exclusively interested in perfecting the technique of schoolmastering. Reverence of the third type is reverence for the undeveloped human being,—for the new generation, for our successors. What is it that we are to revere in a child? Its spiritual possibilities, its latent personality. To bring to birth its personality is the supreme educational end. We show our reverence for the child in the effort to personalize it. Let us consider in brief some of the practical consequences of this idea.

To personalize the individual the first step is to discover the empirical substratum in his nature. There is ever an empirical substratum subject to ethical transformations. The empirical substratum of personality is individuality! Individuality manifests itself in a leading interest of some kind, a predominant bias which indicates the thing which the individual is fit to be and do. To discover the bent or bias is the first step, and the difficulties in the way of taking even this first step are admittedly great. Children and even adolescents often show no marked intellectual preferences whatever. Many adults too appear to be neutral so far as their mental life is concerned. Circumstances ran them perhaps into a certain mould—they might have been run into some other just as well. It is the task of the educator to discover the predominant interest where it exists, and to try to produce such an interest where it does not. What nature has not done in such cases art must attempt.

When the leading interest is found it should next be made the means of creating interest in subjects to which the pupil is naturally indifferent or even averse. I have illustrated the process here implied in a paper on the pre-vocational art school which is connected with the Ethical Culture School. Young persons devoted to art are often unwilling to take up subjects which seem to them unrelated to what they really care for, like science and history. They are obsessed by a single passionate ambition. They are all eagerness to become artists— to draw, paint, model, etc. Time spent on any other subject seems to them misspent. If indulged in this one-sided activity, the chances are that they will not even become competent artists. In any case they will lack breadth and vision. They will lack a cultural background. They will be inferior as human beings. They will not be personalized. For personality, on its mental as well as on its social side, depends on relatedness,—depends not so much on what one does, as on the interrelation between what one does and what other people do.

In order to expand the interest of the young art student, the method employed in the school just mentioned is to present those subjects which appear to be alien in such a way as to bring out the art aspects of them, the contact points between them and art. Thus in history special prominence is given to the age of Pericles, the age of Rembrandt. In science special attention is paid to the theory of color, the chemistry of etching. And all other branches of knowledge are treated similarly. The aim is not indeed to exploit the other subjects in the interest of art, but so to utilize the artistic interest as to lead the mind out to a larger comprehensive interest in other related branches on their own account. Or rather, to put my thought precisely, and thus to connect it with the underlying ethical theory, the aim is to prepare the future artist for the give and take relation between his own pursuit and the activities of men in other vocations. He should be helped to enrich his own life as an artist by drawing upon all that the sciences and the humanities can give him, with a view to eventually returning with interest the profit he has derived. What the artist can do for the scientist, the religious teacher, etc., I have indicated in the previous chapter.

Precisely the same cultural idea should be worked out in prevocational schools of commerce, of technology, of science, etc. In each case the paramount interest should be the starting-point, the center from which lines of interest are to be made to radiate out into the correlated branches.

If this ethical idea is carried out the whole educational system will be remodeled. The caesura in education will then fall about the sixteenth year. Before that the task will be to lay the general foundations and to reconnoiter the individuality of the pupil. After that there will be a system of *prevocational schools.* The college, a legacy which has come to us from a type of society unlike our own, will disappear, and the university will become an organism of vocational schools succeeding the prevocational.[1]

I mentioned at the end of Book I the problem of specialization, the increased necessity of restricting one-self to a limited field in order to achieve anything like the consciousness of mastery, and the inevitable frac-tionalizing of men which is the consequence of this very tendency toward specialization. In the idea of outreach-ing radiations of interest and of the give and take re-lation there is the promise of liberation from the nar-rowness of specialism without the calamity of dilettant-ism. That this idea cannot be fully realized, that no one can actually extend his web of interest so far, that his reactions at best will be feeble, is perhaps a palmary instance of that law of frustration which fatally be-sets all human effort. But the effort will be in the right direction, and the effort counts.

The University

In sketching the ethical or spiritual side of the Uni-versity, initial stress is to be laid on the meaning of the word *universitas.* The term as at present used hardly

[1] Compare with the spiritual conception of culture here outlined Matthew Arnold's "knowing the best which has been thought and said"; and a recent definition of culture by an eminent American as "the knowing one thing well and a little of everything else," without correlation of the little one knows of everything else with the one thing one is supposed to know extremely well.

suggests more than all-inclusiveness. A modern university is an institution in which all the different schools, the school of engineering, the school of science, the school of philosophy, etc., *exist side by side,* under a single governing body, and in which the various branches of knowledge are pursued without any visible systematic connection between them! The spiritual ideal of a university is that of system, of organic connection, for this is what spiritual means.

In looking back on the history of the higher institutions of learning one cannot but be struck by the close correspondence of those institutions to the general ideals of life of the people among whom they flourished. I call to mind the Hindu education with its Brahmanic background; the Mandarin education, with Confucianism as its inspiring principle; the musical education of the Greeks; the theological education of Jews and Mohammedans ; then among the Western nations, the English university a seminary for training rulers of the Empire; the German university, a training institution for the higher bureaucracy; the French university, visibly reflecting the logical tendency of the French mind.

We in America, instructed by the survey of the past, are bound to face the question: In what way shall the American university differ from universities elsewhere? What characteristic shape shall the American university take on? *How can the American university correspond to the American ideal of life?* At present our notions in this respect are in a formative, not to say in a chaotic, condition. The college still survives—an institution designed for the education of gentlemen. Practical tendencies, looking toward materialistic success, prevail in many of our Western universities. The German research idea has come in as a third factor, penetrating deeply in some of our institutions, less deeply in others, but inharmonious everywhere with the rival conceptions that still persist.

The principal circumstance that retards our university development doubtless is that the ideal of American life itself, which the university is to express and to promote, is as yet undefined in the minds of the American people. But without presuming to anticipate what must be the outcome of gradual and prolonged growth, it may still be serviceable to clear our minds as to the goal towards which we desire that the development shall tend. The fundamental ideal of the American people is that of freedom! The notion of freedom is crude as yet, but is capable of being ennobled and refined. To be free is to express power. To be free in the highest sense is to express the highest kind of power. The highest kind is that which is exercised in such wise as to elicit unlike yet cognate power in others. A people is to be called free when all the different social or vocational groups of which it is the integrated whole spontaneously react upon one another, and when in each group each member of it realizes some mental gift of his own. A free people is not one which is merely released from the authority of autocrats. That is only a condition of freedom, not freedom itself. A free people is not one in which strong individuals are permitted to thrive parasitically at the expense of the weak. Nor yet one in which merely equal opportunity is afforded to all in the race for material well-being. A free people is one in which the essential energies of all effectuate themselves unhindered, the life of each swelling the surrounding tide of life, and being enriched in turn by the returning tide. This to my mind is liberty,—the liberation of what is best in each. This is freedom,—the free flow of life into life. The ideal American University is one which expresses and promotes this ideal of freedom.

A university is a group of vocational schools. A truly democratic university is an organic system of vocational schools, one which in the relations that subsist between its schools affords a shining, stimulating example of the kind of relations that ought to subsist between the vocational groups in the state.

The aim of an American university should be to furnish leaders for all the various groups who will undertake the great business of truly organizing democracy.

Education for Adults

Education should be continuous through life. The University Extension movement is endeavoring to meet this demand. It has already to its credit a considerable extension of knowledge, as well as the stirring up of interest in things of the mind among those whom it reaches. But far greater tasks than it has yet attacked remain. The academic method is not suited to the instruction of adults. A method will have to be worked out for teaching a subject to mature minds different from that which is appropriate in introducing the subject to the relatively immature minds of students. The student who has.not yet entered vocational life needs to be put in possession of the principles by which he can lay hold of life. A mature person who is deficient in theoretical education needs to be helped to interpret his vocational experience in such a manner as to find his way back to the principles. In the one case there is the outlook and the emptiness; in the other case the fullness of content without the comprehensive outlook.

Secondly, the stages of vocational development through which the worker has already passed in his vocation are to be borne in mind, and the teaching adapted to the different stages. I have suggested four divisions: that of apprenticeship, that of initial mastery, that of more complete mastery, and the emeritus stage.[2]

Thirdly, it is getting to be increasingly difficult for a specialist in any one branch to keep abreast of the progress made in other branches. Popularization of the ordinary kind does not satisfy. It means, as a rule, diluting the subject-matter, not truly simplifying it. Provision should be made, in any large and generous scheme of public education, for enabling ripe minds to assimilate the ripest fruits produced by contemporary thinkers and writers who work in other fields.

NOTE

A few outstanding points in regard to what is called Moral Education may be added to this chapter.

There should be ethical teaching *in* the universities. The kinds of ethics taught should be adapted to the university period of life, emphasis being put on the experiences of the

[2] See the chapter on "Ethical Development Extending Through Life" in *The World. Crisis.*

student at that time of life,—on friendship, the sex relation, the vocational outlook, etc.

The ethical problems arising in the different vocations should be included in the programme for the education of adults.

Systematic moral education in schools and high schools is advisable. It is frequently criticised on the ground that it is apt to be schematic and unreal. Moral counsels given as the occasion arises are believed to be more effective. They hit the nail on the head and drive it home. The reply to this is that incidental moral advice and exhortation is not excluded, but that it by no means adequately answers the purpose. The occasions for giving the necessary guidance simply do not arise. This kind of moral teaching is apt to be patchy. In the next place, ethical instruction, when rightly planned, has two objects: the one to bring into clear relief the life axioms that underlie the entire home and school experience of the pupil, and secondly, to give to the pupil a provisional chart and compass or ethical outlook upon his future life. Ethical teaching conceived of and conducted in this manner is neither schematic nor artificial. It does not drive home a nail here and there, it constructs a mental house in which the mind of the pupil can be at home,—with windows in it, looking out upon a large landscape outside.

The capital significance of right relations, ethical relations, between the members of the teaching staff has been noted in the text. In every school clubs should be formed consisting of pupils specially interested in any one subject and of the special teachers of that subject:—or if not formal clubs, then at least more intimate personal relations should exist between the special teacher and those selected pupils, the object being through personal intercourse to introduce the young aspirant to a knowledge of the problems on which the older person is intent. There is nothing nearly so educative for the young as to be taken into the counsels of their elders.

The more gifted pupils of the school should be invited to take a personal interest in helping the more backward students. In every school, high school and university there are social misfits,—shy, sensitive, solitary youths who fail to come into easy touch with their fellows, and suffer acutely. They are objects of the most delicate, deferential charity, and the task of bringing them into fellowship offers one of the finest opportunities for ethical education.

A vital system of self-government is to be used as a means of placing real responsibility upon the students under due advice. To exercise responsibility is to acquire character. Self-government is particularly important so far as it relates to the administration of justice in a school. Cases of discipline should be used as means to create the right conception of punishment, the right attitude towards those who have erred.

The relation between the adolescent boy and girl and the parents is of prime significance as illustrating in a way that young persons can understand the general conception of the ethical relation as *reciprocal*. The youth should be shown that he can be not only the recipient but a giver of benefits, that he can be a real help to his parents, chiefly by sympathetically entering into the problems and difficulties with which they have to contend. The parents, instead of being regarded by the young as an earthly providence, existing only for the purpose of bestowing benefits, should be seen in their true light as struggling, and often heavily burdened human beings. At the same time the young son or daughter will in this way gain an invaluable preparation for comprehending the difficulties under which the effort to live must be carried on.

In regard to patriotism, it is important that the errors and mistakes committed by one's nation in the past should not be overlooked or minimized.

The school should furnish to the students various outlets for social service such as they in their period of life are capable of rendering.

CHAPTER VII

THE STATE

THE leading theories of the state should be kept in view for comparison with the ethical theory here set forth—the theories of Aristotle and Plato, St. Augustine and the medieval schoolmen, Rousseau's contract theory, and the German conceptions of the state propounded by Kant, Fichte, Hegel. Moreover, since the ideas actually embodied in governments, in the Persian monarchy, for instance, in the Greek City State, Venice, etc., are not identical with the constructions of the philosophers, the leading facts of the history of politics should be borne in mind as well as the leading theories.

The state has two aspects: (1) It is the balance wheel of the vocational groups included within it. (2) It is the political expression of the national character, and its ethical purpose is to develop this empirical national character into a spiritual character. I shall speak of the first aspect in this chapter.

1. The state exists in order to furnish increasingly from age to age the conditions under which the reactions between the groups described above can take place effectually. In concentrating attention upon the vocational groups as the entities to be harmonized with one another, account is taken by implication of the family and of the individual. The sub-organisms are embraced

within the superior organisms. A more general statement would be that the state supplies the external conditions required for development towards ethical personality by those who pass through the institutions of the family, of the vocation, etc.

The state possesses a spiritual character in so far as it supplies these conditions, and in as much as it has a spiritual character it is not merely justified but ethically required to use force. Force is spiritualized when employed to establish the conditions indispensable to spiritual life. The conditions enforced must be such as in the opinion of the preponderant number of citizens indisputably make for the development of personality. Examples of such conditions are protection of life, property, reputation, compulsory education, the maintenance of the monogamic family, protection against foreign invasion, etc. All the functions of the state commonly enumerated follow from the ethical principle. But over and above the recognized ones, new and nobler functions of the state will appear.

The redeeming thought with respect to the use of force by the state consists in regarding *force as ethical discipline,* and in making the extent to which it is favorable to spiritual freedom the measure and test of its rightful use.[1] When men are compelled to spend the major part of their time in the protection of bare life, as was the case, for instance, in the early days of feudalism, they are to that extent unfree. Freedom consists in energizing the highest and most distinctive human faculties.

[1] *Vide* Appendix II-, on *Force and Freedom.*

The development of the state should proceed in two directions. It should withdraw from many functions exercised by it in the past, notably from such as properly belong to the sub-organisms. At the same time, it should lay its coercive hands upon new ma'tters, imposing new limitations on capricious freedom in the interest of spiritual freedom, as soon as the pertinency of such limitations to the ethical end becomes clear. For instance, the state may, and doubtless will, interfere with marriage to a far greater extent than it has yet done. It will forbid the marriage of the unsound. If a study of character-types should ever become advanced enough—a hazardous conjecture—to make it predictable that the union of certain character-types will lead to infelicitous marriage, the state will be justified in prohibiting such unions.

Law, ideally defined, is the sum total of conditions, capable of being enforced, which are necessary or favorable to the development of personality. The purpose of law is two-fold: to maintain the more developed members of society at the level they have reached, and, by educative penalties, to bring the backward up to the same level. In the article on "Force and Freedom" referred to above, law is compared to such bodily actions as walking, which at first are superintended by consciousness, and then become automatic, thereby setting consciousness free to attend to new and more important business. Similarly, law is designed to render the conditions favorable to personality so explicit that their observance shall become automatic, and that mankind shall be at liberty to discover new and more significant conditions which in their turn are again to become automatic.

Because of the lack of the ethical point of view, the exercise of force by the state has seemed purely arbitrary, and has given rise to a perverted and disastrous conception of *sovereignty*. The sovereignty of the state has two aspects: the one internal, the other external. Sovereignty means supremacy. The state is sovereign, within limits, however, with respect to its citizens. The state is also sovereign, within limits, however, with respect to other outside states.

With respect to the internal aspect of sovereignty some writers hold that citizens have no rights as against the state—only rights accorded by the state. But this from the ethical point of view is a wholly untenable position. There are rights of the individual, rights of the family, rights of the vocational group, which the state does not create but is bound to acknowledge and which its power cannot properly infringe. As against the state the individual has, for instance, the right which is commonly designated as "the freedom of conscience." The family has rights against the state; the law cannot interfere with the intimacies of the marriage and parental relations. The vocational group likewise is only partially subject to public reglementation. I have defined law as the sum total of the conditions. The state can prescribe the conditions, but cannot trace the ways of freedom within the conditions. The state prescribes the enforceable conditions; it has no concern with unenforceable inner processes.

It thus appears that sovereignty or supremacy is an attribute not peculiar to the state, although it looms up larger and more impressive when exercised by the state. Supremacy belongs to the individual in his private sphere, to the family in its proper province, to the vocation, etc. Sovereignty or supremacy belongs to each of the social institutions within its precincts, in so far as the supremacy within that precinct is requisite for the accomplishment of the ethical end to be therein attained. But sovereignty is not absolute in any sphere; neither in that of the individual, nor of the family, nor yet of the state. *The absolute conception of sovereignty is the result of the lack of an ethical conception of the social institutions.* The state is sovereign only so far as the exercise of its supremacy is necessary to the spiritual end of citizenship. On this account and for this purpose it may rightfully constrain the sub-organisms within it, and may also pronounce its *noli me tangere* as against the larger group of states encompassing it. But so far as the spiritual ends to be achieved in the international relations are concerned, the state with respect to these is subject to international sovereignty,—a new conception which mankind is striving to bring to the birth today. The false notion of state sovereignty as arbitrary and absolute, is admittedly today a chief stumbling-block in the way of the formation of an international organization of peoples.

The System of Representation Which Is Required to
Give Expression to the Organic Idea of the State.

The ethical aim of political reformation and reconstruction may be put in a single word, Organization.
*The state and especially the democratic state must be or-
ganized.*[2] This means practically that the basis of representation shall be the vocational group, that vocational
representation shall replace representation by geographical districts.[3] The law-making body on this basis

[2] I use the word Organize in its spiritual sense. The empirical,
animal organism is commonly taken as the type upon which the
notion of organism is modeled. The animal organism, however,
fails to express the implicit idea, for the following reasons: The
number of members is limited; the combination of organs is, so far
as we can *know,* accidental, and the relation is hierarchical,—there
are inferior and superior organs. The spiritual conception differs
in each of these points. The number of members is infinite; the
relation is necessary; and they are equal, that is, of equal worth.
To distinguish the spiritual pattern from the animal type the term
metorganic may be used for the former, in analogy to such terms
as metempirical, metaphysical, etc., and the system of ethics expounded in this volume may be called the *metorganic system of ethics.*

[3] Representation by geographical districts is the logical outcome
of the individualistic conception of democracy. Where this prevails, the state is supposed to take account only of the common interests, those in respect to which all individuals are alike, such as security of life and property, those interests being ignored in respect to
which the groups that constitute society, the farmers, the merchants,
the industrial laborers, etc., differ. Hence any convenient number
of citizens, pursuing their life purposes side by side within a certain
geographical area, may serve as a constituency. The absence of
regard for the real diversity, and often the clash of interests, between persons belonging to such constituencies, is due to the atomis-
tic, individualistic notion of democracy just mentioned. But sheer
individualism is everywhere on the wane, and is bound to become less
and less dominant in the degree that the industrial evolution of society proceeds, and the various groups stand out distinctly as different

will consist of representatives or delegates of the agricultural, the commercial, the industrial, the scientific group, etc. Women belonging to these groups will exercise the franchise within them. There will also be a distinct group of home-makers; motherhood will be recognized as a vocation.

Attention may be called to certain practical advantages of the proposed rearrangement of the representative system. It will tend to bring forward in political life the best citizens, instead of the mediocre or the base. This is likely to come about because there is no distinction that men more ardently covet than that of being considered *primus inter pares;* as, for instance, the first or one of the first of the city's merchants, or one of the most eminent scientists, or an artist whom his fellow-artists select as the fittest to represent them in the great council of city, state, or nation. And if only this much can be gained by the new representative system, that the law-making body shall consist of the most experienced, the most enlightened, the wisest, the actual leaders in the various walks of life, in brief, .that the elected shall be the elect, certainly one of the principal evils with which individualistic democracy is afflicted will tend to be removed.

But other advantages will accrue. This, in particular, that the constituencies, instead of merely delegating their powers, will share in the business of law-mak-

against one another in their functions and in the conditions subservient to those functions. Society is in fact not .an aggregate of human atoms. It is already an imperfect organism, destined to become more and more adequately organized. And the system of representation has got to be remodeled and adjusted to this fact and this ideal.

ing, will be in vital touch with their leaders or representatives, while the latter conversely will politically educate the constituencies. The mode of procedure under the system here sketched will be somewhat as follows:

Take, as an illustration, the group of industrial laborers. They will first meet in a primary assembly, and discuss measures deemed by them important in the interests of their group. The leader who represents them in the legislature will take part in the initial discussions, and exercise no doubt a strong influence in bringing matter finally to a head. He will then carry into the lawmaking body,—which consists of representatives of the various social groups,—the sifted-out demands of the laborers, the measures which they desire to have enacted into law. He will bring forward these measures in the legislature. But there objections are likely to be raised. The representatives of the other groups will discover what the laborers naturally failed to note, that the proposed law or laws, if enacted, will have certain injurious effects on the interests of the other groups. The sifting-out process, therefore, will now begin anew and be carried On on a higher level in the legislature. The representatives of all the various groups will separate the wheat from the chaff in what is proposed by any one group. The next stop will be that the representative of the laborers, returning to his constituency, will communicate to them the difficulties that were raised, the decisions reached, and will thus impart to them the wider vision which he himself gained in the discussions of the lawmaking body. In this way he will be the instructor, the political teacher of his constituents. And the principle by which the value of any new measure will finally be judged will be simply this: that the supposed interests of one group cannot be its true interests unless they are found to promote the interests of all the other vocational groups.[4]

The law-making body should be a council of the groups. It should not be a "Parliament," or "talking body," but a sifting body. Nor yet a body of mandatories commissioned to merely give effect to a public opinion or a public sentiment already existing. In fact, public opinion or public sentiment in the raw is apt to be a poor index of what is really for the public good. Public opinion is apt to be unripe, haphazard, impulsive rather than reflective. Besides, it is often contaminated at its very source, the facts on which the public depend for their opinions being deliberately falsified or placed in false perspective; while the opinions furnished in newspaper editorials are almost inevitably biased. Only on great occasions, when simple moral issues are presented, can the common sense and moral sense of the people be wholly depended on. But such occasions are episodical; and the orderly business of government cannot be carried on by spurts. Government by public opinion may be and in some respects is better indeed than class government; in other important respects it is worse. A class at the head of the state at least as a rule knows what it wants, and proceeds methodically to carry out its purposes. Public opinion, on the other hand, like all opinion, is unsure, unsafe, as Plato has long since

[4] By "interests" I understand fulfilment of the social function with which the group is charged.

made dialectically clear. And public sentiment, like all sentiment, is fluctuating. To build the state on public opinion and public sentiment, as many of our writers on politics would have us do, is after all a good deal like building a house on sand.[5]

Instead of "public opinion" and "public sentiment" let us say public reason and public will!—reason and will to discover in conjunction what the public good really is. For what it really is no one as yet knows. The "public good" is a problem to be approximately solved. The public good will be consummated when the conditions are furnished necessary and favorable to the development of personality in each of the constituent groups of the social body. To study these conditions is the office of the law-making body, and therefore that body must be so constituted as to include these groups in their capacity as groups.

Another advantage to be expected from vocational representation is that the different interests of society, —I stress the fact that they are different, and often temporarily conflicting,—will be compelled under this plan to come out into the open. An industry, for instance, may require the assistance of a protective tariff, in its infant stages, and the agricultural group may rightly be asked to make the necessary sacrifices.

[5] And, as a matter of fact, because this is so, there is no state, no democracy, in which public opinion or public sentiment actually does rule, save by fits and starts. Government is usually in the hands of •more or less selfish coteries, who operate behind the scenes, who .do know what they want and who, like the Piper of Hamelin, are past masters of the art of leading the political children whither they will.

314

In the long run there will be compensation. The agriculturists will eventually benefit by the diversification of the national life. But "in the long run" means that the next generation will benefit, not the present agriculturists, a distinction sometimes somewhat cavalierly ignored. The present generation will be called upon to make a sacrifice, precisely as in the family some of the members may have to sacrifice a part of their income to provide for a weaker member. But the circumstance that the sacrifice is recognized as a sacrifice will serve to put an end to the protection when the special need for it has ceased. Under the present system, on the other hand, the state is supposed to have no concern with the special interests of any group. All the same, there are the special interests, and in consequence that which is for the interest of one group has to be advocated as if it were for the general interest of the entire community. And since general interest is easily mistaken for perpetual interest, the protection is apt to be continued long after its particular usefulness has ceased.[6]

[6] I am not of course discussing the merits or demerits of the protective tariff as such, but am using it as illustration. As such it will serve the purpose.

The practice of "log-rolling" may at first sight seem to resemble the proposed plan. But, in reality, the two are diametrical opposites. By "log-rolling" is meant the kind of concessions made by the shipping interests to the manufacturers by the manufacturers to the farmers, or to the workingmen when the latter happen to be strong enough to enforce their demands. Each group persists in pursuing its selfish aims; only, in order to achieve them it makes concessions to the selfishness of the others. Each follows the path into the Hades of egotism, and throws the necessary sops to Cerberus on the way. The plan outlined in the text, on the other hand,

I am earnestly concerned that vocational representation shall not be regarded as a mere device in the mechanism of politics, like the substitution of the long for the short ballot, or the initiative and referendum. Innovations of the latter kind leave the prevalent conception of democracy untouched, they are merely intended to improve the machinery by which that conception is to be worked out in practice; they are mechanical contrivances, not fundamental reconstructions. Vocational representation, in my view of it, is the appropriate expression of the organic idea of the state. The state is the soul. The soul must have a body. Vocational representation is that body.

Two remarks may here be added. One relates to a question which has given rise to considerable discussion, namely, the question where the state resides? In a monarchy it seems to reside visibly in the person of the king. Louis XIV is said to have declared "I am the state." But where does it reside in a democracy? The chief executive, the law-making body, and even the constituencies, are organs of the state. But where does the state itself have its habitation? The state has no separate domicile. So far as it truly exists at all it exists in the minds of the individuals who truly conceive of it. The object of political life is to educate the citizen so that he may more and more truly con-

has for its object the interlocking of the various social interests, the fitting them reciprocally into one another; or better, the obj ect is to cure each group as far as possible of its selfishness by so modifying its claims, that the granting of them shall become beneficial to the rest.

ceive of the state, so that he may give birth to the state idea within himself. To do this is to pass through one of the necessary phases on the road to personality. In the family the individual is in reactive relations with a few, in the vocation with a larger number. In the state or nation he may be one of a hundred millions or more. Yet it is not the numerical extension as such that constitutes the enlargement. It is rather the diversity of the points of contact, and the complexity of the relations by which the spiritual ideal is more fully illustrated in the finite world in proportion as the circle widens. To engender the idea of the state in oneself is to place oneself ideally into reactive relations with the diverse groups embraced within one's nation. And to do this is a spiritual achievement of no mean order. I should prefer to use the word "stateship" instead of citizenship. Stateship is attained by one who brings to birth within himself the idea of the state, and in whom that idea becomes a controlling ethical force.

A second remark concerns the perplexed subject of the conflict of duties. The nearer duties are sometimes preferred to the more remote, and at other times we are asked to sacrifice everything to the larger whole. We owe our first devotion, it is said, to the members of our family; but then again we must be willing to sacrifice life itself and the welfare of our family to our country when it calls upon us in its need. Largeness alone certainly does not serve as an ethical ground for preference. The quantitative standard implied in such phrases as "the greatest good of the greatest number" is out of place when we deal with ethical relations, which in their very nature are qualitative. Now the account of the social institutions given in previous chapters as successive stations on the road to the spiritual goal may throw some light on this difficult subject. Normally, the claims of the anterior stations are to be preferred—the claims of the family for instance to those of the vocation, because the family is the matrix of the three-fold reverence, and the individual must pass under the ethical influence of family life before he is fit to use vocational life ethically to good purpose. The anterior groups are not merely smaller, they are germinal. The training received in them is the condition on which spiritual progress depends later on. On the other hand, the later groups are the more complete and more explicated expressions of the spiritual ideal; hence if the very existence of one of the later groups is threatened, or is in danger of being denatured of its spiritual use, then the later group is to be preferred to the earlier, the *terminus ad quem,* precisely because it is the *terminus ad quem,* to the *terminus a quo.*

To give a familiar illustration. In our time, which is a time of transition and doubt, many a religious teacher finds himself in sore straits to decide between the claims of the vocation and the family. As a religious teacher he is pledged to teach only what in his heart of hearts he believes to be true; he is especially under obligation to use words in such a way as to convey to others the same meaning that he attaches to them himself. But this may mean exposing his family to serious privations. The situation is full of perplexity and pain, but the line of choice is plain enough. The claims of his

318

high vocation must in this case take precedence. In like manner, when the existence or the integrity of the state is at issue, the claims of the state as the *terminus ad quern* override those of the vocation, the family, and the state, and may even demand the sacrifice of the physical existence of the individual himself.

NOTES

1. The idea of democracy is often neatly put—all too neatly, into the following formula: In antiquity the individual existed for the sake of the state, in modern democracy the state exists for the sake of the individual. Both of these statements as they stand are mischievous and misleading and require to be qualified. It is not true that in antiquity the individual existed for the sake of the state in the sense that his separate existence was extinguished. The citizen class in Aristotle's state, the rulers in Plato's state, and even a member of one of the inferior classes, each in his own way fulfilled a distinct function. He was not suppressed in the state, he expressed his function by the action appropriate to his station. The philosophic rulers might do the thinking and governing. They were the head of the body politic—others the hands and feet. The underlying conception was what may be called spuriously organic, borrowed more or less from the animal type of organism.

The second limb of the formula is no less superficial. In no modern nation does the state exist, or at bottom is it supposed to exist, for the benefit of the individuals who at any time compose it. If this were the ruling conception, how could the democratic state require its citizens to give up their lives in its defense? If the state existed for the benefit of the individuals, the state would be the means, and the so-called good of the individual the end. And in that case it would surely be irrational to sacrifice the end for the sake of the means, in other words to put an end to one's life in defense of the state, a mere instrument for the protection and prosperity of one's own life.

To reply that the state exists for the sake not of one individual but of all (observe however that the formula says "the individual," and is ambiguous and slippery at this point), nor even only for the sake of all the individuals now living, but also for the sake of the millions yet unborn—to say this is once more to introduce an ideal entity which it was the very object of the formula as quoted to banish. The formula was intended to give us, in place of "the metaphysical entities" of the Greeks and the Germans, a very palpable thing—the good of the individual. The good of the individual seemed to be a palpable thing, though in truth it is the most impalpable thing in the world. And by defining the state in this wise we were supposed to come onto solid ground. But now, behold, it is the good of unborn millions which is to be the object of our devotion, and who can *imagine* what this good of unborn millions is likely to be?

The fact is that without ideal entities the conception of the state in any noble shape cannot be construed at all. The organic conception must now take the place of the individualistic. The organic conception indeed as it was worked out in antiquity, or as it lived on in the theories of mediaeval writers, or as it survives in the works of certain German publicists, who use it to defend the feudalistic structure of society, has rightly fallen into discredit,—not because it is organic, but because it is pseudo-organic, that is, based on the type of the animal organism. The individualistic conception of the state at present current in America and in all modern democracies, is a violent reaction against this false idea of organization. The inestimable germ of truth individualism contains is that no such distinction can be allowed as between head and hands or feet in political life, that all the multitudes of "hands" who work in the factories, for instance, must be respected as personalities having not only hands but also heads and hearts. But individualism, though it affirms this idea, belies it in practice, as

320

the actual state of society in America and elsewhere abundantly proves. And it is bound to do so, because personality implies more than material well-being, either for a single individual or for all individuals now living or for all future individuals. Personality implies truly organic relations to other fellow-beings—and this can only be achieved by organizing the society in which men live.

The way taken has been, by reaction from pseudo-organization, to extreme individualism and concomitant materialism. The way out lies in the direction of genuine organization.

2. Certain evils observable in the workings of American democracy may be traced to the following causes:

(a) The people as a whole are still in the pioneer stage. A country enormously rich in material resources stimulates wealth-production. A host of immigrants escaped from poverty abroad are stung into wealth-getting here. The frontier line is now far to the West, but the influence of the pioneer movement still in progress flows back upon the Eastern states.

(b) More important still are the evils due to the crude individualistic idea of democracy just characterized. If the state exists for the good of the individual, and if the good of the individual is conceived to be the acquisition of wealth, then private business will take precedence of the public business. Yet under the democratic system of frequent elections the public business demands constant attention. In consequence, a special class of professional politicians arises, comprising a minority of disinterestedly patriotic men, and a majority of persons whose private business is not sufficiently remunerative to divert them from the public service. The appearance of the political dictator called "boss" is the inevitable outcome of these conditions. This army of professional politicians, and in particular the vulgar figure at their hand, is the chief disgrace of the American democracy, and has been the target of incessant invective by American writers. But it is idle to stigmatize the effect and overlook the cause, to squander invective upon the

321

symptom and at the same time to leave the malady untouched. The malady itself is the individualistic ' conception of democracy, and until this is replaced by a better one, the evil in question may be modified in form but will certainly not disappear.

A way must be found for the citizen to attend to his private business, which is coming to be more and more exacting, and to the public business at the same time. The system of vocational representation offers an opportunity in this direction. Citizens will be voting in their vocational groups for measures intended to advance their vocational interests, but will be taught to advance them in such a way that the related interests of other groups, or the public interest, shall be thereby promoted.

3. Proportional representation, which is at present being tested abroad, and earnestly considered in France, England and Germany, may be a bridge leading over from the present plan of geographical to that of vocational representation. The proportional system itself, it is true, is still based on the individualistic idea. It is a movement on behalf of submerged minorities. It quarrels with the present arrangement for the reason that the will of the greater number of individuals, but not of all individuals, is brought to bear on public decisions. But if adopted it may well offer, without violent change, a way for the collective representation of vocational groups.

4 Citizenship should be graded. A youth of twenty-one is scarcely prepared to exercise the duties of the citizen intelligently. As long as the view prevails that the functions of the state are to be restricted to a minimum, it is-perhaps not wholly absurd to admit a mere stripling to a share in the conduct of government. But the sphere of government is steadily enlarge ing, and its problems are becoming more and more intricate. Twenty-five would certainly be a better minimum age. Under vocational representation there is likely to be an Upper House consisting of members who have served in the Lower House.

Citizens who have attained the age of twenty-five might be empowered to vote for members of the Lower House, those who have attained the age of thirty-five for members of the Upper House, but these are details upon which it is unfitting to expatiate here. The point I have in mind is that citizenship should! he graded.

CHAPTER VIII

THE NATIONAL CHARACTER SPIRITUALLY TRANS-
FORMED: THE INTERNATIONAL SOCIETY, OR
THE ORGANIZATION OF MANKIND

THERE is such a thing as a national character.[1] The national character is reflected in the language, literature, laws and customs, arts, institutions and religion of a people. Even when the religion professed by different peoples is the same in name it is strongly tinctured in the different countries by the national differences. Compare for example the Christianity of Prussia with that of France, or that of England with that of Russia.

The national character, like that of the individual, has its plus and minus qualities, its excellent and its repellent traits.

The national character is to be spiritualized by raising the plus traits to the Nth degree.

To this end, as before, the threefold reverence and especially the third reverence is the means. *The backward peoples of the earth are the paramount object of reverence.* The more advanced peoples are to bring to light

---

[1] See Fouillee's *Esquisse psychologique des Peuples europeent,* also the Chapter on German, English and American Ideals in *The World Crisis.*

the spiritual life latent in the backward. In order to do so, they are to carry out the principle of reverence toward past civilization, to sift out what is vital in the work of previous generations. And further, they are to conform to the second principle of reverence, that toward contemporaries approximately on the same level, *i.e.,* toward the other civilized nations. No single nation is really competent to undertake the great task of awaking the stationary peoples of India and China, of educating the primitive peoples of Africa. A union of the civilized nations should be formed in order that together they may jointly accomplish *the pedagogy of the less developed.* The educational point of view once again appears as the ethical. The relation of the less developed to the more advanced peoples should be analogous to that of the child towards the parents. Just as neither the father singly nor the mother alone can release spiritual life in the offspring, so the different civilized nations, each of which has its own gift, its own plus traits, are to interact for the purpose of jointly awakening the creative energies within the slumbering souls of the undeveloped peoples.

It follows that a nation cannot even be defined ethically except as a member of an international society, and we begin to see the help afforded by the spiritual conception in solving at least ideally the problem of right international relations. Whereas hitherto the notion of the sovereignty of each nation has been a formidable impediment to the formation of an overarching world society, the ethical conception not only permits this expansion of sovereignty, but necessitates it. A nation, ethically defined, is a unique member of the *corpus Internationale* of mankind. As unique it maintains of right its relative independence, as a member it is bound by intrinsic ties to its fellow-members, and is subject to the greater sovereignty including them all alike.[2] A nation indeed cannot even maintain its independence against other nations except by sheer might if it acknowledges none but capricious ties between itself and them, such as treaties, or Hague Conference agreements which can be dissolved at pleasure. There must be recognized an inner ethical tie between nation and nation, and it must receive legal formulation. This ethical tie is the true *vinculum societatis humance* and supplies what has hitherto been absolutely lacking,—an ethical basis for international law.

The ethical relation between nations is founded on the fact that each nation represents a significant type of humanity, that each nation has certain plus and minus qualities, that it is dependent on other nations to supplement its defects; and more than this, that it can expurgate, as it ought, its minus qualities only by striving to evoke the spiritual life in other peoples.

One salient point I must emphasize. The national character with its plus and minus traits is empirical, and

[2] Each term in the series of social institutions is ethically defined by referring to the succeeding terms. The family prepares for the vocation, the vocation for the state or nation, the nation for the international society, and all the successive terms receive their ultimate definition from the infinite spiritual universe which includes them, and broods over them and dwells in each, so that the expanding ethical experience gained at the successive stations is spiritually the *ratio cognoscendi,* not the *ratio essendi.*

the development of the empirical character is not itself the highest aim of the state. The spiritual transformation of this empirical character, as I must take pains to repeat, is the aim.

And herein appears the difference between the point of view taken in this chapter and the political doctrine of the eminent Swiss publicist Bluntschli. He too recognizes the development of the national character as the aim of the state; and in so far as he does this he is in advance of writers who limit the state's functions to the protection of life and property, to defense against foreign aggression, promotion of prosperity, and of power and prestige. Bluntschli has the insight to perceive that a nation is a collective entity, having a certain defined character, and the development of the distinctive national gifts is in his eyes the supreme purpose of national life, the political organization of the state being a means to this end. But he falls into a grave error by identifying the empirical with the spiritual character of the nation, and setting up the former as an end worthy on its own account. The empirical character of a collective entity is in this respect no more worthy of honor, and no more fit to be a ground of obligation, than the empirical character of the individual. And the conclusions at which Bluntschli arrives are a sufficient proof of the ethical inadequacy of his vision. Some nations, a very few he thinks, possess political capacity, and they are to rule other peoples. Here we have the "White Man's Burden"—an obvious violation of the ethical principle of national independence. Further, the world state, which is to include all nations, is to concern itself only with their common interests. Bluntschli thus accepts the uniformity principle in ethics, excluding the idea of the reaction of differences which is of the very essence of the ethical relation; while the ideal future as he sees it is that of nations coexisting peacefully side by side, competing peacefully with each other, and doubtless borrowing from one another the best fruits produced by each. But it is idle to expect peaceful coexistence so long as the strong exist by the side of the weak without there being acknowledged an *intrinsic* spiritual tie between them; and competition between peoples will result, like competition between individuals, in strife and exploitation; while the mere borrowing by each of the fruits produced by the rest omits the vital point, upon which I lay the greatest stress, of the eliciting of the fruits in each by the spiritualizing influence of the rest.

Surveying Bluntschli's doctrine as a whole, it is clear that his empirical conception of the state leaves it a purely secular institution concerned with externals, and not really related to the inner life, certainly not a station in the development of personality. He practically acknowledges as much when he says that the state is man writ large, and the church woman writ large; that the state represents the masculine principle, the church the feminine principle. For the feminine, according to him, is the spiritual principle. The state deals with externals; to the church is reserved the prerogative of entering into and transforming the inner life.[3]

[8] It is true that the state is concerned with those conditions of the spiritual reactions that are capable of being enforced, but in instituting such conditions the spiritual content is inevitably kept in view.

But what shall be the motive force for the creation of an international society? I hold that the sense of national sin, or of national guilt, must supply the motive force. At present all the more advanced nations are to be censured because of their pride. Germany prides itself on its science and its efficiency, England on its political liberalism, France on its logical conception of equality, America on its democratic individualism. Each of the great nations dwells complacently upon its fair traits, and vaunts its special type of civilization as that which should rightfully prevail among mankind generally. The national defects, acknowledged perhaps by the critical few, are glozed over. Indeed the consciousness of a collective national character though latent is not yet distinct. It must be evoked. National self-knowledge must be promoted by the leaders and teachers of mankind, and with it must come, as in the case of the individual, the conscious recognition of deep defects—in the case of Germany the narrowness of the conception of the expert:[4] in the case of England the discrepancy between political liberalism as applied to the white inhabitants of the British Isles and of the self-governing dominions on the one hand, and the "benevolent despotism" exercised over the subject millions of India on the other; in America the effacement of true individualism under the crushing pressure of mass opinion, etc.

Moreover not only will the defects be admitted, but

And in the very process of fitting the body to the spirit, the form to the content, the content itself will be discerned more clearly and explicitly.

* See the chapter in the *World Crisis.*

their detrimental influence on other peoples will have to be frankly avowed—every nation must cry its *Peccavi*— the effect for instance on Europe of the French love of glory, the effect of the efficiency notion of the Germans as it is at present penetrating all other nations,[5] and in the still wider view the effect of Western civilization as a whole on the stationary civilization of China, on Egypt, on the myriads of Africa. The civilized peoples of the earth have sinned their sins and are best seen when we consider:

A. The spoliation and outrages perpetrated by the Western nations, for instance at the time of the entrance of the Allies into Pekin, the wholesale destruction of human life and the mutilations of the natives on the Congo. It has been stated that some ten millions of the natives of Africa perished as victims of the white race. If these acts do not warrant our speaking of the sins of the civilized nations, what kind of human behavior does deserve that name?

B. The effect of European example in practically forcing the peoples of the Orient to adopt militarism and navalism.

C. The effect of Western individualism in undermin-

[5] To myself as an individual I say: look to your radiations, consider the effects you produce on others; if the effects are harmful trace them to faults in your character, and let your desire and obligation to influence others beneficently be the spur to lead you to transform your own character. The same each people should say to itself. For instance the obvious faults of our democracy have retarded the progress of democracy in Europe. Our failure in municipal government is constantly quoted abroad as an argument against democracy. This should Be a real incentive to rouse us out of *our* self-complacency.

ing the religious foundation in Eastern civilization.[6] The spreading of Christianity itself, despite the exemplary influence of the higher type of missionary, must yet be classed, in one important respect, among the detrimental influences exercised by the West upon the East. For Christianity, in the form in which it is usually taught, tends to break up the sense of solidarity which is often strong among the less civilized peoples, without supplying an adequate principle upon which solidarity might be reestablished on a higher plane. Hence Christian teaching in the Orient and in Africa, however friendly and merciful in intention, and however beneficent in many ways, is yet a disintegrating influence.

The great problem of the spiritual education of the lower races will have to be taken up anew. Not only are individual missionaries of broader mental and moral horizons needed, the civilized nations as such must reach a common understanding and establish a union among themselves, the keynote of which shall be reverence for the undeveloped, that is to say divination of what, under right educational influence, they, the undeveloped, may come to mean for humanity. And a union of this kind, consecrated to a noble object, will at the same time be the means of leading the Western world out of the chaotic condition in which it is at present weltering. The object for which nations combine may not be their own peace, their own prosperity. The key to peace between the adult peoples is a common, effectual resolve to win new varieties of spiritual expression from the child and adolescent peoples of the earth. Peace must come inci-

[6] Cf. Lord Cromer's remarks on this subj ect in his book on Egypt.

dentally. The common object must be disinterested, spiritual, because there is a duty on the part of the civilized towards the uncivilized to exercise a spiritual function. The task of humanity in general consists in extending the web of spiritual relations so as to cover larger and still larger areas of the finite world. The family is only partly spiritualized. The vocations, the state, are not yet spiritualized. The international society hardly exists. But what I here endeavor to sketch is the human world as it would be in the light and under the influence of the spiritual ideal. And I set down as the saving task of the civilized nations that of extending the spiritual realm so as to cover backward, undeveloped peoples, so as to embody them in the *corpus spirituale* of mankind.

Some of the Principal Obstacles That Stand in the Way of the Organization of Mankind.

The first obstacle is to be found in the inadequate theories that underlie international law. Seventeenth and eighteenth century thinking is still, strange to say, the theoretical foundation. Grotius and Vattel remain the chief authorities. Grotius's theory is a system of empirical individualism with Christian individualism grafted upon it. to mitigate its harsher features. The right of conquest is admitted. A nation is allowed to punish another, punishment being taken in the crude sense, while what has been permitted under natural law is subsequently modified by counsels of perfection derived from Christian individualism.

Yattel is the intellectual grandchild of Leibnitz. He

332

derives from Leibnitz'through Wolff. Vattel envisages the various states as so many individual entities without intrinsic ties. Peaceful coexistence and unhindered pursuit by each people of its own perfection or welfare with mutual aid to be voluntarily rendered are the ultimate conceptions beyond which this thinker does not venture. And if the root principles are thus infertile, small wonder that the fruit of the tree should be what it is. In any handbook of international law, the preponderant space is allotted to the laws of war, and yet international law has proved impotent to restrain the passion of war, or even to prevent its excesses. International law binds the Samson of war with green withes which the giant snaps in derision. It is plain that we are still in the earliest stages, not only of international practice, but even of international thinking. The problem of the right ethical relations between the nations has hardly been broached.

Another conspicuous obstacle in the way of international progress is to be seen in false hopes. Among the false hopes I class:

A. The hope that increased facilities of intercourse will automatically bring about more friendly relations. To expect this is to forget that closeness accentuates repugnances as well as congenialities, increases antipathy as well as amity. When nations come within short range of each other they resemble antipathetical kinsmen who are compelled to live together. The Czechs and Germans in Bohemia would not hate each other as they do were they not such near neighbors. Spatial rapprochement, for instance, between East and West will

333

not of itself guarantee moral rapprochement—far from it.

B. The hope that science may be relied on to bring the nations together. Science is neutral. Science is subservient to evil as well as good. Science is at present distilling the poisonous gases used on the European battlefields as well as inventing the improved methods of surgery. It has made possible instruments of destruction such as savages might have shrunk from using. Moreover, scientific as well as artistic interests are partial manifestations of a people's life and the ethical relation is between peoples as totalities or collective entities—just as the ethical relation between man and man is between the whole man and the whole man, and not between some partial aspect of the man and of his fellow. Hence it is easy to explain why the scientists and the scholars of the different belligerent peoples were swept away by the war passion like the rest, and in their utterance have even carried animosity to greater lengths, expressing it in language calculated to wound more deeply and to leave more permanent scars. They felt that they belonged to the people as a whole, and when the occasion came for them to choose between their scientific co-workers across the frontier and their fellow-nationals, they sided with the latter.

C. The hope that reliance can be placed on international trade to bring about ethical relations between nations. But trade, like science, is ethically neutral. In its own interest it is favorable to order and security in colonies and dependencies, and when, sufficiently enlightened, to the impartial administration of justice.

The European nations abolished the slave trade in Africa because it decimated the native population, and decreased the supply of labor.[7] On the other hand England in the eighteenth century, even at that time the most liberal country of Europe, did not hesitate to wage war with Spain for the maintenance of the monopoly of the hideous slave-trade, and the Opium War occurred in the "full light" of the nineteenth century. But the most striking example of the ethical neutrality of the commercial mind is to be found in the recent partition of Africa between England, France, the Congo Free State and Germany. The methods which these four nations adopted in the "scramble for Africa" were marked by a perfect disregard of the rights of the native populations of the African continent. Two devices were used—proclamations, and treaties with native chiefs. The Queen of England proclaimed that a certain territory would thenceforth be a British possession, as if proclamation could convey a right to the territory. The German emperor indulged in the same fiction. And there was a veritable race between French and English in the West ; between Germans and English in the East, as to which of the two could outdistance or outwit the other in treaty-making. Karl Peters came in disguise with a stock of blank treaties in his pocket. Forty or fifty treaties were concluded by the French annually for several years in the West—as if a treaty with a native chief, who might be bribed or coerced into lending his signature, could be

[7] See, however, the importation of Indian and Chinese coolies, and the surreptitious resurrection of the slave -trade mentioned by Sir Charles Dilke in his *Problems of Greater Britain.*

the foundation of moral right to the territory occupied by his tribe. The European nations artfully employed the fictions of sovereignty in order to varnish their acts of plunder with a semblance of legality. Of course these proclamations and treaties were not intended to justify exploitation in the eyes of the natives—the natives were not consulted or regarded—but rather to base thereon the division of the spoils between the exploiters. A proclamation or the conclusion of a treaty with a chief was notice given to rivals not to interfere with the spoils reserved for the nation that had issued the proclamation or secured the treaty. It meant "hands off" to competing exploiters.

If it be asked whether this picture is not too dark ?. Whether the civilized nations of the twentieth century in their dealings with the helpless natives were merely selfish? Whether their motives are so sinister? Whether they are not animated by better, more moral aims? the answer is that the commercial mind, and it is the commercial mind that chiefly rules the world today, allays its scruples and justifies its aggressions by the fallacy that to extend trade is to spread civilization, and to spread civilization is to contribute to the advancement of the human race. The interests of trade and of civilization are simply identified. To build railroads, to stretch telegraph lines across the Dark Continent, to launch steamboats on lakes that never heard the whistle of a steam engine before, these are assumed to be the evidences of "progress." Besides are not the natives disciplined in habits of industry, are they not encouraged to cultivate the raw products needed by Europe, and in return to receive the overflow of European markets? The instruments of civilization are thus confounded with civilization itself; the means with the end; while the real object, veiled by sophistry, is nevertheless the material benefit to be secured by the white race. Even the humane treatment of the natives, where it is humane, resembles somewhat too unpleasantly the fattening of the calf prior to its consumption by the owner.

Furthermore, the interests of Trade being supposed to be paramount, it is held that any country the people of which do not sufficiently cultivate the products desired by other peoples, or who close their doors against the industrial surplus of Europe, may be annexed, the land forcibly seized, and the inhabitants subjugated, and moreover that such action is right and proper and in the interests of humanity. So long as this view obtains, there will be no peace on earth. The competition for foreign territories and foreign markets, the scramble between the "civilized" exploiters, will be indefinitely provocative of new wars.

The root disease that afflicts the world at the present day is the supremacy of the commercial point of view. Intercourse and exchange of products is no doubt desirable. The education of backward peoples in agriculture and in industry for their own good and along their own line is indispensable. The fallacy of the commercial mind consists in erecting the means into the paramount end, in brusquing the love of independence which is so strongly entrenched, even among many primitive peoples, and in preventing their development in the direction prescribed by their own natures. All this for the sake of the immediate increase of material wealth. The white race shall have the lion's share of the wealth ; the native population are to be accorded a lesser share, with which they must be content. This is the extent of the concession to humanity. This is, in plain words, what Is .signified by the haughty phrase—"the spread of civilization."

The commercial mind is neither benevolent nor malevolent—as little as science Is. It seems at times to be beneficent ; at other times it seems to be almost fiendish —as in the case of the atrocitics perpetrated on the Congo. It is not fiendish, it is simply ethically neutral or blind.

From this series of reflections, certain conclusions may be drawn as to fundamental points of view relating to international law. The main principle is respect for the total personality of peoples, recognition of them as potential members of the spiritual body of mankind.

The territory of a people is to be regarded as the body of that people's soul. Their independence *is* to fee strictly respected. Expropriation or annexation Is to be characterized as outrage. Intrusion, except for purposes of education, is to be forbidden. The conception which underlies the scramble for Africa and for the Far East—that the material Interests of the advanced nations entitle them to force the backward to become receptacles of the industrial overflow of the West, the producers of raw material for the factories of the West must be abandoned.[8]

[8] As to practical steps -that might be taken to give effect -to this conception of International law., see my published address "The

338

And now the main point may once more be stated. The salvation of the civilized peoples, their spiritualization in the effort to spiritualize the less advanced demands a new turn in the history of humanity. *Union in a common sublime object will overcome the antagonisms and discords that prevail among the civilized nations themselves.* The sword will never be turned into a plow-share until the nations come to love the work of the plow—the work of spiritual *tilth in the human* field. The strong peoples will never cease to harm the weak, and in so doing to harm themselves, until they see in the weak, members of the *corpus spirituale* of mankind, depositaries of potential spiritual life in liberating which they the strong themselves will find increased

Great Role of the United States After the War," in which is discussed the creation of an international law-making body or a Parliament of Parliaments. In connection with the latter, I should attach particular importance to the institution of commissions which may serve as a link between the international legislature and the less civilized peoples—the commissions to study the needs and gifts of those peoples with a view to securing their development along their own lines. In the case of civilized peoples that have until recently been stationary, like the Chinese, the commission representing the Western nations would sit in consultation with the most enlightened leaders of the Chinese people themselves, the common object being to discover the points of attachment in Chinese civilization which may wisely be made the starting point of a more modern and progressive evolution. For instance the filial piety of the Chinese, the rectitude of their merchants, the absence of an aristocracy, and their civil service resting on education (despite its defects). In this manner it may become possible to avoid the abrupt, superficial, and infinitely destructive substitution of modern ideas for the system at present existing, and gradual development will take the place of intrusive and uncongenial change.

life. And the task of uplifting the lower peoples will never be successfully prosecuted until it is seen to be part of the task of humanity in general, which is to spread the web of spiritual relations over larger and ever larger provinces of the finite realm.[9]

[9] I add that this conception will react on the internal life of democracy. Democracy is at present regarded as a relation between equals. In fact, we have in America the negro population, the illiterate and backward immigrants. A truer conception of democracy depends on our realizing that within each people as well as between people and people there is the distinction of the more advanced and the less advanced groups. Democracy rightly conceived will be found to consist in the effort spent by the more advanced in each vocational group to uplift the less advanced, the more advanced themselves coming into possession of their spiritual worth in the degree that they realize this their task of leadership and its great responsibilities.

CHAPTER IX

RELIGIOUS FELLOWSHIP AS THE CULMINATING

SOCIAL INSTITUTION

IN this chapter I shall undertake to sketch the plan of a religious society as determined by the spiritual ideal herein set forth. The religious society is the last term in the series of social institutions, and its peculiar office is to furnish the principle for the successive transformation of the entire series. It is to be the laboratory in which the ideal of the spiritual universe is created and constantly recreated, the womb in which the spiritual life is conceived. No single religious society can adequately fulfill this purpose. The spiritual ideal itself must necessarily be conceived differently by different minds; but the great general purpose will be the same, despite variations in shades of meaning and points of view.

The fellowship of the religious society must be based on the voluntary principle; membership must be a matter of free choice.[1] In antiquity the boundaries of

---

[1] Among other ethical relations based on free election, friendship is the most important. In a separate *Book of Friendship* which I hope to publish, I intend to review the ideals of friendship as they have arisen from time to time in the history of civilized mankind— the ideal of Pythagorean friendship, the ideals presented by Aristotle, Kant, Emerson. And I shall endeavor to show in each case the connection between the friendship ideal and the general philosophy of life. I shall then set forth that ideal of friendship which

the political and religious organizations coincided. The citizen was under obligations as a part of his civic duty to worship the divinities of the state. In modern times a state church is still maintained in some countries and supported out of the public funds, while dissenting and nonconformist bodies exist more or less on sufferance at its side. But this arrangement is harmful, especially so to those whom it seems to favor. Erastianism paralyzes religious spontaneity. The state, it is true, is profoundly interested in the flourishing of ethical idealism, and in the constant rebirth in its midst of spiritual ideals. But it is not competent to determine what the character of these ideals shall be. The moment they cease to be freely produced they lose their life-giving power. The state within limits may enforce actions; it may not even attempt to enforce beliefs.

On the other hand, the "secularization of the state" has given rise to the deplorable impression that the state exists only for so-called secular purposes, and has stripped the idea of the state of the lofty attributes with which the greatest thinkers of antiquity had clothed it. It is the function of the religious society, dwelling uncoerced in the midst of the state, to reinvest the state with the sacred character that belongs to it. I do not of course intend to exalt the state after the manner of

is the corollary of the spiritual conceptions outlined in this volume: the friend being in my view one who assists spiritual development as a spectator. He is the faithful mirror of his friend's progress toward personality, the benevolent yet incorruptible recorder and appraiser. By this token friendship is distinguished from the interlocking relations such as that between partners in marriage, vocational co-workers, etc.

Hegel, as if it were a kind of earthly god or to set it up as an object of religious or quasi-religious devotion. The object of religious devotion is the infinite holy community, the spiritual universe. The function of the religious society is to generate the ideal of the infinite holy community, of the spiritual universe. The family, the vocation, the nation, are sub-groups of this, lesser entities. Even mankind itself is but a province of the ideal spiritual commonwealth that extends beyond it. To concentrate worship upon the state or nation as some propose, would be to usurp for the part the piety that belongs to the whole.

In describing a religious society three main aspects are to be borne in mind:

The teaching, the organization, the worship.

A.   The Teaching

In the religious society as here conceived there is to be worked out a body of doctrine, and there is to be a body of specially designated teachers. An ethico-religious society cannot ignore or dispense with a general philosophy of life and statements of belief. It cannot restrict itself to encouraging practical morality without regard to what are called metaphysical subtleties. A moral society of this kind would soon become ossified. On the contrary, an ethico-religious society should excel in the fertility with which it gives rise to new metaphysical constructions and original formulations of ethical faith. The will cannot be divorced from the intellect. The active volitional life cannot be successfully stimulated and guided without the assistance of the mind as well as of the imagination.

But the relation between philosophy and formulas of belief on the one hand and volitional experience on the other should be the reverse of what it has been in the past. Here there must be a new departure. The doctrine, the formulations, whatever they may be, must not be dogmatic but flexible. Growing originally out of ethical experience, they must ever prove themselves apt to enlarge and deepen ethical experience. By this test they will be judged and they must therefore ever be subject to revision and correction. Every dogma, every philosophic or theological creed, was at its inception a statement in terms of the intellect of a certain inner experience. But then it claimed for itself eternal validity, compressing the spiritual life within its mold, and checking further development. The body of doctrine which I desire and foresee will likewise be an interpretation of ethical experience, intended to make explicit the fundamental principles implicit in ethical experience, and thereby clarifying it, and assisting its further unfolding. But it is not and should never be allowed to become dogmatic. The difference, I take it, is plain: in the one case experience contracted in procrustean fashion into a rigid formula, in the other case an elastic formula adapted to and subordinated to the experience.

Thus much for the body of teachings. There should also be a body of teachers. A teacher in an ethicoreligious society will retain something of the character of his predecessors—priest, prophet, rabbi, pastor. The priest is the mediator of grace; the prophet is the seer of visions; the rabbi is learned in the Divine law, and the pastor is the helper of the individual in securing his individual salvation. But these functions will now be seen in an altered light, and will be radically modified in their exercise. The magical attribute of the priest disappears. The confident prediction of future events, based on the assumption that the moral order is to be completely realized in human society, has ceased to be convincing. The Divine law is no longer identical with the Law revealed in the Scriptures and their commentaries, and the salvation of the individual is to be accomplished by other means.

The religious teacher of the new kind is to resemble his predecessors in being a specialist. The word specialist in this connection may, perhaps, awaken misgivings, and these must be removed. He is not a specialist in the sense of having a conscience unlike that of others, or in being the keeper of other men's consciences. Nor shall he impose his philosophy of life or his belief authoritatively, but propose it suggestively. His best results will be gained if he succeeds in so stimulating those whom he influences that they will attain an individualized spiritual outlook of their own, consonant with their own individual nature and need. But specialists of this kind are indispensable. The generality of men have neither the time nor the mental equipment to think out the larger problems of life without assistance, and the attempt on their part to do so leads to crudities and eccentricities of which one meets nowadays with many pathetic examples among those who have severed their connection with the traditional faiths, and have tried in their groping fashion to invent a metaphysic or a creed of their own.[2]

The preparation of the ethical teacher for his special task consists in making himself thoroughly acquainted with the great religious systems of the past, in which much that is of permanent spiritual value is enshrined.[3] He is to fit himself to revitalize what is vital, not to repristinate what is obsolete. There is required of him a first-hand knowledge of the great ethical systems, and of their philosophical backgrounds: furthermore acquaintance, so far as it is as yet accessible, with the moral history of mankind, as distinguished from the history of ethical thinking; in addition, he should intensively study the economic, social and political problems of the time from the ethical point of view, and the psychology both of individual and national character, so far as that fascinating and difficult subject has been opened up by competent writers. Apprenticeship in the social reform movements of the day, direct touch with the inner life of people, on its healthful as well as on its sick side, is also presupposed.

[2] In certain Ethical Societies abroad, the fear of encouraging the rise of a new clericalism led to the plan of drawing for ethical teachers on professors of universities, and others engaged in various lines of practical activity. These persons could of necessity give only the leavings of their time and thought to the complex questions which they undertook to discuss; and the experiment, as might have been foreseen, proved disastrous.

[3] It has been said that the science of today lives only in superseding the science of yesterday. Whether this be true of science or not it is not true of religion. The religions of the past are not merely superseded. There is much in them that is to be reinterpreted, and thus perpetuated.

Since no single person can be adequately prepared in these various subjects, and since a variety of gifts and talents is demanded, it follows that the teaching function shall be exercised by a body or group of teachers, not by a single pastor at whose feet the congregation are supposed to sit. Some of the persons engaged in this work will excel as public speakers, others as writers, others as teachers of the young, others as leaders of vocational groups. But all these different functionaries must learn to work, not only in harmony, but in organic, reciprocal support, themselves illustrating in their group life the spiritual relation, the knowledge and the practice of which they are to carry out into the world. The guild or group idea must be applied to the religious teachers of the future.

B.   The Organization

Every religion exhibits a certain form of organization peculiar to itself and derived from its controlling idea. The organization of the Buddhist fellowship is dependent on the Buddhist ideal of preparation for absorption in Nirvana. The constitution of the Jewish synagogue reflects the conception of the relation of the Chosen People, as an *elite* corps of the divinity. The organization of the Christian church is characterized by its bifurcation into an *ecclesia militans* and an *ecclesia triumphans,* and further by the idea of incorporation into the body of Christ, a difficult mystical conception as of a typical divine individual including within his body a multitude of other individuals.

The organization of the ethico-religious society has

been foreshadowed in the chapter on the vocations. The society is to be divided into vocational groups. In each vocational group is to be worked out the specific ethical ideal of that vocation. In the groups the general ethical philosophy of life is to be applied, tested and enriched. The so-called ethical teachers will here come into fruitful contact with those who are in touch at; first hand with actual conditions, and are cognizant of the difficulties to be surmounted in ethicizing vocational standards. The members of the groups in democratic fashion will contribute to the advancement, not only of ethical practice, but of ethical knowledge, and thus become on their side teachers of the teachers. The danger of the formation of an ethical clergy will be averted. The teachers will be in certain respects the pupils of the taught, and the relation be reciprocal, that is, ethical.

Among the groups the vocational group of Mothers will occupy the central place. The influence of women, especially of the mother group, must penetrate the religious society through and through, for the purpose of drawing the entire fellowship together into a coherent unity. Women henceforth will take a deeper interest in the ethical development of human society. A main factor, if not the only factor in the ethical development of human society, is the elevation of the vocational standards. The group of mothers will therefore be in close touch with the other vocational groups in order to gain a knowledge of the higher standards therein proposed, in order to appraise them, and to inspire the growing generation with the devoted purpose to carry these standards out in practice.

C. The Worship or Public Manifestation of Religion

The ideal of worship likewise must undergo transformation. It has meant an act of homage toward a superior or supreme individual; it has meant eulogistic affirmation of the power, wisdom, goodness, of that individual ; it has meant prayer or petition for help from that individual. It has also meant spiritual edification.

In all these various modes, religious worship heretofore has focused attention on a single individual deity as one who embodies in himself the sum of perfection. In thus presenting the ideal of perfection, it has encouraged preference for unity at the expense of plurality. The salient feature of the spiritual ideal sketched in this volume is the affirmation, on ethical grounds, that plurality is of equal dignity with unity, and hence that the divine ideal is to be represented not as One, but as manifold; not as an individual, however supereminent, but as an infinite holy community,—every human being being in his essential nature a member of that community.

But can worship be offered to the members of a holy community? In a certain sense one might say, Yes, preeminently so, since worship may be taken to mean Worthship, and the worth intrinsic in our fellowmen is the object of our unceasing homage. At the same time very different associations have gathered about the word. Public worship consists largely of eulogistic singing, prayer, adoration, genuflexion, and these are appropriate only to deity conceived as an individual. We cannot even say with the Psalmist "the heavens de-

349

clare the glory of God, and the firmament showeth his handiwork." For though the beauty and order apparent in Nature is one aspect of nature on which we delight to dwell, yet we cannot disingenuously suppress the counter evidence of disorder, ugliness and suffering which Nature no less obtrudes on our sight. The argument from design implied in the Psalmist's words is no longer tenable. Certainly we cannot any longer pray for material assistance as our forefathers did, or invoke supernatural intervention in situations where human science and human helpfulness are impotent. But worship also aims at ethical edification, by holding up to the mind the moral ideal as an object of imitation, and as a rebuke to man's shortcomings. This indeed is its highest function. Nevertheless the moral ideal, as we conceive it, is incapable of being presented in the guise of an individual being, no matter by what superlative language the limitation inseparable from individuality be concealed. The bare attributes of omniscience and omnipotence are abstract and convey no positive meaning whatever. In actual worship a concrete image is invariably associated with the notion of the individualized Deity, such as the Father image or the Christ image. And as soon as this is done, the vast ethical ideal tends to shrink to the dimensions of a human image; and instead of the ideal in its fullness, only certain selected but inadequate aspects of ethical excellence are presented to the worshiper.

And yet in an ethico-religious society also the public manifestation of religion is indispensable. Of what elements shall it consist?

First, there are to be the public addresses by the teachers, having for their main object to arouse or intensify a certain kind of spiritual distress, and then as far as possible to appease it. Every religion in my judgment originates in a particular kind of anguish, and is an attempt to assuage it. The spiritual distress in which the ethico-religious society has its origin is the agonizing consciousness of tangled relations with one's fellow-beings, and the inexpressible longing to come into right relations with them. He is fit to be a public teacher of this religion who profoundly experiences this distress, who desires nothing so much as to cease to be, for his part, a thorn in his neighbor's side. We are that, each of us, inevitably. The more this feeling is strong in him the more will he arouse similar feelings in others, and thus awaken those who are spiritually asleep, the self-righteous, the self-satisfied, and he will then indicate to the utmost of his power, the way of relief.

The specific ethical ideals of life are also to be presented in public assemblies—the ideals of private ethics, of marriage, friendship, and the rest. These expressions of the specific ideals, charged with feeling, and taking on appropriate imagery, will gradually attain a certain classical fitness—classical at least for a time—and may be used as public readings.

But is there a substitute for prayer?

Among the advantages of prayer is often mentioned this: that in it the soul reaches out towards its source, and in so doing wonderfully recruits its spiritual energy. It finds, ethically speaking, its second wind. It reaches down beneath its utmost strength to find an increment of strength not previously at its disposal. The question is whether this increment of strength cannot be obtained more surely and to better purpose in another way, namely, by concentrating attention on the spiritual need of the fellow-beings with whom we are in daily touch, and by becoming aware to what an extent the finer nature imprisoned in them is dependent for its release upon our exertions. The appeal of the God in our neighbor is the substitute for the appeal in prayer to the God in heaven, the call of the stifled spiritual nature in the men and women at our side, is to draw out of us our utmost latent force, the strengths underneath the strength.

The common life we share with our fellow-members in the religious society demands expression in song and in responsive services. The high wave of this common life welling up in us, rising to the surface, makes the glow of religious meetings, gives them fervor, and a touch of rapture, not indeed the common life conceived as a uniform life, but as the life we live in others, and they in us.

The addresses that awaken and appease spiritual pain, the presentation of the various modes of right living, the songs that lift the individual above his private self and help him to live, not indeed submerged, but rather spiritually accentuated in the life of the whole, these are the public manifestations of ethical religion as I see them. They will contribute to make of the society itself the symbol of its ethical faith. We shall not have an external symbol like the cross: the fellowship itself will be our symbol.

There will also be festivals. Every religion must

have its festivals. In place of Baptism the solemn taking of responsibility for the spiritual development of the child. A festival of vocational initiation, like the ancient assumption of the *toga*. Festivals of citizenship, inspired by the ideal of the national character as one to be spiritually transformed. Festivals of humanity in connection with the commemoration of great events in the history of our race and of great leaders who were inspired in some degree by the ideal task of humanity. Festivals of the seasons, deriving their significance from the spiritual interpretation of the corresponding seasons of human life,—youth, middle age, old age. And a solemn though not mournful festival in commemoration of the departed.

The religious assembly should itself be organized; the members of the different vocational groups should be allocated to different parts of the meeting hall, as were the Guilds in certain of the mediaeval cathedrals.

Besides the public manifestations, the private religion will receive attention. The religious society as a whole is to be the microcosm of the spiritual macrocosm, a miniature model of the ideal society, but care must also be taken for the private communion of the individual with the spiritual presences which the ideal evokes. There should be a special breviary for the sick, a Book of Consolation for the bereaved, a Book of Friendship, a Book of direction for those who pass through the experience of sin, and a book of preparation for those who face the end.

CHAPTER X

THE view of life that man has on leaving it is the final test of his philosophy of life. These are my thoughts: It is time to detach thyself from this earth. The shadows are lengthening. Look around you and note the strange changes that have taken place in the men and women of your acquaintance. Those that you once knew in their prime are now old and wrinkled,— and how many already dead! As you survey the procession of life, how many vacant places are there in it I How many true and loyal comrades have been swept away! Or go into the busy streets of the city, and look at the multitude passing through them. You are still one of this multitude. Presently you will drop out. There will perhaps be a little ripple on the surface, and then the stream will flow on as before. How curious is it to think that this frame of life which sustains such high faculties should crumble into a little heap of dust at the touch of the wand of death! Detach thyself, therefore, relax thy hold by anticipation as thou shalt soon relax it actually. But detachment does not mean cold inattention or unnatural shrinking from the earthly scene, like that of the monk in his cell. Relax thy hold on what is earthly in the earthly scene, and fix thy loving attention all the more on what is *spirit-*

ually significant in it. Regard with a friendly eye the beauty of the natural landscape around thee—yonder lake and yonder noble mountain summit. They are earthly, yet are they also hieroglyphs and symbols.

Still more is this true of thy social relations. Detach thyself means relax thy hold on what is transient in those relations. Cling all the more firmly to what is spiritual in them. The earth is thy foundation, thou art Antaeus as long as thou remainest in contact with the earth. Until the very last thou must lean for strength upon the earthly bases and substrata.

Consider the drive of the human race through the time and space world, and its net result. Thou standest now on a high tower. Lean over the parapet and peer as far out into the future as thou canst. Thou standest as did Moses on Mount Pisgah. Strain thy eyes to catch sight of the Promised Land. But remember that the Promised Land turned out to be a land still of promise, not of fulfilment,—a land in which the prophetic soul of Israel matured its visions of a fulfilment never on earth to be attained.

Remember that as thou art linked to thy ancestry, so art thou linked to posterity. The future centuries of the human race are like the future years of an individual. Thou art keenly interested in what may happen hereafter to the race with which thou art interlinked. But the race, like the individual, will be cut off and become extinct before ever the ideal is reached. Remember, therefore, that the purpose for which humanity exists is achieved at every moment in everyone who appropriates the fruits of partial success and frustration. Whosoever standing on the earth as a foundation builds up for himself the spiritual universe attains the purpose of human existence. There is indeed progress in the explicitness with which the spiritual ideal is conceived, and we are immeasurably interested in the greater light to be attained by our posterity. But the essential fruition of the contact of the infinite that is in us with the finite world is achievable at every moment in every human being. And this gives an entirely new meaning to the spiritual gains achieved in solitude, which seem vain because there are no witnesses. But neither will there be witnesses when the last human beings perish on earth. The spiritual bravery of the shipwrecked man who sinks on the lonely ocean springs from the conviction that though the sea can overwhelm him there is that in him greater than ocean's immensity; a conviction achieved through the experience of living in the life of others. The same is the gain achieved by the sick man who lies in solitude like a helpless log in the darkened room. The altruistic philosophy fails in accounting for the moral grandeur that attaches to the spiritual victories gained in silence and solitude.

Face the terrors of life before you leave life. Be resolute to the last not to cherish illusions. Face the terrors of life, the absence of observable design, the cruelties, the ferocities. Think of William Blake's poem "The Tiger": "Did he who made the lamb make thee?" In your philosophy there is no question any longer of a Creator. Creation is an attempt to explain the coexistence of the imperfect with the perfect, to account for a lower stage in terms of a higher. The ultimate inability of man to understand, to explain, is one of the principal frustrations he meets with, is the crucifixion of man at the point of his intellect.

The radical incompetence of man to grasp with his intellect the world as a "universe," is to be faced by him and accepted without qualification. It marks off this philosophy of life from those philosophies and theologies which have attempted to explain the universe, and which, while affecting humility, are the dupes of an unwarranted self-confidence. Unqualified admission of the incompetence of the human intellect to resolve the world riddle is the determining factor in the more profound humility which characterizes the religion of ethical experience. Agnosticism on the intellectual side is the very condition of the transcending ethical conviction subsequently attained. Without intellectual agnosticism there is no ethical certainty.

Consider now frustration and its supreme outcome, or the various points at which man is crucified. I have mentioned the intellectual crucifixion, due to the incompetence of the mind to understand. I must now speak of still more poignant experiences due to the incompetence of man adequately to fulfill the moral law, or to carry out the spiritual relation in finite terms.

I have reached the bourne, or am very near it. The shadows lengthen, the twilight deepens. I look back on my life and its net results. I have seen spiritual ideals, and the more clearly I saw them, the wider appeared the distance between them and the empirical conditions, and the changes I could effect in those conditions. I have worked in social reform, and the impression I have been able to make now seems to me so utterly insignificant as to make my early sanguine aspirations appear pathetic. I have seen the vision of democracy in the air, and on the ground around me I have seen the sordid travesty of democracy—not only in practice but in idea. I have caught the far outlook upon the organization of mankind, the extension of the spiritual empire over the earth by the addition to it of new provinces, and I do not find even the faintest beginnings, or recognition of the task which the advanced nations should set themselves. I scrutinize closely my relations to those who have been closest to me,—and I find that I have been groping in the dark with respect to their most real needs, and that my faculty of divination has been feeble. I look lastly into my heart, my own character, and the effort I have made to fuse the discordant elements there, to achieve a genuine integrity there, and I find the disappointment in that respect the deepest of all.

These are the various points of my life at which I have undergone the crucifixion. I am like Arnold Winkelried, who gathered the sheaf of spears into his breast, and even pressed them inward, to make a way for liberty. So do I press the sharp-pointed spears of frustration into my breast to make way for spiritual liberty. For these cruel spears turn into shafts of light, radiating outward along which my spirit travels, building its final nest—the spiritual universe.

Consider the new and profounder humility. In ethical experience is revealed the plan of the spiritual relations, but the entities or substances which are thus related are incognizable, unknowable. Did I know them I should be able to solve the riddle of the universe. I should know how it is that the finite exists side by side with the infinite. But I cannot know. I cannot enter into the counsels of the multiform godhead. There are the mighty powers that weave and interweave behind the veil, but the veil between them and myself is down, not to be lifted. Within the palace of light is the solemn and serene assembly of the gods: I, man, stand at the gate.

The world as we know it is itself the veil, the screen, that shuts out the interplay, the weavings and the interweavings of the spiritual universe. But at least at one point, in the ethical experience of man, is the screen translucent. The plan of the spiritual relation is there traced in outline. It is this plan that conveys the certainty as to what verily exists beyond, within, beneath.

As to my empirical self, I let *go* my hold on it. I see it perish with the same indifference which the materialist asserts, for whom man is but a compound of physical matter and physical force. It is the real self, of which the empirical was the substratum, upon which I tighten my hold. I do not assert immortality, since immortality, like creation, is a bridge between the phenomenal and the spiritual levels. Creation is the bridge at the beginning; immortality the bridge at the end. Were I able to build the bridge, I should know. I do not affirm immortality. I affirm the real and irreducible existence of the essential self. Or rather, as my last act, I affirm that the ideal of perfection which my mind inevitably conceives has its counterpart in the ultimate reality of things, is the truest reading of that reality whereof man is capable. I turn away from the thought of the self, even the essential self, as if that could be my chief concern, toward the vaster infinite whole in which the self is integrally preserved. I affirm that there verily is an eternal divine life, a best beyond the best I can think or imagine, in which all that is best in me, and best in those who are dear to me, is contained and continued. In this sense *I bless the universe. And to be able to bless the universe in one's last moments is the supreme prize 'which man can wrest from life's struggles, life's experience.*

I look back upon my life once more, and am grateful for the eternal worth which it was permitted me in this frail vessel of my mortal existence to hold, for the shimmer of the spiritual reality of things which I was permitted to see; grateful especially to those who loved me, and whom I was permitted to love, and who were to me in some measure revealers of the eternal life.

Consider lastly the peace that passeth understanding. Now, if ever, this peace should descend upon me. There is a kind of peace that is accessible to the understanding, and there is the peace that passeth understanding. The peace that can be understood is that which consists in the relief of pain. It arises in various ways. After an acute attack of physical pain how like balm is felt the succeeding absence of pain. After a prolonged sickness, when the convalescent takes his first walk, what a sweet tranquillity fills his mind! There is also the mental relief that comes when some danger has been safely passed; the peace of the sheltered fireside to one who has passed through a storm. Again, there is the peace that follows pecuniary anxiety, or the removal of some carking care, as when an erring son is reclaimed, or an estranged wife or husband is found anew.

But the peace that passeth understanding is that which comes when the pain is *not* relieved, which subsists in the midst of the painful situation, suffusing it, which springs out of the pain itself, which shimmers on the crest of the wave of pain, which is the spear of frustration transfigured into the shaft of light.

It is upon those we love that we must anchor ourselves spiritually in the last moments. The sense of interconnectedness with them stands out vividly by way of contrast at the very moment when our mortal connection with them is about to be dissolved. And the intertwining of our life with theirs, the living in the life that is in them, is but a part of our living in the infinite manifold of the spiritual life. The thought of this, as apprehended, not in terms of knowledge, but in *immediate experience,* begets the peace that passeth understanding. And it is upon the bosom of that peace that we can pass safely out of the realm of time and space.

APPENDICES

APPENDIX I
SPIRITUAL SELF-DISCIPLINE

THE preceding volume in its entirety and in every part is nothing else than a book of spiritual self-discipline. Every religion presents to its followers as real objects that the eye has not seen. The certainty of the existence of these objects, religious certainty, religious conviction, springs from one or other kind of need and distress. The object that the eye has not seen is believed in because it corresponds to that need, and relieves that distress. Furthermore, the conviction is strengthened, the certainty intensified, by two methods: (1) elaboration of the ideas presented; (2) performing acts in the doing of which the existence of the objects is presupposed. Thus the idea of the Heavenly Father corresponds to the childlike need of protection. The elaboration of this idea in theological systems strengthens its hold, every idea being powerful as an active force in proportion as it is worked out in detail and linked up with other ideas. And ceremonies, prayers, acts of worship in the doing of which the reality of the Father-God is presupposed, strengthen the belief in him. Conduct is one of the chief sources of belief. The more frequently a devout Roman Catholic prays to the Virgin Mary, the more firmly will he be convinced that she exists and hears him. These features are common to all religion: unseen objects are presented as real; the belief in their reality is augmented by elaboration of the ideas; and above all their hold is reinforced by practice founded on and presuming the reality of the ideas.

The unseen object which the religion of spiritual experience presents is the unique personality. The lines along which the ideas are to be elaborated have been sketched in the above.

Conduct based on the presumption that the divine nature exists in every human being is the principal means of fortifying that conviction, and this presumption itself rests on the fundamental fact of worth.

The difference in rank between the various religions depends on the kind of need which they seek to satisfy. It may be physical, as when the worshiper prays for large herds and fruitful crops. It may be the urging of a passion, as when a man prays for revenge on his enemies. And it may be ethical. And if ethical, it may be purely ethical, or ethical with non-ethical elements admixed. A religion is neither approved nor condemned because it satisfies a need. The judgment passed on it depends on the kind of need it undertakes to satisfy.

Seek to raise the plus traits to the Nth degree. Seek through spiritual sex interaction to release the spiritual life in the child. Bring to birth in thyself the idea of the state, etc. Every chapter of this volume contains some direction as to the lines of conduct to be followed. The principal self-discipline consists in the effort to follow these lines.

But experience tells us that the effort may be hindered or helped in certain ways. I shall mention a few of the helps and hindrances:

Physical and Mental *Athleticism* ane helps to Moral Athleticism. Ethics is a science of energetics. Bodily and mental energy is favorable to ethical energizing. By mental energy I understand especially the habit of vigorously attacking complex and difficult mental problems.

Right *Asceticism* is related to Ethical Development. I exclude self-abnegation and self-repression practiced as drill apart from any particular occasion requiring them, holding that self-repression should always be incidental to self-expression. This applies especially to the hygiene of the sex passion. A positive ideal of the sex relation, as in marriage, is an invaluable help in ennobling and thereby restraining the passion.

The Ethical Life is the supremely Planful Life. There is a hierarchy of ends of which the ethical is the apex. The ethical

366

end is the supreme end to which all others are to be planfully subordinated. The habit of conducting one's life planfully is favorable to ethical behavior. I say planfully, not pedantically, due regard being always had to spontaneity.

Among hindrances to Ethical development may be mentioned the tendency to be satisfied with the *minor perfections*. The better is the greatest enemy of the best. The disproportionate value set on the embellishments of life is but one illustration of this point.

A great hindrance to the spiritual life is the necessity under which we lie of restricting our actual ethical relations to a *few persons*. We cannot extend our influence to the millions of China and India. We cannot even deeply influence a considerable number of our fellow citizens. On ethical grounds we do acknowledge the claims of each individual, of all these myriads of human beings. Yet as far as any actual good we can do them is concerned, we are powerless, and must leave them to their fate. The tragic aspect of life comes home to us sharply at this point. Intensity must take the place of extensity. Intensive spiritual relations with a few will teach us at least to conceive worthily of those personalities whom we cannot directly affect, and to invest them in idea with the honor which! is their due.

Intimate spiritual relations with a few will also counteract the unethical habit of labeling those with whom we come into casual contact according to the special functions they happen to exercise. Thus a letter-carrier is apt to be thought of as an animated machine to carry letters, a stenographer as a kind of animated machine to take dictation, the servant in the house a machine to render physical service. The more complete our appreciation of personality is in the case of the few, the more we shall be impelled to transfer the concept of personality, at least in its outlines, to all others. In this way our friendships, our close relations, will not restrict our ethical horizon. In the narrower circle we shall engender those ideas which in thought

367

at least we can carry out to the farthest limits of human society.

But among the hindrances to ethical practice the two most conspicuous must not be omitted. They are *pity* and *terror,* pity for the pain suffered by others, fear of pain for oneself. Aristotle regarded it as the high function of the tragic drama to liberate men from these disturbing factors. The two are combined and in consequence exacerbated to an extreme degree in those situations where the pain suffered by another person is at the same time poignantly felt as one's own pain. And the anguish felt in seeing the physical suffering of another is even exceeded in witnessing the moral degradation of another, as of an erring son or an apparently irreclaimable husband or wife. The doctrine of frustration as explained in this volume is intended to show the way of relief in such situations. But it is only by not shirking the pain, by permitting it fully to penetrate, by uncovering the breast entirely to the entrance of the pointed spear that we shall have the experience of the transformation of it into the shaft of light.

APPENDIX II

THE EXERCISE OF FORCE IN THE INTEREST OF
FREEDOM

FORCE is a moral adiaphoron. The stigma attaching to the use of force belongs rather to its abuse. The employment of force is good or bad according as the ends for which it is used are good or bad.

The precept of non-resistance in the Sermon on the Mount is to be understood as a piece of ethical irony.

The right, or to be more explicit, the duty, of society to coerce individual members of it rests on the same ground and holds within the same limits as the duty of the individual to coerce himself. Self-coercion depends on the difference in the quality of one's impulses, on the choice one is bound to make between competitive ends. Self-coercion is of two kinds: stimulative and repressive; stimulative to overcome inertia, repressive to subject wrong to right impulses.

He who denies the duty of self-coercion, to be consistent, must fall back on the position of the Cynics. For the Cynics were indeed consistent. They asserted not only the right of the individual to be free from outside compulsion, but also the right of each individual moment of the individual's life to be lived without regard or subjection to future moments. Hence they rejected civilization and its tasks, inasmuch as the prosecution of any task involves the subordination of the present to the content of some future moment.

But if the coercion of a man by himself be admitted, it fol-

[1] A paper read before the Fourth Conference on Legal and Social Philosophy at Columbia University, November, 1915. (Reprinted from the *International Journal of Ethics,* April, 1916, pp. -120-423.)

369

lows that the exercise of force upon a man by society must in principle be likewise admitted. For we are social by nature; we take an interest in the achievement by each one of his ends, and we regard such achievement as a social-benefit.

As to the limits within which outside interference is to be permitted and welcomed, these can best be ascertained by fastening attention upon the end to be attained. And here the positive conception of freedom seems to be the most helpful,—freedom defined as the release in each one of his essential self, that is, of his distinctive gift and capability, or of that in him which is unique or most nearly so. A society in which such valuable contributions were elicited from each would be the ideal society. Stimulative and repressive social coercion are justified in so far as they provoke energy and check disturbing impulses,—always of course without discouraging spontaneity, which is the very good to be secured.

The antithesis of reason and force common in discussions of this subject seems misleading and inadequate; since reason is a faculty of inference and not of preference, has to do with the adapting of means to ends, and does not of itself afford guidance in the choice of ends.

The concept of freedom as defined is more illuminating. Let freedom and force be contrasted, not reason and force.

The idea of law that would follow from what has been said may be illustrated by comparing the action of law with that of automatism in the human body. The system of co-ordinations by which we learn to walk, or acquire any kind of skill, such as that of performing on a musical instrument, is at first painfully and consciously acquired. Consciousness superintends every step in the process. But after a time the sequences reel off auto* matically. Consciousness retires from the field, ascends to a higher plane, and devotes itself to more interesting and significant business. Law, taking it in its broadest sense, may be regarded as the automatic machinery of freedom. It is the system of stimulations and repressions which the experience of mankind at any given time has found conducive to the attainment of the superior ends of life. In the minds of the more advanced members of the community repressive laws like the prohibitions of murder, theft, etc., have already become automatic. Such a thing as questioning or transgressing these laws never once in a lifetime occurs to them. (Of the stimulative laws, such as the requirement to pay taxes in support of the progressive interests of society, the same is not yet true.) As regards the backward members of society, however, the repressive laws are educative. Just as in certain diseases the convalescent needs to acquire anew the art of walking, which his neighbors exercise without thinking, so the backward members of society have to learn painfully those habits of repression which for others have sunk below the threshold of consciousness.

Social compulsion therefore may be defined as discipline in the interest of positive freedom. We may expect that in future this salutary kind of compulsion will go to even much greater lengths than it has yet gone. Society as organized in the state has undoubtedly the right to interfere in the choice of the sexes by prohibiting the marriage of persons afflicted with infectious disease. If the study of human character could ever be so far developed as to determine what kind of temperaments are radically incompatible with one another (a bare throw in the air of course), it would be within the province of the state to prohibit the conjugal union of such temperaments, and thus to prevent the disastrous effects on real freedom which such incompatibilities are apt to cause.

I am well aware of the perils of this point of view. There is a brutal factor in the action of society, as in that of individuals. A given community is apt to mistake its prejudices for principles, its torpor for conservatism, its superstitions for spirituality. Such apprehensions as those that weighed on the mind of John Stuart Mill as set forth in his *Essay on Liberty* are not to be lightly dismissed. And yet the main trend of his argument was plainly determined by an individualistic conception of liberty which many of us no longer share. It is safe to say that on the whole the benefits of coercion outweigh the detriments. We have only to picture to ourselves a state of society in which these coercions should not exist to realize that this is so. The dangers are real, but are due to the abuse of force and not to the exercise of it under the controlling idea of positive freedom which is here proposed.

INDEX

376

377

www.ingramcontent.com/pod-product-compliance
Lightning Source LLC
Chambersburg PA
CBHW051938090426
42741CB00008B/1184